Reversing the Slide

A Strategic Guide to Turnarounds and Corporate Renewal

James B. Shein

JOSSEY-BASS
A Wiley Imprint
www.josseybass.com

Published by Jossey-Bass
A Wiley Imprint
989 Market Street, San Francisco, CA 94103-1741—www.josseybass.com

Readers should be aware that Internet Web sites offered as citations and/or sources for further information may have changed or disappeared between the time this was written and when it is read.

Jossey-Bass books and products are available through most bookstores. To contact Jossey-Bass directly call our Customer Care Department within the U.S. at 800-956-7739, outside the U.S. at 317-572-3986, or fax 317-572-4002.

Jossey-Bass also publishes its books in a variety of electronic formats. Some content that appears in print may not be available in electronic books.

Library of Congress Cataloging-in-Publication Data

Shein, James B., 1942-
  Reversing the slide : a strategic guide to turnarounds and corporate renewal / James B. Shein. — 1st ed.
       p. cm.
  Includes index.
  ISBN 978-0-470-93324-4 (hardback), 978-1-118-00845-4 (ebk), 978-1-118-00846-1 (ebk), 978-1-118-00847-8 (ebk)
  1. Corporate turnarounds—United States–Management.   2. Corporate turnarounds—United States—Case studies.   3. Working capital—United States.   4. Strategic planning–United States.   I. Title.
  HD58.8.S4798 2011
  658.4'06—dc22

                                                                            2010050247

Printed in the United States of America
FIRST EDITION
HB Printing   10 9 8 7 6 5 4 3 2 1

Contents

Dedicated to my wonderful sons, Justin and Jered, for their encouragement, their senses of humor, and for teaching me what's important in life

Introduction: Conditions and Causes of Distress

Employees at Rhodes Plastics in Linden, New Jersey, trudged through another dreary March day. The plant received its raw materials and supplies at one end of the building, converted them into sterile packaging for the food and drug industry, and shipped them out the other end. The office workers were the first to register shock and confusion when armed sheriff deputies stormed in and ordered everyone out of the building.

"You will take nothing, not even the family pictures on your desks!" one officer shouted. "Not until the bank figures out who owns what."

While locksmiths arrived to change all the locks, the plant workers were ordered out and told to leave even their own tools behind. Unbeknownst to everyone there, the company's top officers had failed to convince the company's lenders that they could turn the company around. Unpaid suppliers and customers with unfilled orders would soon share in the employees' shock.

Although your problems may not be as dramatic, chances are, at some point in your career, you will participate in a turnaround. No matter how profitable you have made your business, or how recession-proof you consider your industry, you will find yourself dealing with a troubled company. Perhaps your own company will need to reinvent itself to deal with new competitive realities, or perhaps a valued customer will begin paying you later and later due to its own internal distress. You may even serve on the board of a nonprofit organization that requires its own strategic, operational, and financial initiatives to remain viable. Whatever the case may be, you will—with near 100 percent certainty—be party to a turnaround at some point in your professional career.

A *turnaround* is any effort to revitalize and make a clear change in the direction of a struggling business of any size. It also applies to improving a business that has simply underperformed its competition. Understandably, many executives are reluctant to admit that their firm needs a turnaround, so I began using the term *corporate renewal* almost a decade ago; they seem to find it a bit less threatening. These terms can apply to an entire company, a subsidiary, or just a division.

The turnaround field relates to companies and nonprofits with clear problems, but also to those who should question whether their employers, customers, or suppliers are on the wrong track. Years ago, I met with the CEO of Siemens Corp., a $100 billion company based in Munich, Germany. The CEO has 700 internal consultants, but still pays out tens of millions of Euros per year on outside consultants, none of whom could prevent the fact that at any given time, at least one of his business units would invariably be performing poorly. He asked me very frankly what "turnaround consultants" do differently than the big consulting firms. This book will answer that question.

Bob Johnson, the highly successful entrepreneur and founder of BET (Black Entertainment Television), asked me to speak to his executives. Although I usually meet with companies in trouble, I met with his staff while they piloted one of the most successful and profitable companies in the country. BET wasn't in trouble— far from it—but Johnson was smart enough to want to know why so many similarly successful companies got into trouble, and he wanted his entire senior staff to recognize the warning signs and avoid similar pitfalls. The saddest cases are those that fail to heed the many early warning signals that they are in trouble, or that a customer or supplier is in trouble, until the damage is irreparable.

I have told my students at Northwestern University's Kellogg School of Management as much for the better part of the last decade in my "Managing Turnarounds" class. The course draws on my three decades of experience helping salvage troubled companies and returning them to profitability, and this book codifies the lessons I have learned in that time and applies them to a broader audience that will surely need them in volatile economic times. I also teach "New Venture Formation" at Kellogg, a pairing that strikes some executives and students as unusual. However, as I explain in the very first class of Managing Turnarounds, turnaround situations often resemble startups in the demands they place upon management. Effective turnaround managers must often become much more entrepreneurial in their approach to any turnaround, and entrepreneurs also should heed the lessons here.

Turnarounds as Entrepreneurship

As already mentioned, one need not work in the field of turnarounds and restructuring to apply the lessons of this book. Turnaround CEOs face many of the same challenges faced by entrepreneurs. In fact, the following ten conditions most frequently encountered by turnaround professionals are also characteristic of entrepreneurial startup situations.

Lack of Cash

Most entrepreneurial ventures fail due to undercapitalization, which prevents a company from gaining sufficient working capital to fund its operations until it can create positive cash flow. Even rapid growth can exacerbate this problem, for as Figure I.1 demonstrates, the gap between cash outlay for salaries and supplies that occurs later in a company's life (G2) typically exceeds that same gap earlier (G1).

Such a cash crunch also rears its ugly head during turnarounds, for it is precisely the lack of working capital that brings a company into crisis. In both cases, turnaround managers and entrepreneurs must carefully scrutinize any expenditure requiring a cash outlay. Both types of managers must quickly and accurately determine which expenditures are absolutely critical to the company's ongoing operations (payment to key suppliers or payroll taxes) and which can be delayed (a new machine or holiday party). Both types of managers must also find short-term projects that generate cash, such as the sale of nonproductive assets. The successful execution of such projects not only frees up incremental liquidity but also restores credibility with suppliers, customers, and employees. Cash is an issue for large as well as

Figure I.1. Cash Flow Timing Across the Organizational Life Cycle

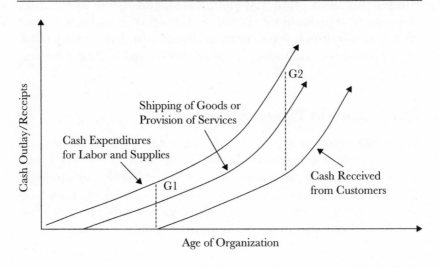

small companies. One of my students, a young entrepreneur who developed a new energy-bar business, found himself running out of cash despite a truly phenomenal growth in new orders. He wound up on the ABC television show *Shark Tank* to raise money from a rather nasty panel of financiers of ventures. He succeeded in procuring financing for his small business, but most do not. At the other end of the spectrum, it was a critical cash shortage that caused Flying J—an $18 billion company—to come to a screeching halt. Best known for its truck stops, they missed payroll only days before Christmas, forcing them to file bankruptcy on short notice. They failed to monitor true cash availability, relying instead on "book" earnings, a subject discussed in more detail later.

Analytical Needs

In a crisis, a turnaround manager often must focus on near-term problems with near-term solutions, typically those related to the cash issues discussed previously. Similarly, entrepreneurs make investment decisions based heavily on the timing of cash outflows to ensure that the fledgling enterprise can remain viable long enough to turn profitable. As a result, entrepreneurs and turnaround executives both have little use for widely used Generally Accepted Accounting Principles (GAAP), as the accrual methods of accounting that they prescribe are irrelevant if a company cannot continue as a going concern. One subtle difference is that turnaround managers frequently must "shock" accountants or chief financial officers out of their historical reliance on GAAP accounting methods, whereas an entrepreneur rarely encounters such problems, if only because of the realization that every dollar is their life blood to survival.

Aside from its manipulability, GAAP provides little value to these managers because it provides an incredibly detailed account of the company's historical performance at a time when the only thing that matters is the accurate forecasting of each of the next thirteen weeks. Both types of executives require up-to-date information about how various strategic decisions—increasing a startup's advertising reach, perhaps, or selling a division of a troubled company—will affect the company's cash balance. The accrual accounting methods of GAAP often mask the cash effects of such decisions, and its assumption of "smoothed" and "matching" of collections and disbursements can project a break-even financial quarter when in fact the company's cash balance will turn negative in a matter of weeks. As such, managers in startups and turnarounds alike have no use for the historical analysis tools provided by GAAP—they must take more of a pragmatic forecasting approach to financial analysis. This concept is discussed in depth in Chapter Four.

The J.A. Jones Construction Company was a highly successful contractor based in Charlotte, North Carolina, with billions of dollars of massive construction projects under way around the world. Jones appeared profitable, because income and expenses were booked according to GAAP. Their projects, including eight new U.S. embassies, hotels, airports, hospitals, and office buildings throughout the world, all came to a halt when the company ran out of cash and declared bankruptcy.

One should not confuse executives' manipulation of earnings reports allowed under GAAP with fraud. When CEO Garth Dabinski changed the depreciation and other schedules at

Cineplex Odeon to make earnings look deceptively strong, those moves were technically permissible under GAAP. While the accounting changes allowed him to show a $40 million profit, in reality the movie theater chain bled over $50 million in cash that year, because he focused on financial engineering instead of on the turnaround tripod discussed in Chapter Three. Dabinski later fraudulently changed accounting records at LiveEnt Company, for which he is now serving a seven-year sentence.

Hiring Difficulties

Entrepreneurs and turnaround managers also constantly face the problem of recruiting and retaining quality employees. Employees naturally gravitate toward stability, something neither a startup nor a distressed company can offer. The entrepreneur must recruit new employees without any guarantee that the company will thrive sufficiently to pay their salaries, while the turnaround manager often finds a staff whose most qualified members have already departed, leaving only those employees unable to find employment elsewhere, often an indication of their productivity. In both cases, the use of equity incentives proves very useful in overcoming this incentivization problem, as employees can typically receive restricted stock or stock options at a low valuation, indicating significant financial upside if the new venture takes off or the distressed company returns to profitability and increased equity value.

In addition to the difficulty of attracting full-time staff, entrepreneurs and turnaround managers also have trouble paying for legal, information technology, marketing, and advertising services. Just when such services can prove immensely valuable, managers in both situations can least afford them. As a result, turnaround executives and entrepreneurs often have no choice but to perform those crucial tasks either themselves or with minimal support.

Disbelieving Customers

Customers also crave stability, not wanting to jeopardize their company or their career if a supplier fails to deliver an order on time, reliably, and of the promised quality. Without a track record, entrepreneurs struggle to convince potential customers that they can deliver, whereas a turnaround manager must overcome a recent negative track record caused by the distressed company's failure to meet customer expectations. One venture capitalist has opined that a successful high-growth startup must offer a tenfold improvement in quality or other important product features over existing alternatives to convince prospective customers to risk relying on an unproven venture. A troubled firm's competitors' salespeople often try to add to potential customers' fears with implicit threats to purchasing executives along the lines of "we'll only supply those who buy from us now" and "you'll look foolish when they don't deliver."

As a result, both entrepreneurs and turnaround professionals find that they can only earn business from less creditworthy customers and those who shop exclusively based on price, thus exacerbating the company's problems with low- or no-margin buyers. Less price-sensitive, more creditworthy buyers can simply wait until the struggling company stabilizes itself by using the advice found in this book. Chrysler faced such problems in 1980 and again in 2009, when consumers and large fleet buyers postponed Chrysler purchases until they could feel comfortable that the company would survive long enough to honor its warranty obligations.

Time Sensitivity

Both startups and troubled companies face a rapidly shrinking time span during which a new opportunity can be exploited or disaster can be averted. With employees working long hours, managers must run meetings focused on specific, detailed "to do" lists rather than as a chance to discuss the company's problems in general. Lacking the luxury of time to conduct detailed analyses, managers must make decisions quickly, often relying on a "Ready—Fire—Aim!" decision-making philosophy. This frenzied pace forces managers to walk a delicate tightrope; they must at once create the sense of urgency necessary to spur an often complacent workforce into rapid, aggressive action, but they must do so in a manner that assuages employee anxiety rather than exacerbates it. Such a balancing act requires a unique blend of charisma, competence, and credibility on the part of the entrepreneur and the turnaround practitioner, shown primarily through how one makes and implements those timely decisions. This concept is discussed in greater detail in Chapter Three.

Steve Miller, author of *The Turnaround Kid* and professional turnaround CEO of six companies, uses this approach.[1] He warns his employees of "paralysis by analysis," whereby they keep studying an issue rather than making much-needed decisions.

Centralized Decision Making

Startups lack organizational structure, thus making it difficult for the entrepreneur to turn to resources inside the company for consultation or delegation. Conversely, such organizational structures may be in place for the turnaround manager, but those same structures' complicity in causing the company's distress makes them an unattractive source of such support. As a result, both situations require a strong, centralized leadership structure rather than a democratic process of decision making until the organization is on an upward course. One need not go to the extreme of "Chainsaw" Al Dunlap, who belittled everyone around him when he took charge of Scott Paper, or "Queen of Mean" Leona Helmsley. Helmsley frequently shouted obscenities at employees just before firing them, and made them beg on their knees for their jobs even for the slightest mistakes, while Dunlap told long-term Scott employees that they were "stupid" for staying so long; both approaches are foolish and short-sighted. Strong management requires at least a short-term focus on centralization which eases as the organization changes course, but leaders must boost morale in the process. Better role models include Jamie Dimon at Bank One, Selim Bassoul at Middleby, or Michael Jordan at EDS, each of whom is discussed elsewhere in this book.

Scarcity of Knowledge and Risk

Both startups and troubled companies operate in an environment of bounded rationality, with limited information and a great deal of uncertainty. Startups lack an organizational history to guide them, while troubled companies are typically troubled precisely because the lessons of their own histories have limited value (see under the heading "Causes of Distress"). Both types of companies lack the institutional knowledge necessary to deal with the problem appropriately, thus making planning and forecasting difficult while increasing the risk of failure. Relying on poor institutional knowledge has caused the downfall of many executives, such as Rick Wagner, the CEO of General Motors, who relied on GM's "If we build it they will buy it" mentality, even in the face of plummeting market share. It wasn't until the U.S. government forced him out that the board faced up to the fact that change was needed. It didn't help much when a longtime GM executive, Fritz Henderson, was named as the replacement, but he only lasted eight months on the job.

At a company that made appliance parts, the CEO finally agreed to a detailed list of steps to return the company to profitability. Months later, when the board of directors confronted him as to why he had not yet implemented any of the steps, he responded that he had split the list in two. They assumed he had created short- and long-term goals, but he took a more practical view of the two lists, declaring that the lists were "those things I don't know how to do and those that I can't bring myself to do." He chose early retirement, and his replacement turned the company cash flow positive once again.

Supplier Problems

Competitors' sales and marketing personnel will invariably extol the weaknesses of a new venture or distressed company, telling potential or existing suppliers that they would be "foolish" to supply such firms given the likelihood that they will not survive long enough to pay for the goods or services provided. Suppliers often feel disinclined to alienate their established customers by selling to the startup or distressed company, requiring an entrepreneur or turnaround manager to exercise almost mystical forces of persuasion to overcome their objections without leverage in terms of price, delivery, or quality. In particular, both the entrepreneur and turnaround practitioner must try to avoid the dreaded "cash in advance" demand from suppliers.

This is a particular problem when there are critical, key suppliers. Fannie May Candies faced this when Bloomers Chocolate

Company demanded cash in advance on all orders. Only Bloomers could produce the exact chocolate mix Fannie May needed to make its well-known Mint Melt-a-Way's™. Unable to pay Bloomers in advance, Fannie May had no choice but to declare bankruptcy when it couldn't come up with the cash.

Lack of Credibility with Lenders

Lenders generally will not extend credit to startups, for they lack the assets necessary to collateralize a revolving or term loan. Similarly, distressed companies have already stretched their lenders to the limit, going so far as to exceed their loan advance rates on accounts receivable, inventory, and other collateral, thereby forcing lenders to enter into an "over-advance." Such a situation allows the debtor access to working capital in excess of the company's collateral in order to finance its turnaround, but it implies that a lender has taken on equity-like risk without equity-like returns, for it stands to lose the entire uncollateralized portion of its advance. Eventually, a lender will require a forbearance agreement or waiver of its foreclosure rights, which typically imposes new restrictions on the company, increases the debtor's effective interest rate, and may even mandate the hiring of turn-around professionals to rectify the over-advance situation.

One company that leased railroad boxcars, coal cars, and containers received multiple waivers on debt defaults from its lenders. When cash flow problems persisted, the lenders, suppliers, and lawyers met to reach an agreement. The meeting started poorly when an argument between the lawyers for the two largest lenders escalated into a full-on fist fight, as both began grappling on the floor over who got to talk first. Each wanted to show everyone how tough they planned to negotiate with each other and with the borrower. It became clear that the company executives probably wouldn't get any additional relief from their creditors.

Great Chance for Equity Gains

When companies start up, it's clear that the equity values are very low, with great opportunity for capital gains. The risk of failure is high, but so are the potential rewards.

Similarly, the stock of troubled companies is valued very cheaply. The difference, of course, is that the stock of a poorly performing company is low because the company is in financial and operating distress. A successful turnaround can thus bring substantial rewards to those who acquire equity even when risk is high.

In the case of the railcar leasing company mentioned above, all the employees who helped with the turnaround received shares valued at fifty cents each. Four years later, the company was sold for fourteen dollars a share: not bad, but there are many stories of investors in troubled companies doing even better, which are discussed in more detail in Chapter Nine. It is interesting to note that one of the lenders represented by the battling lawyers became more cooperative, and was paid in full plus a premium, while the other remained contentious and had his client sell its loan for ten cents on the dollar after months of fighting, thinking he had outsmarted everyone.

In summary, both turnaround managers and entrepreneurs face crisis situations that require the skillful management of multiple, often conflicting constituencies. This requires incredible persuasion and salesmanship in order to overcome their objections and get all of the company's stakeholders working toward a common goal. Ultimately, the two primary challenges are the same: conserving and raising cash, and establishing trust both inside and outside of the organization. Doing so requires a very different skill set than that required of a traditional manager, for mere competence and confidence will not suffice. Startups and turnaround crises demand a certain charismatic zeal[2] in the face of overwhelming adversity to inspire the confidence necessary to invigorate cautious employees and build the trust necessary to assuage nervous suppliers. Therefore, this book is every bit as much about entrepreneurship and innovation as it is about reorganization and corporate recovery.

Causes of Distress

It is important to diagnose the causes of organizational distress, both to help avoid it as well as to repair it. Companies may find themselves in distress from a variety of sources, which can be broken down into the two main categories—internal and external causes.

External Causes

As the name suggests, external causes represent exogenous shocks to all or a significant part of the company, sending management into a tailspin. Here are some common external causes of companies' declines:

Economic Downturns

Economic downturns such as the one recently plaguing world markets can undermine even the soundest businesses. For example, Saks Fifth Avenue's pristine brand equity and strong retail presence in critical markets has historically afforded it significant bargaining power against vendors.[3] Combined with its effective use of technology to streamline its inventory management, this put Saks in an enviable competitive position against other high-end luxury retailers. But even Saks began to struggle in the face of a nationwide collapse in discretionary consumer spending following the macroeconomic crisis of 2008; it watched its gross margin fall an unprecedented sixteen percentage points from the fourth quarter of 2007 to the same period in late 2008.

Such downturns could also come in the form of troughs following waves of financial liquidity. That same macroeconomic crisis of 2008 came on the heels of a tightening in credit markets that kept even healthy companies from financing that could have carried them through. Companies with sufficient foresight, luck, or both to raise funding while credit markets remained loose could ride out the storm, while companies who came too late to the party found themselves unable to close financing.

When Flying J failed to make payroll, they could not raise additional capital on short notice in the face of falling oil prices and frozen credit markets. Similarly, when Circuit City could at last borrow no more to cover the problems it never fixed, it too filed for bankruptcy.

Not all downturns are as far-reaching as the crisis of 2008 and 2009, but regional, or even local, downturns can have a negative impact on businesses. For example, the closing of the Fore River Shipyard in Quincy, Massachusetts, represented a devastating external cause of distress for the nearby restaurants and bars that catered to the shipyard's employees coming off shift from building submarines and tankers.

Industrywide Issues

Industrywide issues, particularly structural ones rather than cyclical ones, may affect not an entire national or regional economy, but instead focus on one industry or vertical. Such changes could come in the form of industry consolidation—such as how the explosive growth of Wal-Mart gave it disproportionate bargaining power against its vendors of clothing, cosmetics, and children's toys, thus crippling supplier margins—or the emergence of new competitive products, such as the eventual devastating effects margarine had on butter producers, or the growing competition steel producers faced from plastic in products ranging from containers to automobiles. Weather can represent another industry issue, as it did when a severe drought devastated coffee manufacturers throughout Brazil in 1999, wiping out some 40 percent of the crop. Changes in commodity prices can also affect entire industries on both the top and bottom lines. For example, sugar processors such as Imperial Sugar faltered in the wake of increased sugar prices in the 2001–2002 timeframe, as they struggled to pass along such cost increases to customers.[4] Similarly, tumbling oil prices in late 2008 slashed revenues at major oil companies, which subsequently rippled through the drilling and exploration industry because it had become less profitable to drill for new reserves. Finally, litigation—particularly class action toxic tort litigation such as that which prompted dozens of bankruptcies among manufacturers with asbestos in their products from the 1980s through today—can represent a widespread external cause of distress to an entire industry.

Shifts in Consumer Demand

Shifts in consumer demand can unexpectedly erode a company's revenue growth. For example, the explosion in popularity of low-carbohydrate diets such as the Atkins, South Beach, and Zone diets weakened many fast-food restaurant chains, notably donut maker Krispy Kreme, which cited the diets' popularity in explaining its expected lower profits to Wall Street in 2004.[5] Similarly, Chapter Nine will demonstrate how Schwinn's failure to recognize the growing popularity of lighter, more agile mountain bikes over its traditionally heavier cruising bicycles presaged its dwindling sales and eventual bankruptcy filing.

Changes in Technology

Changes in technology have disrupted many industries, from the iconic business school example of the buggy whip industry falling in the face of the automobile to significantly more subtle, complicated technological shifts in computing architectures. Today's information technology products and networks have grown so interdependent between software and hardware products and the standards that govern them that a company need not even manufacture the changing technology in order to falter, as did Wang Computer in its failed attempt to hang onto the "midframe" computer market in the 1980s.

For example, Electronic Data Systems found itself lagging significantly behind more nimble competitors like Razorfish, Scient, and even IBM Global Services in the late 1990s, as its historical expertise in legacy mainframe systems created a strategic mismatch with the rapid adoption of the client/server model. The wide-scale introduction of personal computers into the workplace drove adoption of the client/server architecture, leaving EDS with increasingly obsolete mainframe expertise. Though EDS only provided outsourced IT services, its expertise in the disappearing mainframe model (and corresponding inexperience with the client/server model) made it no less a victim of technological change than the manufacturers of such mainframe products. (See Chapter One for more information on the challenges faced by EDS.)

Kodak and Xerox came close to collapse with their belated realization that customers preferred digital cameras and copiers over analog devices. Similarly, it was the Internet as a technical pipeline of information that affected newspapers at the turn of this century, even more than the technical advance in television advertising did in the 1950s.

Government Regulation

Government regulation can send shocks to an otherwise stable industry, most often through deregulation such as that brought about by the Telecom Act of 1996, which sent telecommunications providers scrambling to adjust to the new economic realities of increased competition in the form of competitive local exchange carriers, or CLECs. Bans or restrictions can also shrink market sizes (such as the increase in the legal drinking age to twenty-one from eighteen in many states in 1984) or cut off marketing channels (such as the ban on advertising cigarettes on television and radio enacted by the Public Health Cigarette Smoking Act in 1970). However, regulation need not be so dramatic or sweeping to affect an industry. For example, the push to produce more environmentally friendly fuel prompted the 2007 passage of the Energy Independence and Security Act, which specified levels of ethanol production well above current market demand. This artificially increased demand for the corn used to make ethanol, in turn increasing the price of corn and compressing margins across the livestock and dairy industries, which rely on corn as a primary component of cattle feed.[6] Furthermore, local minimum wage increases can significantly increase operating costs for labor-intensive industries such as retail, as San Francisco's 26 percent minimum wage increase in 2004 drove many Bay Area restaurants out of business.[7]

Changing Interest Rates

Changing interest rates can change the cost of a company's debt, thereby leading to fluctuations in cash outflows. Although the most common example is an unexpected spike in interest rates for a company that has issued floating-rate debt, many financial institutions ranging from investment banks such as Goldman Sachs to credit card issuers such as GE Commercial Finance have complicated balance sheets full of interest rate derivatives, with profitability often predicated on a steady "spread" between floating- and fixed-rate debt. Such institutions can suffer merely from increases in interest rate volatility, even in the absence of a sustained directional move in interest rates. Even nonfinancial companies seemingly *without* interest rate exposure can suddenly find themselves hamstrung by interest rate spikes when customers or suppliers with floating-rate debt find themselves cash-constrained, and begin stretching out payables or demanding stricter cash collection policies, respectively.

Changes in Business Model

Changes in business model can also hamper historically sound businesses. Newspapers are currently facing a drastic shift from their old monopoly-based business models in response to the popularity of reading news on the Internet and their strategic misstep in giving away content for free online. In order to survive, they will have to adapt to these new realities while preserving their historical mission: discovering and presenting the news. As discussed later, they need to rely on their core competencies as "trusted infomediaries."

Internal Causes

Though managers are naturally eager to point to external causes so as to deflect blame, a study suggested that causes of distress coming from within the company are six times more likely to cause a firm's failure. Although there are many examples of such internal causes, the most common—and most deadly—is unquestionably ineffective management, which plagues everything from small, family-led concerns to multinational conglomerates.

Just as Roman writer Publilius Syrus wrote that "anyone can hold the helm when the sea is calm," many management teams can coast along smoothly during periods of stability and economic prosperity. However, executives often fail in the face of adversity simply because they lack the skills to deal with the challenges posed by any of the external causes of distress just discussed. Steven Rogers at the Kellogg School of Management extends this naval metaphor, comparing the revelation of management teams' weakness in times of crisis to a boat that has cruised through a passageway time and again at high tide. When the water level falls, though, dangerous rocks appear suddenly, making navigation unexpectedly treacherous. Always present, the rocks—or management incompetence and organizational problems—lurked innocently below the surface until falling tides or plunging economies reveal the danger that had been there all along. While ineffective management is by far the most common internal cause of distress for faltering companies, it is not the only one. But even when there is another internal problem, like those listed next, management failure usually plays a role, making a bad situation worse.

Blind Pursuit of Growth

Blind pursuit of growth can cause an organization to lose sight of what made it successful in the first place. CEO John H. Bryan took Sara Lee through a reckless strategy of acquisitions for most of the 1980s and 1990s, as the company purchased more than 200 companies, many well outside of Sara Lee's core foods business. This overly aggressive acquisition binge increased revenues from just over $2 billion when Bryan took the helm in 1975 to nearly $20 billion in 2004, a massive growth that hid several underlying problems in the company's management, who fundamentally failed to understand their core customers. Sara Lee had become a complex, decentralized organization with inefficient cost controls, causing Sara Lee to have the highest sales and administrative expenses among its competitors (see Figure I.2)[8] and poor customer relationships.[9]

Blind devotion to "the deal" had many side effects common to poorly managed companies. First, the overriding inclination to buy competitors rather than innovate from within led to insufficient investment in research and development, thus frequently leaving Sara Lee a step behind other competitors and forcing it to play catch-up with "me-too" offerings. Like many companies who overexpand during times of prosperity, Sara Lee's unrelenting pursuit of growth led to inadequate postmerger integration efforts, with management seemingly uninterested in ensuring that new pieces fit together before becoming distracted by the prospect of the next big deal. For example, Sara Lee soon owned nine meat companies, each with a different sales team approaching large grocery chains, an approach that annoyed those chains' buyers who preferred to deal with only one contact. As they so often do, these distractions prevented management from seeing coming changes in the industry, with disastrous results. A host of problems, including slowed growth following the 2001 recession, rising input costs, and pricing pressure from consolidated retail

Figure I.2. Cost Inefficiency at Sara Lee in 2007

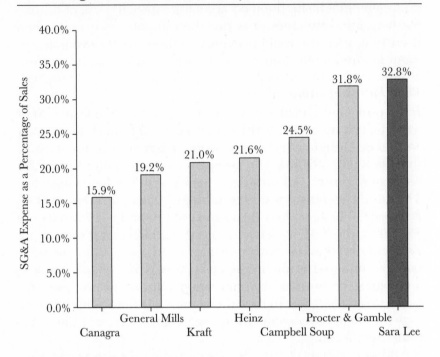

customers, led to the replacement of CEO Steven McMillan in 2004, just four years after he had succeeded Bryan.

Organizations that grow too fast often demonstrate a second example of ineffective management that frequently leads companies further into decline: an excessive reliance on cost-cutting, to the exclusion of more effective alternatives. In the absence of a comprehensive turnaround strategy that pairs a genuine strategic change with downsizing to create a leaner, more focused organization, simply reducing costs by cutting headcount or selling off divisions will invariably fail. In their efforts to turn Sara Lee around, McMillan and his successor, Brenda Barnes, relied heavily on cost-cutting and downsizing. After five years of trying, Barnes still hadn't fully turned Sara Lee around. Sara Lee's turnaround efforts have faltered at least in part due to its reticence in reaching out for help, either from turnaround specialists or from newer, more talented hires lower in the organizational structure. Despite a decade of underperformance, change at the top came slowly, typified by McMillan's moving to the chairmanship from CEO and staying there throughout several failed turnarounds.

In the early 1980s, Frank Lorenzo grew Continental Airlines through the acquisition of four airlines, following a standard protocol of ruthlessly cutting costs at each subsequent target in order to help fund the next deal. Passengers on Continental flights saw a mismatched assortment of seats: some red, some grey, some tall, some short, based on whatever had become available from different planes being stripped for parts. Duct tape secured ancient overhead bins, and on-time performance plummeted. Gordon Bethune, the CEO later credited with the turnaround at Continental, compared this cost-cutting strategy to saving money by taking toppings off a pizza to cut costs; sooner or later, no one will buy it at any price. The key elements to Bethune's successful turnaround are chronicled in Chapter Five.

As noted earlier, Krispy Kreme management blamed the low-carb diet craze for the company's plummeting profits. In reality, many of their problems resulted from excessive growth. As the company first expanded across the country from its home in the southeastern United States, a mystique surrounded their hard-to-find hot donuts, a real treat for many. Soon, however, they appeared in thousands of gas stations and retail outlets, a situation that made them a ubiquitous commodity. The resultant turnaround involved closing some outlets and retrenching, as discussed in Chapter Five.

Overextension of Credit

Overextension of credit in overly indulgent credit markets can sink companies who become too optimistic about their own growth prospects. In boom times, firms often finance acquisitions with debt, naively using "best case" scenarios as base cases for the purposes of financial forecasting. Excessive liquidity can hide severe underlying critical problems at a company the way a fresh coat of paint may conceal dry rot in a building's timbers. Management grows complacent, knowing that they can find an accommodating lender who will let them simply throw money at the problem instead of attacking it head-on. In the face of a downturn, these companies find themselves swamped with debt.

Just one or two bad quarters can lead to depressed profitability and result in tripped covenants, thus forcing these companies to negotiate often expensive forbearance and waiver agreements with their lenders. See Box 1 for examples of frequent covenants that can require such forbearance agreements.

Box 1: Typical Covenants Tripped by Downturns

Although the frothy capital markets of 2004–2007 led to the prevalence of so-called "covenant-lite" loans featuring very few, very lax restrictive covenants, bank loans have historically contained features requiring certain levels of financial performance in order to protect lenders with warning signals. If a company fails to meet one of the covenants at an agreed upon date—typically the end of each financial quarter—the lenders may enforce certain rights, such as a higher interest rate, an additional equity contribution, the divestiture of a subsidiary, the retention of a turnaround professional, or even seizure of the assets. The following covenants have returned to popularity in the wake of the 2007 credit crisis, and are likely to remain so for the foreseeable future.

Fixed Charge Coverage Ratio (FCCR) = Cash Flow / Fixed Charges

The *fixed charge coverage ratio* measures a company's ability to pay its fixed expenses, typically comprising interest expense, the current portion of long-term debt, capitalized leases, and rents. Lenders often insist on a minimum FCCR of, for example, 2.0x, indicating that cash flow divided by agreed-upon fixed charges must equal or exceed 2.0, with cash flow measured quarterly on a rolling four-quarter basis and adjusted for any unusual or one-time items. The rolling calculation means that one down quarter could throw a company previously above the 2.0x threshold below it. The company below, for example, remains healthily above the threshold before a sudden downturn brings it into violation in Q1 2007.

Funded Debt to EBITDA = Funded Debt / EBITDA

Like many such measures, this ratio uses *earnings before interest, taxes, depreciation, and amortization* (EBITDA) as a proxy for cash flow and compares it to the company's leverage as represented by *funded debt,* which consists of outstanding debt, any deferred purchases, and capitalized leases. Unlike the FCCR, banks require that this ratio not exceed a specified maximum ratio. Funded debt to EBITDA is expressed as a maximum ratio, such as 4.0x, indicating that funded debt may not exceed four times EBITDA for a similar four-quarter rolling period.

Current Ratio = Current Assets / Current Liabilities

The *current ratio* measures a company's ability to pay the liabilities it reports as due in the next twelve months, as represented under generally accepted accounting principles (GAAP) by its *current liabilities,* possibly excluding the current portion of long-term debt. It assumes that the company's reported current assets will be used to pay those expenses, so it simply sets a minimum threshold of current assets divided by current liabilities such as 1.5x. As a balance sheet measure, the covenant is typically measured as of a particular day, often the last day of a fiscal quarter. More stringent lenders may instead require use of the *quick ratio,* which uses only the truly liquid portion of current assets (cash, marketable securities, and accounts receivable). It is important to note that both such ratios rely heavily on GAAP, and as we will see in Chapter Four, GAAP is so flexible and accommodating to various interpretations of financial activity (and chicanery) that it is often of limited value in evaluating a company's true health.

Tangible Net Worth = Tangible Assets – Total Liabilities

This figure (also equal to total equity less intangible assets) represents a cushion of sorts for lenders, assuming that assets could be monetized at their book values to cover the company's liabilities. However, as noted here and in Chapter Four as well, GAAP accounting will differ significantly from actual market values, so this covenant should be treated with caution.

Freescale Semiconductor is an iconic example of a company that took advantage of frothy capital markets to take on more debt than it could service. Following its 2004 spinout from Motorola, a private equity consortium including Blackstone Group, Carlyle

Group, Permira Funds, and Texas Pacific Group purchased Freescale in late December 2006, with $9.5 billion of the $17.6 billion acquisition price financed by debt. This resulted in debt being six times earnings before interest and other charges, which became perilous when key end markets such as the automotive industry faced struggles of their own. Though Freescale's borrower-friendly loans have few covenants for the company to violate, it remains to be seen whether Freescale will weather the storm, or whether its private equity backers will have to inject additional capital into the business.

Insufficient Capital

Insufficient capital can be more deadly than excessive capital. If management fails to anticipate downturns in its end markets, it can find itself unable to raise capital precisely when it is most needed, forced to pursue difficult refinancing or the dreaded "consideration of strategic alternatives," which usually means "looking for a buyer." Public companies can find themselves shut off from the public equity and debt markets, leaving the potentially onerous Private Investment in Public Equities (PIPE) markets as its only option. Historically targeted by aggressive, often contentious hedge funds, PIPEs may provide short-term capital, but the equally short-term investment horizon of the highly negotiated, structured securities sold in a PIPE can take a company's stock price on a wild ride, as investors attempt to hedge their exposure to the faltering company through exotic derivatives and short positions. Deservedly or otherwise, such instruments earned a reputation as the financing of last resort in response to the so-called "toxic PIPEs" issued by failing dot-coms such as EToys and Exite@Home, which failed to realize that the terms of the deal allowed the purchasing hedge funds to short its common stock into the ground, causing delisting and further downward price pressure until the equity was essentially worthless, with the hedge fund owning a majority stake for only the price of their initial investment.[10] In this and countless other cases, the company's undercapitalization forced it into draconian refinancing terms that ultimately proved fatal.

After the old Aladdin Hotel and Casino in Las Vegas was purchased and demolished, poor management decisions plagued the

$1 billion replacement project. To save on drainage and construction costs, plans called for the construction of the casino floor nine feet above ground level, accessible only by stairs, with no main Las Vegas Boulevard access to the property, thus making it hard to find and even harder to see from the main hotel strip. Lack of casino operating experience created large losses from operations from the time the company opened its doors in August 2000, and marketing budgets suffered because the company had to use its cash flow to pay down debt. After a year spent pouring in $35 million in additional equity financing resulted in no improvements, GE Capital and GMAC threatened to repossess the slot machines and other gambling equipment, thereby forcing an emergency bankruptcy filing just a year after its grand opening.

Fraud and Dishonesty

Fraud and dishonesty have increasingly come to light in the wake of scandals such as Enron, Tyco, and WorldCom. Such misconduct ranges from the intentionally malicious—such as the rampant embezzlement and corruption that permeated Parmalat USA's Italian parent—to the more subtle manipulation of accounting information. Such creative accounting stems in large part from the flexibility of GAAP, which permits a wide array of interpretations of financial activities. Though designed to accommodate the vast differences in cash collections procedures between industries as dissimilar as cell phone service provision, railroads and skyscraper construction, GAAP's very flexibility renders it vulnerable to a creative manager willing to stuff a portion of next month's bookings into the last days of this month in a desperate attempt to hit Wall Street's earnings prediction and prevent a massive sell-off of his company's shares. Dealing with fraud requires two very different approaches, depending on its severity. As Chapter Seven shows, pervasive and blatant fraud like that seen at Parmalat may require a heavy hand, with public removals of guilty parties serving as repudiations of past malfeasance. Less extreme transgressions may benefit instead from a more balanced approach, with largely symbolic punishments taking a backseat to an organizationwide recommitment to honesty and truth in reporting. Sadly, relatively minor misbehaviors can start innocently enough, such as in the example of a manager under pressure to hit quarterly revenue expectations taking creative advantage of GAAP's liberties by stuffing distribution channels through shipping extra products to wholesalers and others, telling them they don't have to pay until they make the sales themselves. These practices often grow into significantly bolder, more devious deceptions that violate not only GAAP but also loan agreements, local laws, and SEC regulations. In the example of Enron, the company's arguably defensible use of mark-to-market accounting for its energy trading business ultimately incentivized management to exploit its leniency to create artificial paper profits, which in turn encouraged top executives to conceal troubled assets through the use of off-balance-sheet, special-purpose vehicles.[11]

Product Issues

Product issues can create product liability and recall issues, and potentially erode a company's reputation for quality and safety. Fast-food chain Jack in the Box spent years and tens of millions of dollars settling lawsuits for four deaths caused by its *E. coli* bacteria–infected hamburger patties in 1993, all because they failed to manage their supply chain properly. Toyota found how quickly a hard-earned reputation can be harmed when management failed to report acceleration and braking problems until 2010, thus forcing a massive product recall. However, products themselves need not fail to create product issues. Occasionally product portfolio mismanagement can confuse or discourage existing customers, who find the mere repackaging of an old product as "new and improved" deceptive and distasteful.

The mismanagement of the Twinkies brand was one of the elements that forced Hostess' owner, Interstate Bakeries, into bankruptcy in 2004. Management decided to reduce the amount of filling in the Twinkies, discontinue advertising, and create two new products: Teenage Mutant Ninja Turtle pies (two pieces of dough with a green sweet glop inside) and Bear Chomps (a cinnamon bun that looked like a bear's claw had slashed it). To reduce capital expenditures, the company manufactured all three of the products on the same production lines; this required frequent shutdowns, cleanings, and setups, which in turn slashed productivity. In addition, grocery stores balked at management's request for additional shelf space to accommodate these new product lines, thus forcing them to be jammed together on the shelves. Much to management's shock and dismay, the new products sold poorly, Twinkie sales dropped as well, and the cost of production increased.

Similar operations-driven product management decisions plagued General Motors in the 1980s, when executives ordered that the company streamline its manufacturing process by building all of its various brands on the same chassis. Though such uniform processes reduced costs and simplified procurement, those savings were offset by the subsequent brand dilution; each car now resembled the other. The competitive Lincoln Town Car brand launched a successful advertising campaign pointing out that all GM cars came to look alike. In one commercial, owners of Oldsmobile Ninety-Eights, Buick Electras, and Cadillac DeVilles waited impatiently for a valet attendant to find their car, growing confused as to which look-alike car belonged to whom. Finally, a Lincoln Town Car pulled up outside, with the narrator solemnly intoning, "the still distinctive Town Car," as its owner happily reclaimed his keys and drove away from the confused throng.

Product issues transcend mere design problems. When a new, young management team decided to create a more youthful image for Ann Taylor in the 1990s, they completely redesigned their product offerings. Though the new-look products did attract new shoppers to their stores, subsequent research showed that they alienated and lost more than three previously loyal customers for each new one they gained.

Gucci also alienated its customers when Maruzzio Gucci decided to boost margins by using cheaper materials while increasing prices on their products. Only an unusual management coup allowed the company to reverse course from this disastrous strategy; Maruzzio's own wife hired an assassin to put a hit on him, forcing the family to turn to a new management team. Murder is indisputably effective in removing an underperforming CEO, but let's stress right now, *this is not* a recommended turnaround technique. Besides illegality and immorality, it left the organization in shock and forced the new team to deal with even greater morale problems.

Conclusion

Although there are multiple external and internal causes for a company of any size to find itself in trouble, management's lack of foresight is most often to blame. Even when it recognizes the problems, management often fails to act or takes incorrect action. The next chapter outlines these phases and the early warning signs that management and others should have spotted to tell when an organization is in trouble.

Fair warning: Legal concepts are necessarily discussed during any coverage of this book's topics. No legal advice is intended, and one should contact one's own attorney for actual legal advice.

Reversing the Slide

Chapter One

The Phases of Decline and Early Warning Signs

In December of 2009, six partners in the accounting firm Ernst & Young paid $8.5 million to settle long-standing charges that they failed to see problems at Bally Total Fitness. Bally had overstated its stockholders' equity by $1.8 billion and had understated net losses in its business by approximately $100 million in each of several years. The company had recognized revenue it never actually received from initiation fees and prepaid dues. The partners were charged with failure to spot the warning signs at Bally as it slid from profitability to bankruptcy, but the firm itself paid an even higher price.

The longer such problems go unsolved, the harder it is to turn around a company. To determine the effort needed to turn around any organization, one must understand the degree of trouble and how quickly time is running out; an organizational distress curve illustrates this concept. To help determine where an organization is on the curve, there are early warning signs that signal to a board of directors, investors, and management that action is needed.

The Phases of Decline

Regardless of the cause or nature of a distressed company's struggles, it will invariably find itself somewhere on the curve in Figure 1.1, which demonstrates how companies slide down a slippery slope through five phases: the *blinded, inaction, faulty action, crisis,* and *dissolution phases*.[1] If the company cannot fix its problems in

Figure 1.1. The Phases of Organizational Distress Curve

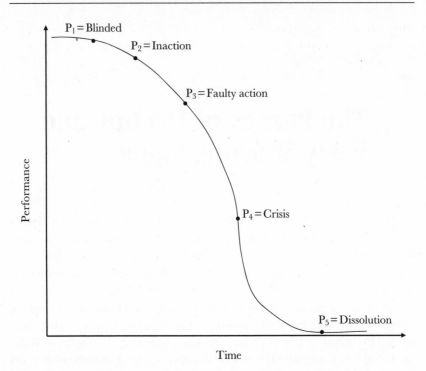

any one phase, they will eventually fall to the next one, with less time to repair the damage and greater effort required to do so.

Companies typically begin in the *blinded phase*. Revenues may have stagnated or even fallen off slightly, but in general, the company has not yet recognized the crisis. Management often writes off one bad quarter—or even two or more—as a blip, only too happy to assume that business will recover in the coming weeks or months. They attribute decreases in sales or profits to seasonal or cyclical variations or temporary customer fickleness, blissfully ignorant of the potentially impending catastrophe. Our examination of Electronic Data Systems in this chapter shows that EDS lay in the blinded phase for years when it overlooked the explosion in popularity of the client/server architecture that would undermine its core competency in the traditional mainframe architectures it served.

Companies in the blinded phase can languish there for months or even for years, as represented by the smooth slope of the curve there. If management fails to take corrective action, however, the company will eventually enter the *inaction phase* when growth continues to stagnate, competitors steal market share, or cash reserves begin to run low. The company is likely to remain fundamentally sound, and may even be profitable, but its problems have grown to the point at which they cannot be denied. Despite the clear need for action, however, companies often linger in the inaction phase, their inertial resistance to change inspiring irrational hope that things will turn around on their own. For example, Pier 1 took years to react to price competition from Wal-Mart and Target. Such managers often invoke images of past recessions weathered, crying, "This company has suffered through far worse than this," hoping that their previous run of luck continues. The examination of the Middleby Corporation in Chapter Four will demonstrate a company in the inaction phase, as the manufacturer of diversified food equipment remained passive throughout the late 1990s despite excessive concentration of sales to a few very large customers and four years of investment in an expensive, unsuccessful product line.

Other examples of inaction include Schwinn management ignoring the growing consumer preference for lighter mountain bikes, insisting that "people want to ride bikes, not carry them."[2] IBM exhibited comparable denial, saying for years that the Internet was "a university thing."[3]

Sometimes those companies do rebound, but they just as often do not, and instead slide further down the organizational distress curve into the *faulty action phase*. At this point, the company's problems have grown in severity to the point that management is spurred to action, but due either to inaccurate information or incompetent leaders, these proposed remedies only make the situation worse.

It is not always easy to distinguish inaction from faulty action. A young friend and fellow turnaround professional who prided himself on fast action, once found himself on a new engagement as a chief restructuring officer (CRO) for a struggling company, and decided to take matters into his own hands. Convinced that employees at one of the plants had gotten lazy, he showed up unannounced during the night shift, determined to ferret out the malingerers. He was convinced his actions that night would solve all the company's personnel problems.

He arrived just before the official break time and saw one young man leaning against the wall, daydreaming while everyone else worked arduously. Furious, the CRO demanded the plant manager stop all work and gather the employees together.

In his anger, he emptied his wallet, taking more than $400 in travel money and jamming it into the hands of the young man. "That," he exclaimed, "is all you'll get in severance pay. You wanna sue me? Go ahead! You'll just lose all your legal bills. Get out. Now!"

The young man glanced around, hesitant and confused, and left. With great satisfaction, the CRO measured the shocked look on the other workers' faces—precisely the desired reaction—before asking the plant manager, "What did that loafer do, anyway? The rest of these people should be able to take up the slack."

"He was the pizza delivery guy," the plant manager replied. "He was waiting for me to bring him a tip."

The story quickly became legend among turnaround professionals.

By contrast, when Jamie Dimon took over as CEO of Bank One in Chicago, he sent a clearer, more effective message to the company's executive team. The executive floor was undergoing an expensive renovation and interior decorating. Dimon ordered all work to stop, leaving several executive offices partly spackled or wallpapered for almost a year. That message rang loud and clear to all the bank's employees: Dimon expected everyone to watch spending. His plan to avoid faulty action worked as he went on to take well-planned immediate action to reduce costs while increasing revenue through more responsive service to the bank's customers.

Sara Lee's failed turnaround efforts in 1997 and 2000 both represent faulty action, as the company remained decentralized in critical product and marketing efforts, causing inefficiencies in achieving scale in purchasing raw materials and winning retail space. Similarly, Blockbuster continued to open stores and even attempted to merge with Circuit City (which later liquidated in bankruptcy court), saying that customers wanted to visit stores to make movie rental decisions despite the growing success of the Netflix model. Borders (a spinoff from Kmart) thought the answer to Amazon was to expand their chain internationally, which proved a painfully regrettable decision. Both Blockbuster and Borders focused on continuing and even expanding their business model in the face of a changing competitive environment. They never reexamined their strategy or core competencies, methods described later in this book.

One most often finds faulty action when executives perform across-the-board downsizing without first reexamining the company's strategy, reengineering, or seeking niche markets. These concepts are all discussed in later chapters.

Sustained faulty action will drive a company into the *crisis phase*. At this point, the company has probably tripped covenants with its lenders and is bleeding cash. Employees are jumping ship, suppliers insist on cash in advance or cash on delivery payment terms, and auditors raise genuine concerns about the company's ability to continue as a going concern. Companies often retain an investment bank to "consider strategic alternatives," or even direct their outside counsel to begin drafting documents for a bankruptcy filing. The examination of Winn-Dixie's 2004 bankruptcy filing in Chapter Six will demonstrate a company "securely" in the crisis phase. American newspapers were also in the crisis phase for years, and still did nothing but cut the people that gather and create its content.

The crisis phase represents a company's last chance to salvage itself and get back on course to profitability. Should all restructuring and turnaround efforts fail, it will descend into the fifth and final *dissolution phase*, which typically requires a bankruptcy filing. Unable to continue as a going concern, the company goes through painful changes or liquidates its assets and distributes them according to the absolute priority rule that is examined in Chapter Six. This is when the sheriff and locksmiths arrive.

These phases present a valuable framework, because study after study has shown that the earlier a company recognizes itself in one of these phases and launches a turnaround effort, the greater the likelihood of its success. As companies slide down the organizational distress curve, they find themselves in a rapidly tightening noose. In order to maintain breathing space for the greatest number of stakeholders, early detection through the monitoring of the warning signs detailed in this chapter in the section "Early Warning Signs" is critical. If a management team recognizes its problems and begins addressing them earlier, it can take action outside of an atmosphere of panic, before a cash crisis severely restricts its options and before employees, customers, and suppliers begin abandoning it.

Moreover, early detection allows a company to monetize assets at greater than fire sale prices. Whether they decide to pursue a sale of the entire company—perhaps to a "greater fool"—or simply sell a division or product line, management will invariably receive a better price if the market does not yet perceive them as distressed. Similarly, if management settles upon additional financing or refinancing as the solution, it will find lenders significantly more receptive to a company having only experienced mild setbacks rather than one in full-on crisis mode.

Perhaps most important, early action limits the likelihood of managers finding themselves personally liable to stakeholders for the mismanagement of the company. Many American courts hold that a board of directors' fiduciary liabilities shift when a company enters a nebulously defined "zone of insolvency." Some courts define the zone as when the market value of a company's assets is less than its book value of liabilities. Others say it's when the company cannot meet its debts when due. It exists when the organization is in the crisis phase even before hitting the dissolution phase on the distress curve.

Previously bound in their duties exclusively to equity holders, the board's duties shift to include other stakeholders—most notably, to creditors and to the "entity"—once the company enters the zone of insolvency. Should the company subsequently enter bankruptcy, courts will examine transactions as much as five years prior to the filing, particularly those dealing with company insiders, and might possibly void such transactions as fraudulent or preferential. Even outside the context of a bankruptcy filing, the risk of director liability has grown in the past decade, with some institutional investors placing "bounties" on directors and officers by offering a much higher percentage contingency fee to lawyers for every dollar of recovery that comes out of the personal assets of corporate executives and directors who are named as individual defendants. The recent economic downturn and foolish acts by executives have even threatened to weaken that panacea of directors and officers accused of wrongdoing: the business judgment rule.

The business judgment rule used to protect almost every decision made, as it assumed each individual used his or her business knowledge, even if the result appeared stupid in hindsight. The officers and directors of Bally couldn't use the business judgment defense, however, when they ignored the warning signs that the company's policies of high-pressure sales tactics and changing accounting practices were leading to serious problems.

Enron's directors also used the business judgment rule as their primary defense, saying they knew nothing of the deceit created by Ken Lay and his staff. That defense fell and the directors paid millions out of their own pockets when the institutional investors paid a bounty to contingency law firms for getting money out of the directors' pockets rather than the company's insurance policies. The motive was revenge for failing to do their jobs and watch for the warning signs.

At a meeting with institutional investors in late 2008, Justice Carolyn Berger of the Delaware Supreme Court suggested that she and her colleagues—the de facto standard for American business law given the concentration of companies incorporated in the state—would also consider limiting the protection afforded by the business judgment rule with respect to questions of executive compensation. This potential threat to executives of troubled companies, who after all, are the only ones typically sued for professional liability, makes it more important than ever to recognize the earliest possible warning signs of distress and take action immediately.

Early Warning Signs

In order to prevent these internal and external causes of distress from festering until it is too late, effective management teams must proactively look for potential challenges, because the sooner they are identified, the greater the likelihood that management can address them successfully. Companies should remain vigilant by using four major analyses: management analysis, trend analysis, industry analysis, and diagnostic and prediction models.

Management Analysis

As the most common cause of internal distress, it should come as no surprise that management of a struggling company should be subject to a rigorous analysis to determine whether it has the personnel and skills in place to handle challenges. First, one should examine whether management is paying attention to critical measures of financial performance, such as true cash flow and working capital management. Without management keeping a keen eye on such metrics, even the healthiest of companies will falter. Many small companies have charismatic CEOs who grow the business through sheer force of will, but who lack adequate financial expertise and all too often resist hiring someone who can provide those complementary skills. Similarly, many middle market companies can coast along through times of prosperity with an absentee principal who prefers to focus on leisure or other business activities. This can put undue stress on middle managers in a downturn or, in a family-held business, on inexperienced second- or third-generation participants in the business who lack the entrepreneur's passion or insight.

Another sign of an unprepared management team is a failure to take responsibility for the firm's performance. If management is constantly pointing fingers at events ostensibly beyond its control, or pitting internal divisions against each other (with manufacturing blaming sales for slow market penetration, sales blaming finance for inadequate funding, and so on), it is probably hiding the real source of problems: itself. Ford and GM were well known for this.

Caterpillar, however, decided to break down the organizational silos, forcing everyone to work together. The silos were based on functional areas such as manufacturing, purchasing, and marketing, each with a senior executive reporting to the CEO. This structure prevented information sharing and individual performance accountability, such that product and plant managers had no idea whether their particular unit or plant was profitable or not. By breaking the silos and scattering the employees into newly created profit centers, behavior changed. Employees were held accountable for results, given agreed-upon profit goals as well as the information and tools they needed, with compensation programs developed to reward them for good performance. As a result, the company went from losing $1 million a day to record profitability.

Constant changes in direction similarly indicate a management team incapable of guiding a company through difficult times. The scattershot acquisition strategy of companies such as Sara Lee constitutes one example of such indecision, which distracts a company from its core competencies. Worse, it obfuscates the company's core principles from stakeholders, such that employees never know which missive from management to follow or whether it will simply be cast aside in six months for a new management fad.

All of these problems tend to be reflected in one difficult-to-measure but critical metric: employee morale. It may require diligent, granular interviews with employees down and across the organizational chart to determine, but once a morale problem is discovered, it must be addressed immediately before it spreads. Turnarounds are challenging enough without the company's best and brightest employees jumping ship for a competitor that they consider more stable.

Trend Analysis

One of the best ways to determine whether a company is heading for trouble is to analyze the trends in its operating and financial performance. In postwar Japan, Dr. W. Edwards Deming used trend analysis as a way to help then-struggling Japanese car manufacturers produce high-quality products, with the key observation that a trend is often more important than the actual numbers. He proved that constantly measuring critical components and gaps between parts can show a trend that signals that adjustments can be made before any faulty cars are produced. His statistical techniques were later applied to many business control areas.

Table 1.1 shows the deterioration of several key financial performance indicators at Sara Lee from 2001 to 2007, during which

Table 1.1. Trend Analysis at Sara Lee, 2001–2007[4]

	2001	2002	2003	2004	2005	2006	2007
Interest Coverage[1]	5.9x	5.2x	5.9x	5.9x	5.0x	3.5x	2.7x
Gross Margin	37.4%	38.5%	38.9%	37.9%	36.2%	37.1%	38.5%
Operating Income Margin[2]	9.6%	8.9%	9.1%	8.4%	7.5%	6.8%	5.7%
EBITDA Margin[3]	10.0%	11.2%	12.8%	12.5%	11.5%	11.3%	10.3%
Net Margin from Continuing Operations	9.6%	5.7%	6.6%	6.5%	3.8%	2.6%	3.5%
Return on Average Assets[4]	14.7%	8.4%	8.1%	8.2%	5.0%	2.8%	3.2%

[1] EBIT/gross interest expense.
[2] Excludes extraordinary items.
[3] Excludes gain on sale of coach brand and impairment charges.
[4] Based on income from continuing operations.

time Sara Lee attempted to rebound from its disastrous acquisition binge. Note that even without comparing these figures to comparable companies in the same industry, an astute observer can discern that the company is in trouble, for with few exceptions, the figures all began slipping in 2002, stabilized or recovered slightly in 2003, and then resumed their slide for the next four years. Many companies slide much faster.

For public companies, of course, share prices and volumes can indicate growing concern in the marketplace. Large blocks of shares dumped on the market immediately following upticks caused by positive news releases can indicate faltering faith in the company's prospects by institutional shareholders who wish to reduce their exposure. However, share price itself is typically a lagging indicator of distress rather than a leading one, so investors must look deeper within the company to determine its outlook.

The ratios referred to in Box 1 serve as a solid starting point for trend watching. Because in a turnaround one must "manage to cash" as opposed to using GAAP principles, the more stringent cash flow and quick ratios are typically more representative of a company's true liquidity. However, even these metrics are not immune to manipulation, for an aggressive manager can artificially increase accounts receivable (increasing the quick ratio) by stuffing the distribution channel, by selling to less and less creditworthy customers, or by simply changing accounting assumptions.

Regardless of how close to or far from its lender-stipulated thresholds a company is, consecutive quarters of declining current ratio or increasing funded debt to EBITDA should cause concern. The strength of such trend analysis is that it compares a company's performance to its own history, rather than to competitive companies whose idiosyncrasies may make them less than perfectly comparable. For example, a computer or copier manufacturer that also provides post-sale maintenance and repair services to its customers will have higher asset utilization ratios as compared to a pure-play manufacturer in the same industry, for the services component of its revenues may require significantly fewer hard assets to remain operational. Trend analysis uses internal metrics to ensure that all comparisons are made on an apples-to-apples basis over time.

In addition to the metrics frequently used for covenants listed in Box 1, managers should carefully monitor the following profitability and asset management metrics:

Profitability indicators

- *Gross margin declines* should raise immediate red flags; they require examination into whether they occur at the company, divisional, or product-line level. Eroding margins can indicate a larger problem such as increased competition, increasing returns or product failures, or growing consolidation among customers. It's especially important in a turnaround situation to look at *actual* gross margins rather than merely the margin reported by the sales or accounting departments. Short-sighted sales representatives giving back-end discounts, improper allowances for returns or volume incentive rebates, and inaccurate allocation of shipping or overhead costs can distort the company's perception of its true gross margin, thus masking such declines.

- *Profit margin declines* may result from a decrease in top-line revenues, or an inability to pass on increased input costs to customers. In addition, they could result from a negative change in the product mix, with demand shifting from higher- to lower-margin products, possibly indicating cannibalization by the cheaper product.
- *Sales declines* can result from a general loss in market share, competitive pressures, changes in customer preferences, or quality problems.
- *Negative cash flow* quarters are also a significant cause for concern, as they can quickly cause liquidity shortages. It is important to look to true cash flow rather than EBITDA or a GAAP proxy for cash flow, for it is too easy to use such measures to hide the company's true ability to generate cash.
- *Declining tangible net worth* indicates a company's dwindling asset base, or a stagnant asset base outpaced by the company's growth in additional liabilities. By stripping out intangible assets such as goodwill, noncompete agreements, and trade secrets, a manager can get a clearer picture of the company's actual cash-generating assets.

Asset management indicators

- *Growth in accounts receivable* faster than real sales increases can indicate a host of problems, as it implies that a company is incurring costs in manufacturing and delivering products without the corresponding inflow of cash to keep the company afloat. This could result from slower turnover when struggling customers try to extend payment terms to conserve their own cash, or from an increase in receivables dilution. So-called "big box" retailers such as Wal-Mart have earned a notorious reputation for finding the slightest problem with shipped goods—a label out of place or a pallet missing the proper identifying tags—to shave off as much as 10 percent of the agreed-upon price for the shipment. This taking of discounts after the fact is known as dilution, and it can strangle a cash-hungry company. Meanwhile, growth in accounts receivable exceeding a company's sales growth can indicate that sales staff are selling to less and less creditworthy customers, perhaps desperate to move product out the door. Finally, aged receivables (those older than, for example, ninety days) can point to serious problems lurking around the corner, such as deadbeat customers, customer disputes regarding product quality, or even fraud.

- *Inventory levels* must be monitored religiously to ensure that existing inventory has not become obsolete. Frequently, companies fall in love with their own products, seemingly content to let them sit on the plant floor taking up space even if the company has overproduced a certain model, received a high number of returns on a defective product, or customer preferences have shifted to a new competitor. Such companies may be afraid to liquidate inventory because it could result in a write-down, particularly if they are personally compensated based on GAAP measures such as net income. Managers must pay close attention to changes in the rate of inventory turnover and in inventory composition, and make the necessary adjustments both to the balance sheet and to the physical location of the inventory. For example, Schwinn's inventories exploded despite flagging sales, partly because its Budapest plant's low quality killed sales. Schwinn's local advertisements, translated into Hungarian, read, "Buy Schwinn bikes: They're not as bad as you think." Under Hungarian law, the plant had to remain operational regardless of sales, so workers simply threw the poorly made bikes into the river behind the plant.

- *Accounts payable* that increase faster than sales and total cost of goods sold indicate a company has begun stretching out its payments, which could make it more difficult to retain suppliers in the future.

- *Revolving loan* balances can show a company's ability to finance itself through cash generation instead of borrowing. If the company's revolver balance is increasing (and it is not related to or is greater in magnitude than the usual seasonal increases) and it is faced with decreasing availability, then a near-term cash crunch is highly likely. As shown in Chapter Three, Sunbeam's increasing revolver balance should have served as a warning that CEO "Chainsaw" Al Dunlap's claims to have sold large numbers of outdoor gas grills during the winter was false.

Industry and Product Analysis

In addition to monitoring trends in a company's own performance, managers should use benchmarking to see where a company stands in relation to its peers. Though no set of comparables will ever be perfectly equivalent, it is valuable to see how a company is performing compared to the best, mean, or median performers in its field. For example, Figure I.2 in the Introduction clearly shows that Sara Lee's sales, general, and administrative overhead costs (SG&A) as a percentage of sales had grown to among the highest in its peer group, suggesting that it should examine ways to reduce corporate overhead. While it might not ever reach the 15.9 percent figure attained by Conagra, it should certainly aim to reach the median range of 21 to 24 percent achieved by Kraft, Heinz, and Campbell Soup.

Other industry analyses can determine the likelihood of performance deterioration by measuring the concentration of customers' buying power and the company's sensitivity to increased input costs. Typically, a Porter's Five Forces analysis serves as a solid groundwork, examining supplier power, technology development, buyer power, new market entrants, and competition. Note that a company's distress makes it increasingly important to conduct the analysis not as a snapshot of the industry in time, but rather one that looks to the next twelve months.[5]

Diagnostic and Prediction Models

Finally, several diagnostic and prediction models exist to assist in the analysis of a company's situation. Naturally, these models work on a "garbage in, garbage out" basis, so any inputs, such as financial data, must be heavily scrutinized to ensure that they drive the proper conclusions. (See Box 2, this chapter, for an example of how creative accounting information can skew reported results.) This can be especially difficult at private companies, where accounting controls are often more lax, and cozy (or even familial) relationships between the board and the CFO can slow or block the flow of information.

Once the reliability of financial information is verified, managers can use the most famous predictor of financial distress: the

Z-score, developed by Dr. Edward Altman, a professor of finance at New York University. Altman created this analytical tool by running a massive logistic regression of various financial data against a binary variable to indicate whether a firm would file for bankruptcy protection. Altman's work ultimately resulted in the following equation, which produces a single "Z-score" that predicts the likelihood of the company filing for bankruptcy within two years.

The Z-Score Formula

$$Z = 1.2(X1) + 1.4(X2) + 3.3(X3) + 0.6(X4) + 0.999(X5)$$

where

X1 = Working capital divided by total assets

X2 = Retained earnings divided by total assets

X3 = EBIT divided by total assets

X4 = Market value of preferred and common equity divided by total liabilities (book value acceptable if market value is unavailable)

X5 = Sales divided by total assets

Altman has since added to this original model, tailoring it to privately held companies, with the following result:

$$Z = 0.717(X1) + 0.847(X2) + 3.107(X3) + 0.420(X4) + 0.998(X5)$$

As you can see, each of the five components (X1–X5) of the Z-score represent internal ratios measuring the company's liquidity, leverage, profitability, market valuation, and asset turnover. The final outcome is the Z-score, which practitioners can apply to the matrix in Table 1.2 to determine the likelihood of bankruptcy.

Altman has since determined that U.S. businesses have grown more risky than when he first created the Z-score in 1968, and so he has fine-tuned this three-zone model into one that assigns a bond rating equivalent (BRE) to a range of scores. These scores have changed over time, as pictured in Table 1.3.

The power of the Z-score stems from its basis on empirical data, which has fueled its popularity as an indication of financial

Table 1.2. Original Z-Score Interpretations

Z-Score Results and Interpretations	Score		
	Publicly Held Manufacturing Company	Privately Held Manufacturing Company	Non-Manufacturing and Emerging Market Companies
Low Probability of Bankruptcy	≥3.075	≥2.90	≥2.60
Company Requires Monitoring	1.875–3.075	1.23–2.90	1.10–2.60
Insolvency Likely Within 12 Months	≤1.875	≤1.23	≤1.10

Table 1.3. Revised Bond Rating Equivalent Z-Score Interpretations

Rating	2004–2005	1996–2001	1992–1995
AAA	5.31	5.60	4.80
AA	4.99	4.73	4.15
A	4.22	3.74	3.87
BBB	3.37	2.81	2.75
BB	2.27	2.38	2.25
B	1.79	1.80	1.87
B–	1.34	1.31	1.38
CCC+	0.90	0.82	0.89
CCC	0.45	0.33	0.40
D	−0.19	−0.20	0.05

Source: Cole-Gomolski, Barb, "Client/Server Outsources Changing Pricing Methods," Computerworld, June 28, 1999.

Box 2: The Effects of Financial Shenanigans

Despite the reform efforts of Sarbanes-Oxley in the wake of the Enron and Arthur Andersen accounting scandals at the turn of the century, GAAP remains a set of accounting rules so flexible as to allow for significant manipulation without violating its tenets. In a turnaround, a manager must therefore "manage to cash," or focus entirely on the activities that denote actual cash flowing into or out of the company, instead of on noncash expenses that can inflate or deflate GAAP earnings. In the example company in Table 1.4, creative accounting allowed the firm to misstate its true financial position without technically violating GAAP rules.

Sales Miscategorization

Management categorized $117 million on the sale of properties as revenues, rather than one-time divestitures and decreases in PP&E (property, plant, and equipment). Instead, they artificially boosted top-line sales by some 20 percent.

Changing D&A Assumptions

During a rough fiscal year, the company lengthened its depreciation and amortization schedules, decreasing those expenses to boost earnings before interest and taxes (EBIT) by $131 million and asset values, and retained earnings by $14.3 million.

Off-Balance Sheet Liabilities

This company used significant off-balance sheet liabilities to finance operations, thereby increasing the book value of equity while decreasing short-term liabilities by $52.5 million and total liabilities by $112.8 million.

Aged Receivables

Management's refusal to write off receivables much older than 90 days—in some cases those owed by companies already in Chapter 11—resulted in a reported accounts receivable figure some $20.4 million higher than the amount it could reasonably expect to collect.

(Continued)

Box 2: (Continued)

Capitalized Expenses

In an effort to boost EBITDA, management decided to capitalize customer acquisition costs rather than expense them. This creates an artificially high asset base, EBIT, and retained earnings.

Correcting for these shenanigans paints a very different picture of the company, as represented in Table 1.4.

Table 1.4.

		Adjustment	
Current Assets	227.0	(20.4)	206.6
Current Liabilities	167.7		220.2
Working Capital	59.3		(13.6)
Total Assets	905.0	(34.7)	870.3
Retained Earings	197.1	(131.3)	65.8
EBIT	157.2	(131.3)	25.9
Book Value of Equity	16.8		(130.7)
Total Liabilities	888.2	112.8	1,001.0
Sales	695.8	(117.0)	578.8
	Reported		Adjusted
X1	0.066		−0.016
X2	0.218		0.076
X3	0.174		0.030
X4	0.019		−0.131
X5	0.769		0.665
Z	1.737		0.772

stability. The metric has become so widespread that Bloomberg terminals now list Z-scores for every company that files its financial statements publicly, and Altman himself testified before the House Financial Services Committee during the hearings on whether General Motors required a governmental bailout. Upon running his Z-score analysis, Altman determined that upon

Figure 1.2. DuPont Analysis

$$\text{ROE} = \frac{\text{Net Income}}{\text{Equity}} = \frac{\text{Net Profit}}{\text{Pre-Tax Profit}} \times \frac{\text{Pre-Tax Profit}}{\text{EBIT}} \times \frac{\text{EBIT}}{\text{Sales}} \times \frac{\text{Sales}}{\text{Assets}} \times \frac{\text{Assets}}{\text{Equity}}$$

| | Tax Burden | Interest Burden: 1.0 for a company with no interest-bearing debt | Operating Profit Margin | Asset Turnover | Leverage Ratio |

emerging from bankruptcy under the restructuring plan then on the table, General Motors would be likely to file for bankruptcy again (so-called "Chapter 22"), so the reorganization plan was supposed to be expanded and improved until the reformed entity would be more viable in preparation for an initial public offering (IPO).

Practitioners can also use the DuPont analysis to examine the sources of a company's return on equity (ROE) to reveal both strengths and areas of weakness. This calculation is pictured in Figure 1.2.

Each of these five components provides helpful information as to how well the company performs a financial task, particularly in conjunction with the trend analysis and benchmarking already described. If a disproportionate amount of the company's ROE is coming from the leverage ratio, for example, it is poised to suffer disproportionately in a downturn. Similarly, an asset turnover ratio below industry norms would suggest that the company is using its assets inefficiently, and should either devise a way to use them to drive additional revenues or strip out the assets that do not support sales.

A related measure of profitability is ROA, or return on assets, which is simply calculated by dividing net income by total assets. A downward trend obviously signals impending peril and should be compared to other companies in the same industry. A general rule of thumb for *all* industries, however, is that ROA should exceed the company's weighted average cost of capital (WACC). If ROA falls below WACC, the company must determine whether it makes sense to continue in certain business lines or to undergo an organizationwide overhaul and refocusing.

Performing such analyses would have revealed looming financial difficulties at Canadian cinema chain Cineplex Odeon in the late 1980s. Careful review of the company's financials shows that CEO Garth Drabinsky was steering the company toward bankruptcy and hiding it through a variety of financial shenanigans. The company's board of directors ignored the warning signs of accounting method changes, plummeting ROA, low Z-score, and others, and the company later went into bankruptcy along with another theater company with which it had merged. A colorful character who once barbwired the entrance to a competitor's office building under cover of darkness, Drabinsky was later indicted for "cooking the books" at Live Entertainment and will serve seven years in prison for fraud and forgery.

Finally, there are several other indicators that can identify a company entering a period of distress. Excessive staff turnover suggests that employees are fleeing a sinking ship, and unfortunately, those who leave are typically the best, most qualified employees because it is they who can most easily find comparable positions elsewhere. Aside from the costs of plummeting morale that result from good people leaving, such turnover can create a painful cycle of lost organizational knowledge, thus making it difficult to train new hires to replace those who have left. In addition, newly constructed lavish headquarters during a period of declining profitability should serve as a red flag by indicating that management has become complacent, distracted, or overly concerned with perquisites rather than creating shareholder value.

Companies who have recently changed accounting firms also deserve scrutiny, as such changes often result from a quarrel over the veracity of the company's financial information. The auditor may have gone so far as to notify the company that they would have no choice but to issue a letter questioning the firm's ability to continue as a going concern, thereby prompting their dismissal. Threats of delisting are another obvious sign of distress for public companies, as they result from failing to meet minimum share price and volume levels.

There are many examples of companies that slide down the entire distress curve, in spite of warning signs along the way. Chapter Six of this book examines a number of them. By contrast, there are companies that manage to stop the plunge, even if it takes multiple tries. One example is EDS.

The Turnaround at EDS

Launching the company in 1968 with a $1,000 loan from his wife, Ross Perot received seventy-eight refusal letters before landing his first client for Electronic Data Systems. He persevered, and the company's success resulted in its $2.5 billion acquisition by General Motors (GM) in 1984.

After years of success, EDS began a multiyear slide down the distress curve. EDS's historical expertise in legacy mainframe systems and their programming languages created a strategic mismatch with the rapid adoption of the client/server model in the 1990s[6] and blinded management to the wide-scale introduction of personal computers into the workplace. GM spun off EDS in 1996, signing a ten-year, below-market contract with its former subsidiary.

During the Internet explosion of the late 1990s, EDS quickly came to represent a plodding, technologically backward relic of the dismissively labeled "old economy." EDS also failed to move quickly on the massive outsourcing contracts awarded to address the problems anticipated from reaching the year 2000 to avoid causing computers that abbreviated years with double-digits to malfunction.

Competitors swooped in to take advantage of these strategic blunders. This competitive pressure resulted in steady market share declines for EDS. In response, EDS began bidding more aggressively on the increasingly frequent multibillion-dollar "mega-deals." Lack of bidding discipline by EDS management— particularly CEO Les Alberthal—had focused on just getting contracts signed, no matter what the profitability; they would worry about red ink later.[7]

Causes and Warning Signs Under Les Alberthal

Several warning signs should have alerted observers that EDS faced an upcoming crisis in the mid to late 1990s; these can be grouped according to the four types of analysis that could have been used to detect them.[8]

- *Management analysis.* The most common cause of internal distress is weak management. The complexity of EDS's operations clearly overwhelmed Alberthal, such that he overlooked critical changes in the marketplace. Moreover, his detachment from the workforce grew, as exemplified by his inexplicable decision to cut the phone lines in his office to prevent distractions or complaints.
- *Trend analysis.* EDS significantly underperformed during one of the greatest sustained bull markets in history, at a time when competitive technology services providers thrived. Operating cash flows stagnated and operating margins plummeted to 6.6 percent despite a booming economy during this time. Meanwhile, debt increased at an 18 percent annual rate and accounts receivable increased at a 20 percent rate, both much faster than any growth in sales. These trends clearly denote an organization on the decline.
- *Industry analysis.* Due largely to weak, disconnected management, EDS completely missed critical industry changes such as the emergence of the client/server architecture, the run-up to the Y2K bug, and the Internet explosion. As a result, EDS's market share plunged to just 7 percent in 1999.

In response, the California Public Employees' Retirement System (CalPERS), a large shareholder, added EDS to its annual list of the worst corporate performers based on corporate governance and stock performance, and began publicly questioning the board's role in EDS's governance.[9] With morale tumbling and shareholders crying out for a change, EDS's board of directors decided a new CEO was needed. Questions should be raised as to why the board failed to take action sooner, for it took a revolt by shareholders to prompt Alberthal's removal.

The board then hired Richard Brown as CEO. Brown came to EDS from Cable & Wireless PLC, where he had negotiated and integrated twenty-one merger transactions in just twenty-nine months as its CEO. Brown's aggressive pursuit of acquisitions had left Cable & Wireless's cash flows flat during his tenure despite a 27 percent growth rate in top-line revenues and a 7 percent growth in net income, as acquisitions depleted the company's cash balance by some $2.5 billion during his tenure. None of this bothered the EDS board at the time.

At EDS, Brown found an organization whose rapid growth had created a sprawling, inefficient operation with forty-eight distinct business units. The company's internal complexity frustrated employees and confused clients, who often found themselves receiving sales calls from several different units with duplicative and sometimes conflicting offerings, thus revealing EDS's failure to go to market with a clear, cohesive strategy.

Brown found that he could not access monthly financials because of poor internal systems. He even found e-mailing all of EDS's 140,000 employees impossible, as haphazard growth had led to their using sixteen different e-mail systems, including free online services such as Hotmail and client systems.[10]

Amid the chaos resulting from his ironic efforts to bring a technology company kicking and screaming into the Internet age, he described his four-point plan to return the company to profitability. First, he vowed to push EDS's revenue growth. Second, he would pair this growth with nearly $1.4 billion in cost-cutting, including laying off employees, selling half of its corporate aircraft, and eliminating its 2,000-vehicle executive car program.[11] Third, he would personally oversee the GM contract and stabilize its decreasing margins. Fourth, he would focus on organizational change.

Already depressed by EDS's fall in its traditional IT outsourcing business, employee morale suffered further as Brown laid off a total of 15,300. Meanwhile, short-term financial performance suffered as Brown's turnaround resulted in more than $1 billion in recorded restructuring charges and asset write-downs in 1999 alone.

However, just as Brown tried to lead the company back to growth and profitability, storm clouds brewed on the horizon, with critical mistakes by the new CEO ultimately undermining EDS's competitiveness, plunging EDS down the faulty action phase of the distress curve. EDS failed to anticipate the growth of Indian outsourcing and allowed new entrants to gain significant footholds in a market that demonstrated explosive growth both before and after the turn of the millennium. By overlooking the rise of offshoring, Brown's EDS found its market share slipping in the face of brutal pricing pressure.

On October 6, 2000, EDS won the largest IT outsourcing contract in the history of the U.S. federal government: the Navy/Marine Corps Intranet, or NMCI. The eight-year, $6.9 billion project sought to integrate 400,000 workstations, 500,000 laptops, and 1,000 internal networks across one secure, integrated voice and data platform, with universal sign-on capabilities and a single, unified help desk.

Unfortunately, warning signs emerged even before the project's launch. Eager to win such a high-cachet project, Brown had insisted on a razor-thin 4 percent margin, cutting the initial $8.6 billion bid by $1.7 billion despite the CFO's admonition that the NMCI contract would not be profitable. Even more ominously, the revamped bid included deferred payment terms that required Navy approval for any disbursement. In effect, EDS would have to invest $1.9 billion in infrastructure merely to begin the project, would pay out cash for many years after that, such as buying and holding thousands of laptops for two years (during which time they became obsolete), but could not receive payment until the Navy expressed its satisfaction with end-user systems.[12] In order to fund these payments, EDS levered up its balance sheet, increasing total debt from $1.2 billion at Brown's hiring in 1999 to $5.4 billion in 2002.

Then the project's execution went awry. Many end users expressed such frustration with the project's delays and unfriendly user interface that EDS created that they relied on commercial e-mail services for official communiqués rather than their NMCI-issued accounts.[13] As you might expect, an organization as security-conscious as the Navy was not shy about expressing its dissatisfaction with EDS's performance.

Other projects also went wrong. EDS's eleven-year $6 billion network services arrangement with WorldCom left it with significant exposure to the telecom's bankruptcy. A Texas attorney general's report concluded an EDS subsidiary had violated its contract with the Texas Medicaid program and had engaged in improper accounting, double-billing, and inappropriate payments to providers,[14] which called into question EDS's ability to retain contracts with the sixteen other state Medicaid programs it listed as clients. There were also market concerns over the company's exposure to the airline industry's collapse—particularly a complicated airplane leaseback arrangement with United Airlines that unraveled when the airline filed for bankruptcy in December, costing EDS $40 million in write-downs.

Brown refused to acknowledge even the possibility of problems, going so far as to single naysayers out as "quitters." Delivering bad news to Brown met only with denials and reprisals. While Brown seemed blinded to the problems, in reality his mismanagement led the company further down the organizational distress curve by taking faulty actions that exacerbated problems.

Causes and Warning Signs Under Brown

- *Management analysis.* Much of the blame for EDS's failure to anticipate and respond to the growth of the outsourcing market falls at Brown's feet, as does the blame for EDS's overlooking the growth of the Business Process Outsourcing (BPO) market. Furthermore, the emergence of overly aggressive accounting policies suggests weak managerial control and a refusal to listen to and deal with bad news. Finally, Brown's obsessive pursuit of zero- or even negative-margin mega-deals crippled the company. Brown's insistence on winning the NMCI contract can be considered his Waterloo, a fatal misstep that is not without irony, given the lessons EDS should have learned about market share grabs under Alberthal.
- *Trend analysis.* The effects of Brown's mismanagement were masked slightly by the explosive growth of the IT market from 1998 to 2001. Once the tech bubble burst, however, EDS went into free fall, with operating margins falling to 2.9 percent in 2003, while debt climbed.
- *Industry analysis.* As previously stated, the growth of competitors represented a seismic shift in the industry, one to which EDS failed to respond properly or in time. EDS was bleeding cash and customers when the industry was growing at a rapid pace.

Based on these warning signs, EDS found itself deep in the faulty action phase of the organizational distress curve, with its debt load, negative cash flow, and customer discontent pulling it into the crisis phase of the organizational distress curve. When the board appointed Brown as CEO, it knew that Brown had negotiated twenty-one merger agreements in just twenty-nine months as CEO of Cable & Wireless PLC, which should have undermined

his credibility as the right person for the job of uniting a sprawling, inefficient organization. Also, one should question the board's
governance role throughout Brown's tenure at EDS, for it appears
that the board failed to take its fiduciary duties seriously. For
example, it surely had to approve the aggressive bidding on the
NMCI project and its required $1.9 billion in capital expendi-
tures, with no corresponding cash inflows expected for years.

With shareholders again threatening to revolt, EDS's board of
directors finally took action, announcing in March 2003 that it
would replace Brown. After paying Brown's $30 million severance
package, EDS hired Michael H. Jordan to right the ship.

Jordan set about fixing the dozen problem contracts that it
designated as critical accounts and immediately reassigned some
of EDS's best engineers and managers to the NMCI group in
order to restore accountability. Jordan renegotiated contract
terms in an effort to speed agonizingly slow cash collection, and
exited others.

Management under Brown had allowed the company's costs
to spiral out of control, adding to the pressure that overly aggressive bidding put on its margins and undermining its ability to
compete for other contracts. Jordan made drastic changes: he
centralized EDS's procurement activities, reduced surplus labor,
and moved jobs—including EDS's own employee help desk—
to India and Eastern Europe. He moved to standardize and
automate processes and tools, thus reducing costs across the
board and resulting in savings of more than $1 billion a year
through better purchasing, $1 billion through more efficient data
center capacity utilization, and $1 billion through more than
20,000 layoffs.[15] He further restructured sales team processes,
replacing Brown's mantra of pampering the client at any cost with
a philosophy of charging additional fees for any customized
service outside of EDS's standardized product offerings.

Jordan also took the opportunity to raise cash and pay down
the debt Brown took on by exiting myriad business units and
subsidiaries that did not fit in his vision of EDS's future core business strategy, such as the divestiture of A.T. Kearney, the fourth
largest management consulting firm in the world, acquired by
EDS for $600 million in 1996. The envisioned synergies failed to
develop. Kearney had negative $10 million in operating income,

so Jordan cut EDS's losses through a buyout by the consulting firm's partners in 2006. Although it raised only $52 million in cash, it eliminated an underperforming division and refocused EDS on its core businesses. Between 2004 and 2006, Jordan raised more than $2.8 billion from divestitures, which eased the company's liquidity crisis and reduced its leverage significantly.

Finally, EDS focused on working capital improvements such as shortening its receivables collection period, which drove a steady increase in free cash flow. As of December 31, 2006, the company had total positive liquidity of approximately $3 billion, a stark contrast with the $5.3 billion in debt under Brown's tenure.

In order to grow the IT outsourcing business and catch up to low-cost competitors such as Wipro and Infosys, Jordan announced that EDS would pursue a "best-shoring" approach, which incorporated a combination of offshore, onshore, and near-shore services in client contracts. Jordan refocused EDS's remaining employee base on its core outsourcing business, stating that "the concepts of low cost and high value must be present in every action we take, in every service we provide, in every piece of new business we pursue."[16]

Conclusion

EDS's twin turnaround efforts created an unusual situation wherein the company descended down the organizational distress curve into inaction, at which point the board replaced CEO Alberthal with Brown. As the case illustrates, Brown righted the ship temporarily—although one could argue that the go-go atmosphere of the late 1990s contributed as much to EDS's brief resurgence as did his leadership—before his mismanagement led the company onto a new organizational distress curve, where it became blinded to new problems, remained inactive in the face of them, and even began taking faulty actions that exacerbated those problems, such as repeating Alberthal's mistakes of overbidding for "mega-deals" that boosted the company's stock price by means of razor-thin margins on top-line growth only. As such, EDS actually rode two different organizational distress curves, as illustrated in Figure 1.3. Despite leading the company out of inaction on the first organizational distress curve to a record-setting 2001,

Figure 1.3. EDS's Twin Organizational Distress Curves

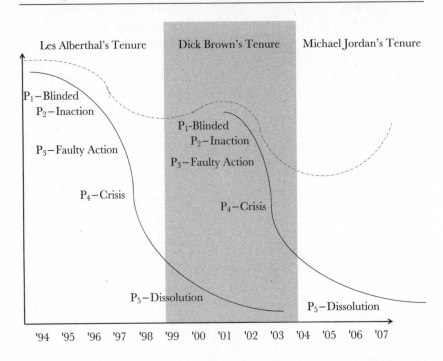

Les Alberthal's Tenure   Dick Brown's Tenure   Michael Jordan's Tenure

P_1–Blinded
  P_2–Inaction

P_3–Faulty Action

    P_4–Crisis

P_1-Blinded
  P_2–Inaction

P_3–Faulty Action

    P_4–Crisis

P_5–Dissolution

P_5–Dissolution

'94   '95   '96   '97   '98   '99   '00   '01   '02   '03   '04   '05   '06   '07

Brown's overbidding on the NMCI contract and aggressive
accounting policies led the company down a second curve into
faulty action, such that only his replacement with Jordan could
return the company to stable growth (and ultimately its acquisition by HP). Had Brown been permitted to remain as EDS's CEO,
it seems possible that the company would have slid further down
the curve into crisis, and possibly even dissolution.

Any organization that gets into trouble, even if just underperforming compared to its peers, goes through several phases, some
at a much faster pace than others. Understanding where one is
on the organizational distress curve gives one an idea of how long
a company has to fix its problems and what resources must be
brought to bear in order to do so. Recognizing the warning signs
and taking the correct actions are critical to stopping the slide
down the curve. The next chapter examines the three elements
necessary to begin any successful turnaround process.

Chapter Two

The Turnaround Tripod

"Even CEO Can't Figure Out How Radio Shack Still In Business," the headline read. The article went on to quote Radio Shack CEO Julian Day as saying, "There must be some sort of business model that enables this company to make money, but I'll be damned if I know what it is."[1]

Though it appeared in the pages of the satirical news publication *The Onion*, the article represented a case of art imitating life, coming as it did on the heels of a turnaround effort by recently named CEO Day that got well ahead of itself, focusing entirely on cost-cutting before developing a coherent strategy for the reorganized company.

Founded in 1921 to sell radio equipment, Radio Shack was acquired out of bankruptcy by leather goods manufacturer Tandy Corporation in 1963. Under Tandy's management, the consumer electronics chain grew to more than 7,000 retail outlets across the United States in the mid-1990s. However, weak managerial controls damaged Radio Shack's performance at a time of rapidly rising competition in the retail consumer electronics space. As category killers such as Best Buy emerged, garnering market share through superior pricing, variety, and customer service, Radio Shack failed to adopt to a shift in purchasing behavior or develop an effective strategy for wireless product sales. The company proved incapable of effectively managing its inventory levels in a rapidly changing marketplace, and did little to differentiate itself from competitors with stronger brands. In early 2006, CEO David Edmonson initiated an operational turnaround effort focused on closing unprofitable stores and replacing dated product lines such as metal detectors, but just months into the turnaround,

Edmonson admitted his distortion of his academic record and his involvement in several alcohol-related driving incidents, thus leading to his dismissal.[2]

Reeling from the Edmonson scandal and the company's faltering cash flow, Radio Shack's board brought in Julian Day as CEO, based on his success in leading Kmart out of bankruptcy in 2004. Day continued the turnaround launched by Edmonson, which focused on cost reductions by closing 480 unprofitable stores in 2006 alone, closing or selling three distribution service centers, dissolving European and Canadian operations, and reducing payroll and commission expenses by $135 million, down 17 percent. However, the plan contained little or no provisions for a change in strategy, aside from the disposal of slow-moving inventory (which allowed the company to save $329 million and increase inventory turns from 2.8 times in 2005 to 3.5 times in 2008) and rebranding the company as "The Shack" in conjunction with launching new higher-margin technology products across the stores.[3]

As of this writing, Radio Shack has amassed an $870 million cash balance from cost-cutting, but management has failed to identify attractive investment opportunities to drive growth. Years too late, Radio Shack finally created an online sales presence, but it remains negligible, while online retailers and competitors' web platforms have consistently stolen share. Best Buy, for example, has built a web-based platform accounting for $2 billion in sales. Ironically, it remains entirely possible that if shuttered stores had refocused upon the higher-margin products Radio Shack eventually introduced, they might have proven profitable, but the hasty drive to reduce costs made the point moot; by the time any sort of strategic refocus could be evaluated, many of those possibly profitable stores had already been closed. Though facetious, the *Onion* article hints at a darker truth; the Radio Shack turnaround focused entirely on operational changes in the name of cost-cutting, without identifying a clear go-to-market strategy that could create a sustainable business model. Speculation abounds that the only strategic end game for Radio Shack is to sell itself to a competitor, predicated on the perhaps faulty "bigger fool" assumption that someone out there will acquire a company lacking strategic direction.

Radio Shack therefore represents a classic example of focusing on operational fixes to a turnaround when a more holistic approach is needed. They did buy time, but there are many cases in which a focus solely on cost-cutting or financial engineering only delayed the demise of a company. Turnaround practitioners should instead follow a roadmap with three elements, which I consider the three legs of the Turnaround Tripod: strategic changes, operational changes, and financial changes. Like any tripod, all three elements are necessary for a successful turnaround; take away one leg by, for example, failing to make operational improvements, and the tripod tips over, thus making a successful turnaround less likely.

A company must first recognize its core competencies in order to determine the new strategic vision of the company going forward; strip out the assets that no longer support the footprint for that strategy and monetize them in order to rationalize the company's balance sheet and short-term financial position; and make operational changes to improve the efficiency and productivity of the assets that remain in the company. This three-pronged approach will invariably produce greater results than a one-dimensional turnaround such as the one at Radio Shack.

Which Comes First: Strategy, Operations, or Finance?

While any turnaround decisions must take into account the strategy of the organization as a going concern, that may not be the starting point. To clarify, it is strategy that is always needed, but it is finance that is appropriately used to determine where an organization is on the crisis curve. As covered in the Introduction and Chapter One, first look at

- Trends
- Thirteen-week cash flow forecasts
- External signs
- Internal signs
- Benchmarking
- Z-score
- A return on assets (ROA) exceeding the company's cost of capital

(Continued)

If a company is in crisis phase, in particular, there will be pressure to stop the bleeding of cash quickly. This is particularly true if bankruptcy looms large. Strategy decisions will then be made quickly, on an ad hoc basis, while cutting costs and looking for sources of cash. This means the optimal future strategy must be delayed in order to survive today.

If in an earlier phase, there is time to do things the right way: to determine strategy before undertaking cost-cutting, downsizing, or any other operational or financial changes. In any phase of the curve, however, there must be *some* decision as to strategy. It will be done rapidly and more on instinct if the organization is running out of cash, but is still just as important as saving cash.

Strategic Restructuring

Ultimately, most turnarounds should begin with identifying the company's strategy going forward. Although a full discussion of business strategy is beyond the purview of this book, readers unfamiliar with the topic will benefit from a brief introduction to the concepts of core competencies, competitive advantage, Porter's concept of the Five Forces that shape industries, and SWOT analysis (strengths, weaknesses, opportunities, and threats).

Core Competencies

Turnaround managers must identify a company's core competency,[4] which will necessarily determine the strategy for the future that best allows the company to exploit that core competency. Conversely, if a company lacks a core competency—that is, if it doesn't do any one thing sufficiently better than its competitors that it can win business from them or charge a higher price—then it is likely that the company is not worth turning around. Without a core competency, a company becomes the dismal black box described by classical economists, competing solely on price in a world with zero economic profit.

An example I use in classes with executives is to hold up a plastic bottle of a popular cola, then ask: "I make this. What might be my core competency?" Eventually, the following are the correct answers they offer:

- Creating the brand of the product
- Making the liquid
- Printing labels
- Making bottle caps
- Applying bottle caps
- Making plastic bottles
- Distributing drinks
- Sourcing ingredients
- Filling

The answer could be just one or a combination of the list above. The key is to break down what a company does into finite steps and ask which step(s) make(s) up the core competency. Executives should be asking this question as part of setting strategy every year, even if not in trouble.

The identification of a company's core competency is frequently an interactive and iterative process, requiring senior management engagement. Managers must remain intellectually honest with themselves; the claims made in a company's marketing materials regarding quality or service rarely correspond to the company's actual core competency. In fact, a company's core competency may lie in an unusual or unexpected area, such as a manufacturing company who realizes that it holds no competitive advantage in the production of its products but realizes that its reputation for on-time delivery is considered the best in the business. Such a company might go through a transformational turnaround whereby management strips out the manufacturing assets and refocuses the business on executing the fulfillment strategy for its former competitors to leverage its core strength in logistics.

Known by generations of video gamers as a creator of popular games, Atari, Inc. discovered its core competency under a great deal of pressure and at great cost. The company still had some popular titles in its portfolio, such as *Dragon Ball Z*, *Test Drive*, and *Alone in the Dark*, but most of these top sellers had resulted from outsourcing or licensing. In continuing to believe it could return to the days of producing such hit games in-house, management ignored Atari's true core competency: its game distribution system to almost all of the mass merchants in the United States, Mexico, and Canada. Even various competitors paid Atari to use its supply chain management systems as a way to sell their games efficiently to the big box stores and to large Internet sales organizations. It was that core competency that led to the buyout of struggling Atari by Infogrames, a French producer of games late in 2008 who realized the potential of the distribution channel. In effect, the company's management failed to identify its core competency and instead had it brought to its attention by the strategic buyers who lined up to purchase its highly valuable distribution channel into thousands of retailers worldwide.

When Northbrook Corporation found itself in bankruptcy, it had to determine its own core competency in order to survive. As a full-service lessor of railroad freight cars and truck trailers, Northbrook acquired and financed the equipment, maintained it, paid multistate taxes as the equipment moved around, and found lessees for thousands of pieces of equipment, while competing with dozens of companies from very small mom-and-pop operators up to and including General Electric. The bankruptcy of its then-public company parent caused Northbrook to declare its own Chapter 11, which uncovered a seemingly unsolvable mess. Northbrook owed $400 million but had less than $50,000 in unencumbered assets, not enough to cover their lawyers' requested retainer. After suppliers learned that they might get one to two cents on the dollar they were owed, they weren't too keen on working with the company any longer.

Northbrook executives didn't give up. They realized their core competency was in the management of the equipment and in the relationships they had with customers such as Cargill for grain-hauling cars, Peabody for coal-handling cars, and other corporate users of rail and truck equipment. Those customers valued Northbrook's rapid-response maintenance teams and payment-settlement process with the railroads and taxing authorities. Management convinced the lenders, who now owned the equipment, to leave it with Northbrook, with the owners responsible for all costs. Northbrook would take 20 percent of gross income on the cars as a management fee. They even convinced competitors, such as GE, to give them part of their underutilized fleet to manage. As described later in Chapter Nine, Northbrook went on to acquire and turn around other underperforming companies, eventually paying off all of its creditors in full.

Porter's Five Forces

Having identified a company's core competency, the manager should then analyze industry or industries in which the company competes to identify its structure and how it drives market forces. In his seminal work on the subject, *Competitive Strategy: Techniques for Analyzing Industries and Competitors,* Michael Porter described the five forces that shape industries:

- The threat of the entry of new competitors
- The availability of substitutes to the company's product
- The bargaining power of suppliers
- The bargaining power of customers
- The intensity of competitive rivalry in the industry

Generally speaking, the higher each of these five metrics, the less attractive the industry will be. Consider, for example, the airline industry. Since deregulation of the industry, the threat of entry of new competitors is high because it is relatively easy to acquire the planes and permits necessary to launch a new airline. There are many substitutes owing to the industry's excess capacity (not to mention the frequent consumer option to drive or take a train). Many suppliers have bargaining power because airlines cannot operate without critical inputs such as petroleum. Customers have bargaining power because aggregators such as Kayak.com, Expedia, or Priceline have made pricing transparent and allowed them to choose the absolute lowest possible fare for any flight. And the industry has a high degree of competitive rivalry because there is excess capacity in a situation in which an unsold seat represents an asset that depreciates to zero once the plane takes off. The pressure to sell that seat gives airlines more incentive to cut costs to win a sale at any cost, thus resulting in an aggressively competitive rivalry. Although certain providers in the industry have carved out defensible niches, these five factors collectively make the airline industry a very difficult industry in which to operate profitably. Not surprisingly, airlines are repeat customers of turnaround shops and bankruptcy attorneys, and they will likely remain so until one of frequent bankruptcy filings by airlines results in a liquidation instead of a reorganization, thereby eliminating some of the industry's excess capacity and restoring some pricing power (i.e., reducing customer bargaining power) to the operators that remain in business.

By contrast, the pharmaceutical companies have historically enjoyed significantly higher profitability margins than airlines. Intellectual property laws eliminate the threat of new entrants during the life of a drug's patent, thus allowing drug companies to enjoy almost monopolistic pricing power. Suppliers have little bargaining power because the inputs to most drugs are commodity chemicals, readily available from any number of manufacturers. Customers similarly have very little bargaining power, because a patient requiring an expensive chemotherapy treatment has little option but to purchase it, or more accurately, require her health care insurance provider to purchase it on her behalf in accordance with the terms of her health care coverage policy. The enormous cost of bringing new drugs to market generally means that there are few substitutes for a given product, and even when substitutes exist, a small number of very large competitors will split the market in a sort of oligarchic pricing structure. Finally, a never-ending supply of new customers with new ailments and new therapies with which to treat them—as well as the aforementioned bar to competition frequently provided by patent protection and laws preventing the government from negotiating volume discounts—reduces the competitive rivalry within the industry to moderate levels. Clearly, the pharmaceutical industry offers a significantly more attractive industry structure than does the airline industry . . . at least in 2010. Industries change rapidly, and the liquidation of one or more airlines could reduce the competitive pressures in that industry significantly, while major changes to health care regulations around the world could put downward pressure on the margins of pharmaceutical companies. An analysis of Porter's Five Forces is therefore a snapshot in time, and should come with the acknowledgment that industries naturally evolve over time, both for the better and for the worse.

Porter's Five Forces in a Turnaround Context

Porter's Five Forces suggest that companies in crisis typically face scenarios very different from those of their healthy competitors. In the pharmaceutical industry, which we have established as having an attractive structure, a struggling company will find its suppliers holding greater bargaining power, as management can ill-afford the distraction of seeking new suppliers even when such alternate providers are plentiful. Knowing that their business has taken on a disproportionate level of importance to the company's survival, customers will attempt to exercise similar bargaining power by pushing for price reductions, citing the increased risk of doing business with a company that might shut its doors. Rivalry in the industry may increase as well, for competitors may attempt more aggressive short-term price reductions in the hopes of forcing the company into liquidation, thus leaving them with one fewer competitive threat going forward. A company in crisis will therefore face *at best* the same Five Forces of its healthy competitors, and at worst may find itself at a significant competitive disadvantage even in industries with attractive structural factors. A company must, whether or not using the Five Forces model, audit the environment in which it operates.

SWOT Analysis

A popular tool to audit the business environment for an organization is SWOT analysis. It is also useful to help guide the choice of strategy. The acronym stands for strengths, weaknesses, opportunities, and threats. Strengths and weaknesses are used to evaluate *internal* factors. Opportunities and threats are viewed as *external* issues.

Examples of strengths are

- Core competencies
- Patents

- Brand recognition
- Distribution network

Weaknesses could be

- Products that do not differ from competitors' products
- Quality problems
- Poor reputation
- Higher costs

External opportunities might include

- Outsourcing
- A different pipeline such as the Internet
- Joint ventures
- New technology
- Strategic alliances
- Market niche in unfilled customer need

Threats could be

- The potential for price wars
- Competitors with better quality or products
- Competitors with better distribution channels
- Substitute products emerging
- Possible regulatory changes

Management must be realistic when using SWOT analysis, being as specific as possible, especially in making comparisons to competition. Where possible, focus this analysis on a specific market segment, which may look different from that of the entire company. Any SWOT entry that cannot generate a change in strategy is not important.

The key is whether an executive group can think like entrepreneurs. As outlined in the Introduction, the environment is similar. Matching strengths with opportunities can yield a new strategy. Another approach could be to find ways to convert weaknesses or threats into strengths or opportunities.

Harley-Davidson's major bout with financial distress came in the 1960s when foreign-made cycles penetrated the U.S. market. Honda, Kawasaki, and Yamaha invaded the country and drew buyers to the lighter-weight, higher-quality, and cheaper bikes that were made in Japan.[5] Harley's quality problems made things even worse. A team of former executives came in and acquired the company to save it from bankruptcy with only $1 million in equity and $80 million in bank debt. The team now focused on converting two of its weaknesses (quality and cost) into a strength by improving quality, even going so far as touring a Honda plant to seek out improvement ideas. There the team learned about the Total Quality Management (TQM) process, which actually was invented in the United States by Dr. W. Edward Deming but previously rejected by American manufacturers. By putting TQM into use along with just-in-time inventory and employee involvement in the process, the break-even point for Harley's operations decreased by 40 percent, thus making them more cost competitive. The executives mitigated the threat of strong competitors by lobbying President Reagan to increase import tariffs on motorcycles with engines 700 cubic centimeters and over to 45 percent. The tariff took effect in 1983, and though it was only scheduled to last five years, it gave Harley time to recover. In the meantime, the company utilized one of its only strengths, a loyal customer base, and created the Harley Owners Group, known as HOGs, and they organized rallies to strengthen the relationship among its stakeholders, which of course included customers. Today there are over 750,000 members of the HOGs, which include accountants, lawyers, and doctors, both male and female, who spend on average 30 percent more than other Harley owners on apparel and special events.[6]

This refocusing on its core competencies proved so successful that with great fanfare, Harley management requested that the tariffs be lifted in 1987, a year before they were due to expire. "We no longer need the special tariffs in order to compete with the Japanese," announced CEO Vaughn Beals.[7] During a decade where many American manufacturers struggled to compete with lower-cost Japanese imports, the gesture proved to be a smashing public relations coup, prompting President Reagan to visit the company's plant in York, Pennsylvania, and call Harley "an

American success story." In reality, the tariff actually had little effect after 1984, when Harley's Japanese competitors completed the retooling necessary to manufacture 699cc "tariff buster" motorcycles, thereby avoiding the tariff by one cubic centimeter.[8] By then, Harley's problems were fixed.

By contrast, Montgomery Ward filed for bankruptcy in 1997 because it could not convert its weaknesses and threats. It was overleveraged and could not compete with Wal-Mart and other retailers that emphasized price. After a financial restructuring financed by a group led by GE Capital, it emerged from bankruptcy saying it would go for "the niche" between Sears and Wal-Mart. That strategy announcement drew a collective "Huh??" from retail professionals, who were right when they predicted Wards would end up back in bankruptcy court, liquidating soon thereafter. Just saying you have a strategy does not make it the right one. Montgomery Ward management did not realize that it had no real core competency, and instead suffered from a poor reputation without any real product differentiation.

The *Chicago Tribune* used the wrong strategy when they fired investigative and other experienced reporters as a cost-cutting move, the new owners failing to notice that their subscribers wanted information not mere "fluff pieces." Substantial numbers of subscribers voted with their (and the *Tribune*'s) money by cancelling their subscriptions. The phrase most commonly heard was "they dumbed down my favorite paper." To their credit, management saw the results of their change in strategy and have tried to refocus on in-depth stories, a change that has slowed down the defections. Newspapers failed to react to the main threat, the Internet pipeline, until they were bleeding cash. The strength they fail to lever is that of a "trusted infomediary," a concept discussed in Chapter Ten.

Strategic Repositioning

Armed with these analyses, managers can then determine the strategic vision that best exploits the company's core competencies, based on the resources needed to implement that vision, the timing of the change, and how the company plans to measure the effectiveness of the change. A fresh set of eyes is often very helpful, as incumbent management can struggle to reexamine an industry with which they have become very familiar. "That won't work" is a common refrain from such insiders, which can prove a destructive attitude in the kind of brainstorming necessary to identify an effective strategy that diverges from the status quo. As a result, outside resources can prove very helpful, such as a turnaround specialist or new management team, because they lack slavish devotion to "the way it's always been done."

The identification of a new strategy is an inherently innovative process, requiring an open mind and a willingness to defy convention that we often associate with entrepreneurs. My colleagues Robert Wolcott's and Mohanbir Sawhney's work on the twelve dimensions of innovation is relevant to this process; they argue that while we typically think of innovation as the creation and introduction of new products, there are actually many ways in which firms innovate new ways to provide value to their customers:[9]

- Offering innovation—the actual development of new products that companies bring to market, such as Apple's introduction of the iPad and iPhone, which helped it accelerate away from highly competitive computer manufacturers
- Platform innovation—the use of common components to build a platform that allows for the rapid creation of derivative offerings, such as the way Nissan uses a common engine platform to reduce the cost of bringing cars with very different styles to market
- Solutions innovation—the combination of a suite of products, services, and information to solve a customer's problem in a novel way, such as UPS logistics services' Supply Chain Solutions, a freight-forwarding subsidiary that acts as a market maker for transportation capacity by purchasing it from carriers and reselling it to customers
- Customer innovation—the identification and targeting of previously underserved customer segments, such as Staples' identification of small businesses as potential customers, which created the big-box office supply business
- Customer experience innovation—the redesign of the customer interaction with the company, such as the outdoor

sporting goods shop Cabela's adding set pieces and even aquariums to stores to provide an entertainment experience

- Value capture innovation—the redefinition of how a company gets paid, such as struggling law firms now offering fixed-price securities work, rather than billing by the hour
- Process innovation—an improvement of efficiency through redesigning the way a company goes about building a product or providing a service, such as some auto parts companies retooling in a way that allows shorter parts runs and quicker line changes to help just-in-time manufacturing for their customers
- Organization innovation—the redesign of organizational form or how an organization interacts in its marketplace, such as Cisco's partner-centric networked virtual organization
- Supply chain innovation—the reconception of sourcing and fulfillment, such as the way retailer Wal-Mart utilizes data exchange with suppliers to minimize costs and rapidly match their actual sales with reorders
- Presence innovation—the creation of new distribution channels or new ways of leveraging existing channels, such as Starbucks using its real estate at the point of millions of customer interactions to sell music CDs in addition to flavored coffees and teas
- Networking innovation—the creation of network-centric intelligent offerings, such as CEMEX's launch of an integrated fleet of GPS-guided trucks to optimize fleet utilization and cut delivery times for ready-to-pour concrete to 20 minutes
- Brand innovation—the application of a brand into new verticals, such as Virgin Group's branded venture capital expanding into the travel, entertainment, and media industries

Turnaround managers should brainstorm along each of these dimensions in attempting to find the revised business strategy that best exploits the company's competitive advantage. An article by McKinsey & Company suggests that a "portfolio of initiatives" to refocus the company's strategy is best. Although any group of initiatives must be consistent and complementary to avoid the trap of attempting to be "all things to all people," the McKinsey study suggests that revising the company's strategy on multiple dimensions provides a quantity and diversity of tactics that collectively improve the likelihood of survival for any one of them.[10]

Strategic Error: Stretching Core Competence

Donut maker Krispy Kreme's strategy relied on a loyal customer base that stemmed from the product's unique taste, the novel customer experience of receiving piping hot fresh donuts, and scarcity. Krispy Kreme's cult following had customers lining up at locations where they saw the illuminated "hot donuts now" signs. That scarcity disappeared when management created easy accessibility to the product through factory production and ubiquitous locations and outlets, thus tarnishing the brand's mystique.[11] Suddenly, Krispy Kreme could be found everywhere from retail outlets to grocery stores, gas stations, kiosks, campuses, and even prisons. In the midst of this overly aggressive expansion, Krispy Kreme sacrificed its core competencies of quality and traditions in exchange for growth. Customers soon felt like they were being cheated out of the fundamental Krispy Kreme experience: fresh, hot donuts.

In a misguided attempt to combat the growing popularity of low-carbohydrate diets such as the Atkins diet, the company further compromised its core strategy by tampering with this core competency by announcing the release of factory-made low-carb donuts. The resultant backlash of bad press delayed the product's release and antagonized loyal customers. Many of these blunders resulted in part from Krispy Kreme's decision to go public, which subjected an ill-equipped management team to the constant pressure from Wall Street analysts to hit forecasted quarterly earnings numbers.

Krispy Kreme's most disastrous move came when its large factory stores began selling to 20,000 grocery and convenience stores, a decision that severely damaged the products cachet and the company's differentiation from competitors. Further expansion into these distribution channels meant Krispy Kreme could not directly control the quality or presentation of its donuts, while cannibalizing existing store sales, commoditizing the product, and cheapening the brand. This represented a critical strategic error, for it annihilated the company's core competency and instead transformed it into a mass-produced donut supplier. Krispy Kreme also failed to diversify its product portfolio by promoting complementary high-margin products such as coffee, which accounted for roughly half of Dunkin' Donuts' revenues but just 10 percent of Krispy Kreme's. After input costs rose, wiping out Krispy Kreme's profit margin, several franchisees went bankrupt, and many analysts speculated that Krispy Kreme would do the same, until the board finally took action and brought in a known turnaround consulting firm, which crafted the refocused strategy that management had failed to produce. It eliminated underperforming franchisees in unprofitable markets while repositioning the company as a focused regional player to take advantage of its strong support in the South.

Even big, successful companies can stumble. In the mid-1980s, when Pepsi made slow but steady market share gains and claimed that it outscored Coca-Cola in blind taste tests, Coke executives were scared into marketing a "new formula" with a sweeter, more citrusy flavor. The company failed to anticipate the sheer outrage consumers expressed at the change of a flavor from their childhood, which they perceived (rightfully or wrongfully) as the repudiation of the memories they associate with the familiar red can or bottle. "New Coke" proved a disastrous miscalculation of a company's core competency by its own managers, who quickly backpedaled, withdrawing New Coke from the shelves just seventy-seven days after its launch and reintroducing the original formula as "Coca-Cola Classic."[12] Cans of New Coke are still available from time to time on eBay or at antique fairs, an ironic knickknack that serves as testament to one of the greatest corporate strategy missteps in history.

Operational Restructuring

A strategic refocusing represents the first and most important leg of the turnaround tripod, and once completed, should be followed by operational and financial restructuring efforts. In addressing a company's operations, managers should focus on completely reengineering its processes. Once again, fresh eyes are invaluable, for outsiders are less reluctant to challenge the status quo or take certain truths to be self-evident, and will instead question every aspect of the company's operational footprint.

Laying off employees is one effective but overused effort to reduce costs. We examine reengineering and downsizing in more detail in Chapter Five—specifically how to manage morale during challenging periods with layoffs—but managers should keep in mind three general rules. First, downsizing should only take place *after* the company has revised its strategy, or it will run the risk of having laid off the wrong workers in the wrong departments or divisions. Companies making this mistake frequently must hire back those laid-off workers as consultants, often at twice their previous salary! AT&T discovered this in each of several rounds of downsizing; for example, across-the-board layoffs led to a loss of IT and sales executives. The same result occurred from voluntary layoffs, during which only the most talented employees left. Second, managers must resist the urge to appear "fair" by simply declaring that every department must cut its workforce by 10 or 15 percent. There is a natural inclination to want to spread the pain around so that everyone seems to have borne a burden, but this is rarely the most efficient allocation of resources. In all likelihood, some struggling divisions may need to be gutted entirely while profitable divisions may actually require additional employees. Finally, morale suffers far more when companies announce multiple rounds of layoffs. Uncertainty makes for a gloomy, unproductive workforce, as employees spend less time actually working and more time updating their résumés and speculating when the next axe will fall, and upon whom. It is far better to conduct the appropriate analysis to identify which groups of employees to let go, so as to ensure that another round of layoffs will not be necessary, and then make one announcement before taking steps to salvage the morale of the workers who will remain with the company throughout the turnaround.

Overall, management must adopt a brand new approach to their operations. Gone are the days of ambitious expansion plans; instead, managers must adopt a relentless attention to cost reductions across the board without destroying the company's brand. As I explained in the Introduction, Continental Airlines' Frank Lorenzo made precisely that mistake in mismatching seats on

Continental's airplanes. Though it did result in slightly reduced maintenance expenditures, it corroded Continental's brand, undermined consumer confidence, and destroyed top-line sales.

Throughout these changes, managers must listen to the employees below them. Companies often get into trouble when a bureaucratic hierarchy flourishes and managers build fiefdoms. Turnaround practitioners can respond by flattening the organization, reducing the number of levels between the CEO and the lowest employee on the shop floor. Very often, the lowest-ranking employees understand the fundamental problems facing the company, and their proximity to its actual operations allows them to see the forest for the trees instead of getting bogged down in reams of conflicting data. In one turnaround, for example, line-level employees knew that productivity had fallen precipitously at a plastic film plant because the three-foot-wide rolls of film would gradually grow thinner and thinner, until they would snap, requiring a costly delay as a maintenance worker was called to reset the jammed machine. For just $200 each, we purchased a handful of micrometers to measure the tape's gauge. A few times every shift workers would verify that the gauge had not fallen below the threshold ordered by the customer. Costly shutdowns and change-overs were reduced. The line employees were also trained to make adjustments to the machines' controls as needed so that there was no need to track down supervisors each time a change was needed. The former management team had no idea that such simple problems were killing productivity, but the information was found by listening to and empowering line employees.

Part of operational restructurings can focus on firing customers. When Core Technologies realized they were losing money selling components to a certain appliance manufacturer, they decided to fire them. They did it, however, by raising prices on their injection molded parts by 40 percent. Rather than leave, the customer agreed to pay it because Core had first done an excellent job of turning its weakness of poor quality into a strength by becoming the most reliable producer of critical parts.

One must also prune products that are bringing down the performance of the company. The toughest part sometimes is convincing sales personnel that a product has to be eliminated. They often claim that even a low-volume item is needed, because customers won't buy without a full offering. When manufacturing ten colors of plastic film for duct tape at one plant, we did an analysis to show that certain colors were losing money, particularly white because of the high cost of titanium resin. When sales personnel fought to keep making it at a loss, another analysis proved how rarely the very expensive white tape was actually ordered, which contradicted the guesses of the sales team. We then outsourced this low-volume item to another vendor, who could buy the white titanium resin at better prices, thus avoiding additional setups and downtime. Similarly, the elimination of Bear Chomps and Teenage Ninja Turtle Pies at the Twinkie bakeries saved significant money by reducing the downtime needed to change out the manufacturing lines each time a different product was run.

Inventory reductions are often needed. When I visit a facility, I often point to inventory, whether in process or finished goods, and ask what those things are. I always get a long answer describing the actual inventory. My response is then to say, "No, it's cash you've tied up." There are analytical tools that help determine optimal inventory. One of the first steps, however, is to get rid of obsolete inventory for cash. As noted in the next chapter, managements are often reluctant to take those accounting hits to their financial statements, even though needed cash is acquired, as well as space.

Suppliers must also be evaluated, even when you are having trouble paying them. As discussed in the next chapter, the key is to first rate them as critical, or as needed but eventually replaceable, or as immediately substitutable. The latter could be an office-supply chain you might stall paying and switch to another. A critical vendor, such as Bloomers' Chocolate was to Fannie May Candies, required more extensive negotiations and a debt offering.

In today's modern business world, the information technology department plays an interesting role in many turnarounds. First, an improper IT strategy can sometimes act as an internal cause of distress, such as when a company makes a poor choice of technology vendor. Buyers of Wang Laboratories' computers immediately before the company filed bankruptcy, for example, faced significant switching costs and were therefore stuck with a hardware provider that had stopped innovating.[13] Alternatively, the IT department can be a symptom of greater difficulties, such as when Solo Cup's payroll and accounting systems had yet to be integrated with those of the competitor it acquired more than a year after the close of the merger. Most often, however, IT expenditures represent a cause of distress simply by proving twice as expensive and half as effective as initially promised, with hidden costs, lagging implementation, and user resistance to new technologies.

Whether IT has played a role in causing a company's distress, it can almost always play a role in its recovery. As a major line item expenditure—IT spending represented approximately 3.4 percent of corporate revenues in 2009—it is often rightfully seen as a short-term opportunity for cost reductions as managers freeze hardware purchases, delay software upgrades, and outsource non-core IT functions in order to conserve cash.[14] In the long term, however, changes to a company's IT strategy should result naturally from the reengineering of its business processes, possibly resulting in *increased* IT expenditures in order to drive the operational restructuring, or even assist in a change of strategic focus.

By benchmarking all the factors just mentioned against "best in class" rather than direct competitors, management can set goals for almost every aspect of the business. Mark Hurd, former CEO of Hewlett-Packard, did this rather than benchmarking only against other printer manufacturers, most of whom weren't doing much better than Hewlett-Packard.

Financial Restructuring

Companies in crisis frequently have "upside-down" balance sheets, meaning that the company's total debt amounts to more than the company's total value. In such cases, equity holders are "out of the money," making their shares worthless unless the balance sheet can be rationalized.

The first step to a financial restructuring is to perform a cash flow analysis to identify the company's liquidity situation. As I explain in Chapter Four, this requires ignoring the generally accepted accounting principles (GAAP) that so many CFOs have been trained to treat as gospel, and instead focus exclusively on the cash flows in and out of the company's bank accounts. GAAP not only focuses on smoothing that distorts the actual daily cash inflows and outflows that are a company's lifeblood, but it is also focused on past results, thus making operating according to GAAP like trying to drive a car only by using the rear-view mirror.

Instead, managers should build a thirteen-week cash flow forecast, enough to identify the company's cash needs over the coming quarter, and update it on a rolling basis to ensure that the company has visibility into its liquidity going forward. This requires a strict attention to detail as to exactly when cash will arrive from customers and depart to pay suppliers. Very few CFOs do this correctly—a lifetime of working in a GAAP-focused world makes it difficult for them to switch out of an accrual-based world—so an outside consultant is often necessary.

Financial restructuring moves must be integrated with the strategic repositioning by incorporating the predicted short-term and long-term cash flow needs of the company into the available strategic alternatives. Once management has determined the cash resources needed to execute these repositioning efforts—the cost of a rebranding campaign, for example, or the severance payments required to shut down an unprofitable division or product line—they can go about fixing the balance sheet.

The first step in rationalizing a balance sheet often comes with renegotiating the company's debt structure. This can take any number of forms, such as swapping junior debt for equity, or convincing a company's lenders to waive certain covenants or extend the terms of repayment. Such suasion can prove very difficult, particularly when lenders feel that management lacks credibility in promising that the turnaround will prove successful and the company will be able to make these delayed, typically increased payments.

Companies can also rationalize an upside-down balance sheet by selling nonproductive assets, such as divisions or product lines that no longer fit with the refocused strategic vision for the company. Though buyers can often sense a company desperate to raise cash quickly and bid accordingly, such divestitures can provide the injection of capital necessary to meet short-term liquidity requirements, particularly if the divested divisions were at or below break-even or represented a distraction to management because they were not a real fit with the rest of the company's business. Creativity can prove valuable here, as there are often hidden assets on the balance sheet that can be monetized. For example, distressed debt investors rallied around both Playboy and Steinway & Sons despite eroding financial performance in early 2009, recognizing that both had significant assets not fully reflected on their balance sheets. Playboy owned the Playboy Mansion free and clear of any liens, in addition to a difficult-to-quantify but certainly valuable trove of never-before-published photographs of celebrities such as Marilyn Monroe. Musical instrument manufacturer Steinway & Sons similarly suffered when the economic downturn depressed sales of high-end pianos and brass instruments, but savvy investors knew that the company owned the office building housing its showroom floor in downtown Manhattan, as well as significant real estate on Long Island. Such assets were listed either on the balance sheet at cost (a cost paid, in Steinway's case, nearly a hundred years ago) or at zero; in the event of real trouble, management easily could have divested such assets without undermining the companies' core operations. The sale or licensing of intellectual property can similarly provide a capital infusion, such as in situations where an investor may want to revive a brand that still holds some mindshare among consumers.[15]

Finally, management should take a hard look at its management of working capital to reduce the liquidity pressures on the company. Reducing a company's cash conversion cycle (its inventory holding period + its receivables collection period – its payables collection period) frees up cash immediately without requiring permission from or difficult negotiations with already frustrated lenders. Benchmarking can be very helpful here, for often a company need only return to its historical levels of inventory, receivables, and payables outstanding in order to ease the cash crunch. Suppliers may combat this by refusing to extend trade credit and insisting on Cash in Advance (CIA) or Cash on Delivery (COD), but turnaround managers can find some leverage in these discussions if the company is a critical customer of the supplier in question.

Creativity can help a company's working capital situation by how it deals with aggressive creditors demanding repayment just as the company is trying to stretch its payables in order to ease liquidity pressure. While assisting in the Fannie May turnaround, I received a phone call from an aggressive collection agent who had clearly been hired by a supplier on a contingency fee to collect a past due payment. I held the phone away from my ear for a few minutes as he threatened to file a lawsuit, pursue a judgment lien, and even storm down to the company's manufacturing facility to begin seizing equipment to recoup the amount of the supplier's claim.

"Oh, you don't want to do that," I began drawing on my experience in long meetings at Fannie May's headquarters. "You're just going to put on 10 pounds."

"WHAT?" he bellowed.

"They make candies. Every few seconds, a freshly made chocolate or roasted nut candy comes spilling off the conveyor belt, and they put bowls of 'em in every office, on every conference table. Trust me, don't go down there, you'll just put on 10 pounds. I put on a few every time I'm there. Then you'll just be fatter when they throw you out, and all you've learned is that they're honestly trying to fix the place."

After a pregnant pause, he broke out laughing. "I've been doing this a long time, but I haven't heard that one. OK, I'll back off for a while."

Solo Cup: A Three-Pronged Turnaround

Long a family-run institution, the Solo Cup Company ran into immediate difficulties in attempting to integrate the acquisition of rival Sweetheart Company in 2004. The merger more than doubled Solo's size to $2.1 billion, making it the largest disposable foodservice manufacturer in the country, but the Hulseman family that dominated the management team failed to realize the anticipated synergies that would justify the company's vastly increased debt load. These managerial problems led the company to the brink of bankruptcy, thereby prompting Moody's Investors Service to downgrade Solo Cup's publicly traded debt, suggesting "poor standing . . . subject to very high credit risk."[16] When input costs rose by more than 55 percent in 2005, Vestar Capital—the private equity firm that had taken a minority position in sponsoring the acquisition—exercised the underperformance clause in its purchase agreement, jettisoned the founding Hulseman family, and hired David Garfield at Alix Partners to support new CEO Robert Korzenski in executing a three-pronged turnaround known internally as the Performance Improvement Plan (PIP). The PIP called for a new strategic vision of the company going forward, the monetization of any assets that did not support that new vision in order to rationalize its balance sheet, and operational improvements to improve the efficiency of the assets that Solo retained. Undertaken just as credit markets began to contract and GDP growth stalled in early 2007, the PIP had to focus on quick results driven primarily by cost reductions rather than revenue growth. With a mantra of "the dollars are in the details," Korzenski and the consulting team began poring over the vast, jumbled data sets containing millions of transactions spread across tens of thousands of products and thousands of customers.

Strategic Repositioning

Despite the time pressure imposed by impatient creditors, Korzenski and AlixPartners, the consultants, took a fresh look at Solo Cup's positioning in the industry to examine whether it was going to market with a clear, coherent strategy. Solo decided to shed noncore businesses and assets to allow the company to reduce debt and focus attention on a narrower set of operations. For example, they determined that most of Solo's private label brands—particularly Hoffmaster, a legacy of the Sweetheart acquisition that produced disposable tableware and other special occasion consumer products—contributed little to the company's profitability while presenting what Garfield called a "classic management distraction."

"Hoffmaster used a completely different set of equipment, and they had two plants in Wisconsin pretty much dedicated to that product line," Garfield said. "It was clearly non-core, it didn't have any overlap with the company's core competencies, and it was a separable business, so it was a logical divestiture."[17]

Solo's well-intentioned move into the Asia-Pacific region had similarly backfired, as the division had failed to implement the broad range of products necessary to service its typical foodservice and retailer customers in the region, and instead sold mainly drinking straws and milk bottle caps. On the contrary, the flow of competition had gone in the opposite direction, with Asian competitors entering the U.S. market rather than the other way around. As Korzenski noted at the time, "Our production in Japan is narrow in scope and not well-aligned with our core disposable foodservice business."[18]

Perhaps the greatest strategic repositioning effort came in the form of a product portfolio streamlining, as significant analytics were brought to bear on Solo's impossibly complex array of 35,000 different products or stock keeping units (SKUs). They sold directly to a foodservice operator in some cases, or through a distributor in others, so there were many different contract types, some of which were multiyear contracts on large portfolios of products. Some of these products were being phased out to customers that required different service levels. Meanwhile, some products had a competitive advantage in the marketplace—such as superior design—resulting in different pricing power.[19]

The PIP team first focused on making a rationalized, consistent pricing scheme based on the product and geographic areas where Solo offered a competitive advantage. It required complex analytics to integrate data from divergent reporting systems.[20] Working hand-in-hand with the operations-focused team members assigned to the sourcing, manufacturing, and inventory management challenges Solo faced, the pricing team identified a number of products that Solo simply could not offer at a positive margin, such as the uncoated white paper plates known as "penny plates." The company made a strategic decision to exit this commodity product line and focus its attention and investment on its decorated and coated white paper plate business.[21]

Financial Restructuring

Rationalizing the company's balance sheet became a top priority for the CEO, the board, and the consulting team, with several large debt payments looming. Solo's strategic repositioning had identified assets that did not support the long-term strategic vision of the company, and with the help of Goldman Sachs' M&A team, they set about monetizing them as quickly as possible. Solo Cup sold Hoffmaster to Kohlberg & Company for $170 million in September 2007, including its entire product line, two manufacturing facilities in Wisconsin, a distribution center in Indianapolis, and a sourcing subsidiary in Hong Kong. These sales and other closures resulted in a streamlined North American manufacturing footprint that reduced costs while "right-sizing" the company. At the time of the sale, Solo also announced the sale of the white paper plate business to AJM Packaging Corp for an undisclosed sum.[22] Finally, Solo divested its Japanese subsidiaries, Yugen Kaisha Solo Cup Asia-Pacific and Solo Cup Japan to Yugen Kaisha PC Rose, an affiliate of Japanese investment fund Phoenix Capital, for approximately $48 million.[23]

Divestitures were not the only balance sheet measures undertaken as part of the restructuring plan. In June, the company announced the sale and leaseback of six manufacturing facilities in Texas, Illinois, Georgia, and Maryland. The $130 million transaction allowed Solo to pay off its second lien term loan completely, as it entered into a twenty-year lease with four five-year extension options at each facility. Meanwhile, the company's distress had become clear to landlords at other leased facilities, who begrudgingly renegotiated unfavorable leases rather than risk losing Solo as a tenant entirely in the case of liquidation, or having to pursue a claim for breach of contract in a broken lease, or as an unsecured creditor in a potential Chapter 11 bankruptcy filing. Collectively, these efforts raised a combined $370 million in 2007, allowing the company to reduce its debt burden significantly.[24]

Operational Improvements

Though these strategic and financial changes refocused the company and rationalized an upside-down balance sheet, the critical components of the Solo Cup turnaround came from the basic "blocking and tackling" of the PIP's operational improvements, which dictated the decisions behind the sale of divisions, the closure of plants, and the discontinuation of product lines. Critical to these efforts was a change in company culture, driven from the top by Korzenski.

Korzenski and the board pressed a theme of fostering a "culture of performance and accountability" in order to improve performance by making every employee individually accountable for his or her performance. The wide array of simultaneous initiatives—which included improving the company's competitive position, paying down significant debt, and rationalizing pricing to return to profitability—relied heavily on such accountability.[25]

Instituting accountability in a company that for decades had not made it a priority proved challenging, but the team's objective analytical work made it possible. These analytics involved the construction of several proprietary forecasting and pricing tools, such as a Planner's Dashboard, that provided clear direction to all of Solo's supply chain managers to optimize inventory management.

The company also revised its incentive program, which problematically gave plant managers conflicting objectives. In an effort to provide high-quality customer service, plant managers were rewarded for on-time deliveries and high-quality products, which incentivized costly inventory buildup and overstaffing. Despite these incentives, Solo had just a 75 percent order fill rate, thus indicating that roughly one-quarter of ordered products arrived late or not at all, which infuriated customers.[26] Recognizing that this more competitive marketplace demanded both high quality *and* efficiency, Solo revised its incentive plans to align with the company's needs.

Dovetailing with their strategic repositioning efforts, Solo Cup took a long hard look at its pricing scheme, finding in several instances that it had failed to take into account "hidden" costs like specialized packaging in determining its breakeven price on certain products. This flawed analysis made it look like only a very small percentage of certain divisions' sales were loss leaders, when in fact Solo had significantly underpriced a majority of its projects. Management had thought their product portfolio produced a weighted average contribution margin of 13 percent, but when the consulting team examined improperly allocated costs, the weighted average was much closer to 0 percent.[27] In response, Solo raised prices to levels where it made sense to continue providing each product, and it clarified to customers exactly what drove the cost of their purchases by region, by customer, and by facility, which often resulted in the "firing" of unprofitable customers. The company shrank its sales by tens of millions of dollars to large customers who hadn't seen an increase in four years, a period during which Solo faced raw materials pricing increases, which cost it $50 million in 2005 alone. "We learned that you can't manage every customer the same way," Korzenski said. "We reviewed the strategic customers where we knew we were under-pricing the market, and we just matched the market, even though we lost a portion of our customer base. But we understood that they were a drain on the company, so we had to. The other thing about pricing is that there's a lot of 'bleed' that occurs, lots of deals had side actions where sales representatives would add a little service to close a deal to hit his number, but it would end up costing us. We focused on cleaning those up and getting our sales reps in line."[28]

Individual Solo managers were also paired with consultants in each of the company's major functions to produce savings across the cost structure. In the manufacturing department, complex models optimized the process of worker utilization, adapting the level of labor to the level of production through better arrangement of full-time and part-time workers. Solo also redefined production processes to optimize labor and resources allocation, and shifted production to more efficient plants. Given the company's spike in cost of goods sold (COGS), the reduction of material scrap proved particularly helpful, as the team shaved 2 percent of resin materials out of the company's manufacturing processes, thereby saving millions of pounds of raw materials. Finally, the consultants and management completely revamped Solo's procurement operations by shifting toward lower-cost materials and sourcing more strategically by geography and by product.

Solo also attacked its working capital management, incentivizing customers to pay invoices early and stretching vendors to improve its cash conversion cycle. The company also integrated its separate IT systems, introducing an SAP order-to-cash system that for the first time allowed Solo to operate on a "one order, one truck, one invoice" basis. The system brought greater clarity and account information to sales representatives, and allowed for higher-level analysis to ensure that Solo approached its customers intelligently and with a coherent pricing scheme. These PIP measures proved incredibly successful, saving $7 million from more efficient sourcing efforts, $30 million from streamlined manufacturing processes, $35 million in superior inventory management, $13 million in reduced SG&A, and $10 million in improved sales and marketing in 2007. These measures helped Solo Cup reach $68 million in net income and $142 million in EBITDA, the highest figure in the history of the company.

The company and AlixPartners won recognition for the speed and success of the turnaround, winning both the Industrial Turnaround of the Year award from M&A Advisor in March of 2008 and the coveted Large Company Turnaround of the Year award from the Turnaround Management Association in August. As with most successful turnarounds, however, the efforts aimed at streamlining the company did not stop upon the return to profitability. Solo would go on to close additional plants in 2008 through 2010, demonstrating its ongoing focus on operational efficiency at other U.S. plants, while pursuing new growth opportunities such as a partnership with nonprofit educational organization Sesame Workshop to create a branded line of paper plates, bowls, and cups.

Conclusion

In true turnaround situations, there is no quick fix, no silver bullet such as a wildly successful new product that someone simply forgot to launch or an unprofitable lease that someone forgot to cancel. Companies must go through the sometimes painstaking process of identifying a core competency and determining the revised strategy that will best exploit it, before stripping out the assets that no longer support that vision and making operational changes that allow the company to execute it. Focusing on only one leg of the tripod without first identifying a refocused strategic plan will lead to decisions that management will regret, thus reducing the likelihood of a successful turnaround and leading to bankruptcy or a distressed sale.

Chapter Three

Leadership in a Crisis

Even the best turnaround plan, modeled to incorporate the strategic, financial, and operational legs of the turnaround tripod, will fail if the company cannot execute it. This execution requires the key ingredient that causes teams to pull together and overcome adversity: leadership. Important even in times of prosperity, effective leadership becomes far more critical in times of crisis, when its demonstration comes with a significantly higher degree of difficulty. While much has been written on the broad topic of leadership, I find that great turnaround leaders must demonstrate three main characteristics in order to convince skeptical stakeholders to follow them: courage, decisiveness, and credibility. These then lend themselves to a change in culture within an organization.

Captains Courageous

Courage in a turnaround means facing up to people who are very opposed to what you want to do and sometimes requires personal sacrifice. Occasionally, it requires physical courage, as the turnaround leader will need to be present in many tense situations.

A colleague of mine had a difficult experience while engaged as the chief restructuring officer for the U.S. operations of a major European food manufacturer. After conducting a frenzied situational analysis to identify a new strategic focus for the company's domestic subsidiaries, he received a phone call instructing him that he could meet the company's union representative that evening at a famous steakhouse in an outer borough of New York

City. Upon arriving—looking forward to starting negotiations— he found himself approached by a large man who ushered him through the kitchen, out the back door, and up a shadowy stair- case to a small office upstairs. With two very large gentlemen standing silent guard in the back of the room, the union head lit a cigar and asked to hear the details of the plan. As the CRO began detailing the divisions that would be sold, the plants that would be shuttered, and the union contracts that would require renegotiation, the union head nodded silently before launching his own inquisition.

"And what about my sons? And my cousins? Will they keep their jobs?" he began.

"Well, that depends," the CRO replied, "on what division they are in. What do they do, exactly?"

"They don't do nothin'," the union head responded, glancing none-too-subtly at his two colleagues in the back. "They don't do nothin'. Are they gonna stay on the payroll?" And then he men- tioned the names of the wife and children and the home address of the CRO to show that the union knew where they lived.

Telling the story years later, my colleague chuckles at the memory of the smoke-filled room and the implied threat of physi- cal violence that loomed over the meeting. "It was like something out of the *Godfather*," he laughed. "I said I would look into it, and got the hell out of there as fast as I could. I knew that couldn't intimidate me, however, or I'd never get the place fixed." In the end, the two met a number of times and negotiated major changes both sides could live with, gaining mutual respect for each other.

Situations like this, though somewhat extreme, illustrate the first rule of leadership in a corporate crisis: leaders absolutely must display courage. In times of distress, diverse sets of stake- holders will invariably come into conflict, and they will fight for their goals by using any means necessary, even, as in these cases, the implied threat of violence. It also could take the form of shareholders who threaten lawsuits. It takes courage to bring contentious stakeholders together and convince them all to pull in the same direction.

Courage is always needed to challenge "the way we've always done it" in a large organization, especially if it's an executive who has been there a long time who is now faced with a turnaround situation. Simply put, new people often succeed because they are willing to do things that the old ones can't or won't. I was once involved in a group that had purchased a struggling appliance parts manufacturer that was breaking even but benchmarking terribly against its competitors. In my first meeting with the CEO, I discussed our turnaround plan with him, breaking down all of our intended changes into three lists: strategic, financial, and operational strategies. A month later, I noticed that none of them had been implemented, so I sat down with him a second time to find out why. "Well, I took your lists," he began. "And broke them into two new lists: those I don't know how to do, and those I can't bring myself to do." His proximity to the situation and his commitment to the status quo made it impossible for him to make the changes we needed, so we quickly agreed on his retirement plan and brought in an outsider whose fresh eyes and ears allowed him to implement the plan without reservations.

Decisiveness: Ready, Fire, Aim!

Courage serves as a bedrock for the next critical requirement for leadership in a turnaround: decisiveness. I regularly explain to my students that the further down the organizational distress curve a company finds itself, the more urgent the need for decisive action. Paradoxically, the level of distress inversely corresponds to the amount of time available for data gathering, debate, and analysis, so turnaround managers often must follow the "Ready, Fire, Aim!" approach to decision making. There simply is not enough time to conduct a rigorous, bottoms-up analysis for the company, so managers have to use an 80/20 rule; if 80 percent of the data to make a decision can be gleaned quickly, one cannot wait for that exhaustive last quintile of information, particularly if a company is already in the faulty action or crisis phases. Sometimes one must ask: How outrageous must the last bit of undetermined data be to make us go in a different direction? If it appears the odds are that a full 100 percent analysis probably won't change what we already know, stop analyzing and take action. Fortunately, if a leader demonstrates the courage necessary to make difficult decisions quickly, employees and lenders will be more likely to respond well should a change in course become necessary down the line. As Steve Miller, CEO of several successful turnarounds (and author of *The Turnaround Kid*) noted, it is more important to get everyone at a company pulling rapidly in the same new direction, even if it later becomes clear that it was the wrong direction. The willingness to admit error and then change direction yet again based on results is important. Companies often reach that crisis phase because of infighting, misaligned incentives, or differing ideas on how the company should do business, so eradicating those internal conflicts is the necessary first step to returning the company to health. Paralysis by analysis is a deadly situation in an underperforming company. As Miller points out: "Don't study things to death. Most of the choices you need to make are clear, and decisiveness breeds confidence. Listen to you customers because they know more about what's wrong and right with your company than anyone, and listen to your people, from the boiler room at the plant to the executive suite."[1]

Credibility

Finally, turnaround managers must project a certain level of credibility in order to inspire their charges to pull together. While incumbent management can on occasion offer that credibility, such as was accomplished when existing Caterpillar management broke down the company's siloed structure, struggling companies are often where they are because of management's failed leadership, so fresh faces can often bring more to the table. Experience is key; a turnaround manager who has been through the process several times before and knows the steps that companies must take in order to right themselves can often convince employees accustomed to riding a rudderless ship that they have what it takes to turn things around. Even a "strong" CEO can create an intolerable situation by refusing to change course. New leadership often provides "fresh eyes" to see things differently and "fresh ears" to listen to everyone in order to determine changes needed. In initial meetings with employees as part of an overall situation analysis, mentioning past engagements or relevant comparable experience—in the same industry or the same type of transaction (a 363 sale, for example, which we explore in Chapter Nine) or the same size of company—can inspire faith that the company is finally in the hands of someone who can help. Sometimes a simple "I've sweated payrolls before" tells people you are experienced and understand their pain.

The most important trait that brings credibility is honesty. Unfortunately, we've reached the point that too many business people believe lying is "just business." In a turnaround situation, it's an unforgivable sin. Turnaround managers face a first test of that credibility and honesty when first meeting with employees, creditors, or incumbent management. As the old saying goes, you only get one chance to make a first impression, so it is important to project confidence and competence in these initial meetings, where a manager probably has not had a chance to formulate a strategic plan for the turnaround but must nonetheless inspire confidence among those key stakeholders. The second test for credibility comes after the plan has been implemented and the first data become available to test whether the plan is meeting its targets. As explained in the next chapter, the thirteen-week cash flow model is a critical diagnostic and forecasting tool that can help ensure that managers formulate rational expectations, communicate them throughout the organization, and meet the expectations they have created. For example, the model will clarify whether a supplier can be paid on time, and if it cannot, the manager must use it to determine and communicate when the supplier can be paid, and then must *meet* that target date or risk losing credibility both inside and outside of the organization. Meeting targets for lenders—such as returning to compliance on covenants—is especially important, as those key stakeholders are typically fatigued by an extended track record of broken promises and underperformance. Winning their confidence by hitting the promised targets will buy the company the time needed to implement the chosen turnaround plan.

In succeeding John Akers as the CEO of IBM in 1993, Louis Gerstner exemplified these traits by demonstrating a willingness to make difficult decisions to unite a fragmented company. In the early 1990s, IBM's seemingly unlimited resources made it better-positioned than any competitor to take advantage of the growing computing revolution in client/server architectures and the Internet, but the organization's silo structure and reward system incentivized managers to protect their own fiefdoms rather than support a cohesive go-to-market strategy. As a result, they refused to cannibalize the sales of mainframe computers—long IBM's core strength—by introducing more technologically-advanced replacements, with one manager labeling the Internet "a university thing; we're doing serious business here."[2] Meanwhile, several product lines remained incompatible with each other, particularly those legacy mainframe products, thus aggravating customers and destroying the company's gross margins and market share.

With IBM losing money for the first time in 1991, discussions about a potential spinoff of the PC division led to the CEO talking about completely breaking up the company into thirteen pieces. The uncertainty created an atmosphere of suspicion and empire-building, as management became distracted from fixing the company's underlying problems and worried instead about retaining control of the largest possible piece of any post-breakup entity. Most of the turnaround attempts involved downsizing of employees and plant closings, without looking at the strategy that customers would require. Upon taking control, Gerstner found a culture of bureaucracy and groupthink, where decisions were made by committee and meetings were largely ceremonial. In an astonishing example of this bureaucratic inefficiency, executives frequently held lengthy "pre-meetings" of their own before actual meetings, to ensure that the data presented was in accordance with each department's expectations so that no one would lose face or present contradictory opinions. (I have personally found that executives whose strongest skill is to make great presentations are more suited to be good TV newscasters than good decision makers.)

As the first CEO ever hired from outside the company, Gerstner faced a great deal of resistance in attempting to change IBM's culture of complacency and conformity. He shocked managers simply by attending an annual IBM conference for their largest customers and making personal contact with customers' CIOs. Rather than skirting issues facing the company as his predecessors had, he addressed problems head-on, such as finding out what those important customers really wanted. His open and engaging communication style made his strategic priorities clear to employees, frequently through notes sent to the entire company. Upon discovering that European country heads were rewriting his notes to make them less critical, Gerstner attacked this resistance to change, firing the head of European operations and making it clear that anyone committed to preserving the status quo would be shown the door.

Ultimately, Gerstner's courageous decision to cut through IBM's red tape and restore accountability to managers gave him the credibility necessary to invigorate the company, a feat made doubly impressive by IBM's sheer size and scope. Particularly in such massive companies, inertia is a powerful force, so once an enormous firm starts sliding down the organizational distress curve, it is more difficult to change direction than it might be for a smaller, more nimble organization.

By changing IBM's culture, departments were able to implement his strategy of meeting customers' needs by going to market as "one IBM," finally with cross-department cooperation. The operational changes required to do this also included reengineering key processes, a last round of downsizing done all at once, benchmarking to eliminate $7 billion in costs, and simplifying the organizational structure to speed up customer responses and new product development.

Communication in a Turnaround

Communication plays a critical role in uncovering the true problems causing distress and addressing them. Because companies typically slide through the blinded and inaction phases of the distress curve before realizing the scope of their problems, information flow in troubled companies is often very poor, and employees may be afraid to bring bad news to management for fear of being blamed. One first critical step for turnaround managers is to make themselves visible in the company and interact with employees across the organizational hierarchy. As mentioned in the previous chapter, my meetings with employees at a tape manufacturer allowed me to identify poor production methods that caused frequent down time when the tape would thin to the point of tearing. Such interactions need not take place in the context of formal meetings; simply making oneself accessible to employees by eating lunch in the plant cafeteria, for example, can make them more comfortable in bringing problems or new information to the manager's attention. Steve Miller, when he was CEO of Delphi, personally answered all his e-mails from employees. Free flow of information is absolutely critical in a turnaround; it is hard enough to solve problems you know about, but you absolutely cannot solve problems that you have yet to identify.

The turnaround manager should not limit his communications to those inside the company, but should also meet with stakeholders both upstream and downstream from the company in the supply chain. Suppliers will likely be frustrated with extended payment periods, and may be threatening to put the company on Cash in Advance (CIA) or Cash on Delivery (COD). A turnaround manager who can meet with such suppliers and placate them by convincing them that the turnaround plan will allow them to be paid on time once again will prove very successful. Meeting with customers is also critical; if cash flow is the lifeblood of any business, then the customers who provide it are the company's heart, so meeting with customers should take a high priority to learn what they want (and are willing to pay for). Managers should also contact players even further downstream, such as end users of the product that includes a component made by the company, in order to get a clear picture of how the company is perceived by the marketplace, unclouded by the myopia or denial of incumbent management and employees.

Having met with these stakeholders, the turnaround manager should focus on building support within the company. Early efforts should focus on individuals and small groups rather than on companywide meetings, as this allows the turnaround manager to receive feedback in private, learn the company's cultural norms, and see what will and will not work. Sometimes one has no choice but to deliver news to a large group, but it should be done in a way that the executive sticks around to answer all questions honestly.

Another colleague of mine in Florida decided to take his senior executive staff and representatives of his unhappy bankers and his bondholders out for golf. He chose the famous "Blue Monster" course at the Doral Country Club, hoping everyone would bond and get to know each other better. He warned them several times beforehand that "this is a very tough course." They all gathered at the first tee to watch the first foursome tee off. As the host, my friend took the honor of being the first to tee off. After several practice swings he carefully took his stance. A good backswing, a mighty swing and follow through—and he whiffed, completely missing the ball. With that, he turned to the assembled executives and creditors and said, "I told you this was a tough course." They were laughing so hard they could barely tee off themselves. The group did bond, but to this day my friend won't admit whether or not he missed the swing intentionally as an icebreaker. They went on to work well together as a group, making tough compromises in the best interests of the company.

Most turnaround plans are likely to involve some difficult decisions that may not immediately enjoy popularity in a company that has grown accustomed to the status quo, so early efforts should focus on identifying key employees and winning their support in person. Every company has "thought leaders" who for whatever reason—be it longevity at the company, technical expertise, or simply charisma—hold disproportionate sway among their coworkers; and they are not necessarily C-level executives. In one turnaround effort, one of my colleagues quickly identified the CEO's secretary as precisely such a power broker whose loyalty to the company allowed her to see the situation clearly. This secretary had recognized that the CEO's profligate spending and the refusal to share information with the bank-recommended chief restructuring officer had led the company to ruin; the CEO even refused to allow the CRO to visit any plants. Using her connections within the organization, the secretary filled out the paperwork to have the CRO hired as a temporary in one of the company's manufacturing facilities. With this cover story, line-level employees felt comfortable communicating with him honestly, and he was able to identify several basic operating weaknesses that they might otherwise have been reluctant to bring to management.

Just as important as identifying the key stakeholders and winning their support is identifying those who will oppose it and isolating or outmaneuvering them. In this same turnaround, the CRO discovered that the main plant's shop steward steadfastly refused to discuss any changes in manpower in the plant. Somehow, however, the CRO convinced the steward that the banks and the company's CEO were demanding performance evaluations of each employee, which was allowed under the contract. Inexplicably, the steward produced those evaluations, and the CRO promptly fired the bottom 10 percent. Identifying the steward as someone who would oppose the implementation of the turnaround plan and outmaneuvering him allowed the CRO to act before the steward could foment internal strife and resistance to the plan.

As an interim CEO, I have attempted to overcome such objections by listening to every viewpoint, even those that I believe to be incorrect or overly committed to the status quo, and only explain our plan of action after I have heard and evaluated all of these viewpoints. Often, employees will reveal themselves as obstacles when they then voice their objections a second time, perhaps more vociferously. I listen again, but then explain a bit more firmly that this is not a democracy, and there will be no recounts or second votes. Management by consensus may work in some settings, but a turnaround is not one of them. This may lead to a situation described by Professor John Whitney at Columbia, one of the first professors to teach a dedicated turnaround course to MBAs, when he suggested that turnaround CEOs often have to make examples of people in order to get rid of the naysayers, as Gerstner did with the rewriters of European memos at IBM. After determining the course of action, a manager may need to eliminate someone who persists in undermining that plan, particularly if he or she is very senior. As stated, this requires courage: not a huge ego, per se, but confidence and a willingness to stick with a decision.

It is very important to understand each stakeholder's incentives as well; for example, this shop steward clearly wanted to retain as high a level of employment as possible, so the CRO's recognition that he would block any attempts to pare payroll dictated his strategy. On other engagements, I have also seen executives who seem far less risk-averse than one might expect, until I see a capitalization table showing that they own a potentially valuable equity position and are therefore willing to throw the proverbial hail mary in the hopes of preserving some value for equity holders or even their jobs. In another famous bankruptcy case, the CEO of a large food manufacturing company was a significant equity holder, but also began purchasing the company's subordinated notes at a discount, eventually amassing a position that gave him some leverage in driving the reorganization plan (and making it less important from his standpoint that the equity class recover any value). It is critical to understand the motivations of each stakeholder in order to address and encourage them properly.

Let us be very clear here, leadership is required by more than the CEO. Many national union officers are just as self-interested as CEOs who are only driven to protect their jobs, a nasty trait also seen in most politicians. Meetings with lenders can take a negative turn, even when just one of them won't cooperate, if they think they have to look tough to keep their job even if it means the bank loses more money because of it and the company goes out of business. The best turnaround people are great mediators, effectively secretaries of state who have the ability to persuade even warring stakeholders to agree on a course of action.

Only once key stakeholders have been won over and the ideal messaging approach determined should one then proceed with mass communications, such as "town hall" meetings and companywide missives. The support of these key employees will ensure that the message is communicated clearly and coherently throughout the organization, and will make employees' acceptance and buy-in far more attainable. Once again, it is imperative that it not be an e-mail or any other cowardly way to deliver bad news without being there to answer questions. Turnaround managers should also recognize that most employees will have limited familiarity with the turnaround process, and that they must therefore act as a teacher and counselor in these times of crisis. The more a manager communicates with all stakeholders, initiating contact rather than waiting for problems to be brought to her, the more likely she can eliminate surprises, calm jittery employees and lenders, and produce a superior outcome.

I have found that employees often respond best to these communications when they include military or medical metaphors. The concepts of war or medicine seem to connote the urgency of the company's situation and the "win-at-all-costs" nature of the necessary response. In turnarounds, managers often refer to "stopping the bleeding" or "conducting triage," and talk of being "in the trenches" or needing to "take that hill." It may seem overly simple, but these metaphors resonate immediately with employees, who find themselves in a highly emotional situation with uncertainty and fear swirling around them. They want someone to lead, and by invoking easily-accessible stories, a manager can help employees understand the situation quickly and thoroughly.

Culture plays an important role in implementing any turnaround plan, but some executives can't seem to understand that. Tom Ridge was an invited guest at a Turnaround Management Association conference shortly after he was named the first Secretary of Homeland Security. Considering that dozens of completely different federal departments, in administrative, protective, and investigative branches, were joined with hundreds of thousands of employees, he was asked what culture he would try to create there. We expected him to say something about efficiency, willingness to share critical information, cooperation— something. Instead, he seemed shocked at the idea, saying "culture is something grown in a Petri dish," informing us he had no intention of trying to create anything other than more bureaucratic layers. Without that needed change in culture, years have gone by without many necessary changes in the federal government.

There are those that say "culture eats strategy for breakfast." Does that mean everyone can take whatever hill they want because it's a culture of change? Do you just ricochet from one strategy to another? Absolutely not. Fostering a culture that will survive the present and the future means creating an environment where everyone is listening to new ideas from within as well as from customers and has a willingness to change. It means that each department head will quickly make whatever changes are required to get the strategy implemented, particularly all needed operations and financial changes. The right culture has everyone in the organization feeling free to make suggestions for improvements, whether small or massive, and moving quickly to implement those improvements.

Chainsaw Al

Market observers saw two sides of Albert Dunlap and the turnaround he engineered at Scott Paper. On one side, Dunlap—and a Harvard Business School case on his exploits—argued that he led "one of the most successful, quickest turnarounds ever." His critics claimed instead that Dunlap gutted Scott Paper's long-term prospects in order to pretty the company up for a sale, which he eventually engineered to Kimberly Clark for $9.4 billion in late 1995, pocketing more than $100 million in the process.

Scott's board hired Dunlap after he had earned the nickname "Chainsaw Al" for his work slashing payroll at Crown Zellerbach. Labeling Scott a "beached whale," Dunlap took less than two months before announcing his slash-and-burn restructuring plan, which would eliminate 35 percent of the employee base, divest noncore units, and cut R&D. Many of the details of the turn-around are subject to strenuous debate; with his typical bragga-docio, the abrasive former West Point cadet claims credit for all of them, while company insiders claim that many of the opera-tional measures were already in the works well before Dunlap was hired. Of note, however, is that the greatest disagreement on Dunlap's behavior seems to stem entirely from what the witness's relationship was to Scott Paper.

Scott shareholders adored Dunlap. During his tenure at Scott, the company's stock price rose by 225 percent, creating some $6.3 in shareholder value that was realized upon the sale to Kimberly-Clark. To hear them talk about Dunlap is to hear the exalted reviews of a turnaround maestro, a legend in his own time.

Nearly every other stakeholder in Scott Paper feels differently. In fact, in his memoir written immediately following the Scott sale, Dunlap referred to the very concept of "stakeholders" as "the most ridiculous term heard in boardrooms these days," asking how much those stakeholders had paid for their stake. He went on to belittle companies like Ben & Jerry's and the Body Shop for their employee programs and for supporting social causes, arguing that "the notion of other interests and other constituencies becomes an excuse for flaccid management and poor results."[3] Those spurned stakeholders took note. Downsized employees lament not only his decision to enact mass layoffs, but the hostile attitude with which he did so. Upon hearing that one of the workers leading him on a tour of a Scott plant had been at the company for three decades, he reportedly sneered, "Why would you stay with a company for 30 years?"[4] He also antagonized the company's community, discontinuing all of the company's corporate gifts and going so far as to renege on the final $50,000 installment of a $250,000 pledge to the Philadelphia Museum of Art. Nonshareholders' descriptions of Dunlap always took on a very different tone, one that accused him of gussying the company up for a fast sale that essentially represented a transfer of wealth to Scott's shareholders from its other stakeholders, particularly the pain he proudly caused employees.

I use the case of Chainsaw Al in my class to ask the question: To whom does a management team owe duties? While some more compassionate students will argue that the company owed a duty to its other stakeholders, others know that management only owes duties to equity holders, with a few specific exceptions.

Before we examine those duties, however, the Chainsaw Al story has an unhappy postscript. After the sale of Scott, he was hired to enact a similar turnaround at home appliance manufacturer Sunbeam, and the stock market soon rewarded the company with a stock price at an all-time high. In the meantime, he penned a blustery memoir entitled *Mean Business: How I Save Bad Companies and Make Good Companies Great,* a wildly self-promoting tome filled with hyperbolic braggadocio. It has not aged well, and in light of subsequent events, reads a bit like a pre-Watergate autobiography of Richard Nixon.

Forensic accounting by analysts covering Sunbeam soon revealed questionable revenue bookings, in which the sales of seasonal items like backyard barbecue grills somehow magically spiked during the winter season to cover anticipated revenue shortfalls. In addition to this channel stuffing, a massive SEC investigation revealed that Dunlap had counseled the company's controller to be as aggressive as possible in his accounting interpretations, exaggerating the company's loss (an example of the "big bath" financial shenanigan) in 1996 to make the 1997 recovery look all the more impressive. The board fired a disgraced Dunlap, and Sunbeam soon filed for bankruptcy. In his settlement with the SEC, Chainsaw Al paid $500,000 in fines and was forbidden from ever serving as an officer of a public company, and later settled a suit with Sunbeam shareholders for $15 million. In 2009, Portfolio.com named him the sixth-worst executive of all time, noting that the obvious glee he took in antagonizing his critics and embracing his reputation for cold-heartedness made him "the middle finger of the free market's invisible hand."[5]

Board Accountability and Fiduciary Duties

History will not be kind to Chainsaw Al, but until he ran afoul of the SEC at Sunbeam, he did nothing wrong from a legal perspective at Scott Paper. As an officer of Scott Paper, his only duties were to the company and thus shareholders, and Scott's directors had those very same duties, so they were right to support anything that maximized shareholder value.

Directors are not always so aligned with a CEO in turnaround situations, when they must decide whether to support incumbent management or clean house with someone who can return the company to health. The decision of whether or not to replace a CEO is *the most difficult* decision a board ever has to deal with, and not surprisingly, one that comes up frequently when companies are in crisis. Naturally, after years of working with a particular CEO, directors can grow reluctant to replace him or her even as a company slides into insolvency; they may live in the same town, play golf at the same country club, or otherwise have personal connections that unduly influence their professional interactions, particularly in the case of closely held family businesses. In my work on several boards, I am often called upon to explain to other directors exactly what duties we owe to the company, to management, to shareholders, to employees, and to creditors.

A gentle reminder that the author is not giving legal advice but summarizing legal concepts and answers given general situations. The general answer is that under U.S. corporate law—which is a function of the state of a company's incorporation but generally follows Delaware corporate law—directors owe primarily two duties to the companies they serve. The first is a duty of care, which essentially requires that directors and officers act in good faith, in an informed and deliberate matter. That means doing one's homework. Potential violations of the duty of care could include waste, such as engaging in a transaction so obviously one-sided that no reasonable person could decide that the company received adequate consideration for whatever it exchanged. A famous case[6] involving a company that executed a leveraged

buyout also established that the board of directors was grossly
negligent for failing to make reasonable efforts to remain
informed regarding the company's situation, making a rapid decision to agree with the CEO, and doing nothing to be sure they
weren't accepting an offer to sell the company well below fair
market value. (Because the Delaware Supreme Court's holding
explained that merely consulting with a financial advisor or valuation expert would have constituted reasonable effort, the case
has become jokingly known as the "investment banker full employment act.")

However, violations of this duty of care are difficult to prove
in court, because most courts have accepted the Business Judgment
Rule (BJR), a blanket protection that presumes that directors
performed their duties in good faith, with the level of care that
an ordinary person would exercise under similar circumstances,
in a manner they reasonably believe to be in the best interests of
the corporation. In effect, the BJR places a high burden of proof
on the plaintiff to prove that a director or officer has violated this
duty; even a stupid decision can be protected by the BJR if directors can show they took time to study the issue, hired and relied
on outside experts, and used their business judgment to make the
call. Only gross negligence overcomes the protections it offers,
and the standard for meeting such a blatant dereliction of duty
is so difficult to prove that plaintiffs (typically the shareholders of
a company) rarely meet it. It is interesting that when shareholders
sue the company in what is called a derivative suit, management
is responsible for defending the corporation; any damages are
usually paid by the corporation itself, thus limiting their effectiveness because the shareholders ostensibly already owned any assets
used to pay damages.

The second major duty directors and officers owe the companies they oversee is the duty of loyalty, which requires that they
prioritize the company's well-being over their own personal gain
from company decisions. Although transactions between the
company and the director or officer are permitted, they must be
transparent and considered reasonably fair to the company; a
director cannot engage in a transaction with the company that is
profitable to her personally but not to the company. Situations
that violate this duty include flagrant diversion, where an official

essentially steals corporate assets for her own benefit, engagement
in a transaction on her own with a third party that the company
could have profitably engaged in (the "corporate opportunity
doctrine"), insider information, or failure to disclose information
in a timely manner to shareholders. Note that the BJR will not
apply if there is a breach of the duty of loyalty. In general, the
duties are owed to shareholders. Normally, creditors are only
owed whatever duties are spelled out contractually.

These duties to the corporation exist at all times, but additional duties have been interpreted to arise when companies
approach what is known as the "zone of insolvency."[7] Different
courts use various legal tests to determine after the fact whether
a company was in this zone, such as a balance sheet test that
determines whether the company's liabilities exceed the market
value of its assets, a cash flow test that determines whether the
company has the necessary cash flow to meet its financial obligations, or a capital test to determine whether the company has the
capital necessary to obtain or support financing for its operations.
A company that trips covenants with its lenders, is overdrawn on
its revolver, faces chronic liquidity problems, or knows it's impossible to pay its looming bondholder payment, is likely in the zone
of insolvency. From a practical standpoint, any time a company
may be approaching the zone of insolvency, directors should
protect themselves by contacting an experienced restructuring
attorney, assuming that these additional duties have arisen, and
acting accordingly. As a result, boards are generally very careful
to note in their meeting minutes that any difficult decisions were
made "after a great deal of study and advice from professionals"
and "keeping in mind any potential duties we may owe to creditors" and "after considering the motives of various stakeholders."
The key is that you may not yet be declared insolvent, but it's
coming.

When in the zone of insolvency, directors' duties expand to
include not only the company and its shareholders but perhaps
its creditors. Courts have compared directors in such situations
to trustees administering the company's assets for the benefit of
creditors as well as shareholders, such that they must maximize
the value of assets that may be needed to pay the debts of the
company. Generally, maximizing a company's enterprise value

meets this duty, but in so doing directors may not unfairly favor the equity holders over creditors, who according to the absolute priority rule that we discuss in Chapter Six have a first claim to the company's assets before the equity holders receive any consideration. To be clear, the directors do not have to take orders now from creditors, other than contract or loan negotiations. The duty is to maximize the value of the entity.

Some courts have also considered a "deepening insolvency" theory, where directors may be held liable for negligently prolonging the life of a corporation by taking on high-risk projects that increase the likelihood of there being some value left over for shareholders while decreasing the amount that creditors could be paid. For example, if a company is producing sufficient cash flow to justify a $400 million pre-debt valuation but has $450 million in outstanding debt, the company is insolvent and equity holders are "out of the money" by $50 million. A negligent board might approve a risky new product launch that costs $100 million and has a 10 percent chance of producing an extra $500 million in valuation. While equity holders would support such a product launch—as its unlikely success would be the only way their shares would be worth anything—creditors would recognize that with 90 percent certainty, it would reduce the amount distributed to them from $400 million to $300 million. Courts have recognized such deepening insolvency generally in situations in which there were more egregious acts, such as when directors falsified financial statements to obtain additional financing, or concealed a company's insolvency from creditors to prevent them from seizing their collateral. However, thus far, no court has found liability exclusively under a theory of deepening insolvency, but rather only in situations where the deepening insolvency liability occurred in conjunction with violations of the duty of care or duty of loyalty.[8] Shrewd directors and officers—and even turnaround consultants hired by the board—should maintain rigorous documentation of the care taken in all material decision-making processes in order to avoid such allegations of liability.

Revisiting Chainsaw Al for the moment: Despite the company's struggles, Scott Paper was probably not in the zone of insolvency when Al began stripping out assets. Even if the company was found to be in that zone, however, its sale to Kimberly-Clark made all of its creditors whole, so there would probably be no reason for them to file a lawsuit based upon some breached duty. One might argue that things would have been significantly worse for Chainsaw had the sale failed to go through and the company been left insolvent, but this was not the case. It might also have been a different situation in one of the states that allows a corporation to declare that it owes duties to whatever stakeholders it chooses. Some of these states establish that the company's articles of incorporation may lay out exactly what order of priorities the company wants to follow. Barring any state statute requiring that other stakeholders be considered, however, no such duties will arise unless the company has entered the zone of insolvency.

One other exception can arise where a director or officer may owe duties to someone other than the company's shareholders or creditors, and that is in the case of various whistleblower statutes. In the event that a subordinate reports wrongdoing within the company, a CEO cannot use his or her duty of loyalty as an excuse for illegal activity, such as suppressing a whistleblower or interfering with the whistleblower's attempt to support an investigation.

With regard to examples we have already considered, one can pose legitimate questions as to why the boards at EDS overseeing Dick Brown or at Sara Lee under John Bryan waited so long to replace clearly ineffective managers. If anyone sued them for breach of fiduciary duty, they would probably escape punishment by pleading the Business Judgment Rule; they simply made poor decisions in a situation with leaders exhibiting a great deal of hubris that they refused to replace until substantial outside pressure mounted. Boards should learn from these mistakes, and act more aggressively when a number of the early warning signs discussed in Chapter One suggest that a regime change is in order.

Leadership Examples

There are unlimited examples of leadership, many of which are briefly described in this book. Two of my favorite extremes are the CEOs of Schwinn and J. Crew. Apple is a good addition to show how entrepreneurship can trump bureaucracy.

Schwinn

Hubris is the biggest enemy of any leader, whether a CEO, a union head, or a politician. When a leader believes he can do no wrong, he usually is wrong. He stops listening. He thinks the rules apply to others but never to him; self-sacrifice is not an option. Such executives are dangerous in a turnaround situation as they are the least willing to change or even admit anything went wrong due to their decisions or lack thereof.

An example of negligent leadership in a turnaround situation is instructive. Schwinn Bicycle Company dominated the American bicycle manufacturing industry for nearly 100 years, passed down through four generations of the Schwinn family until 1979, when Edward Schwinn Jr. took over as CEO. Ed, as he was known, immediately created a schism between the old guard of marketers who had taken the company to great heights in the 1960s and a new flock of MBAs who answered only to him. His bristling arrogance—as a Schwinn, he considered himself bicycle and corporate royalty—prompted him to fire longtime executives or banish them to undesirable subsidiaries, such as when he exiled the number-two man in the company—Al Fritz—to the company's exercise bike division in a distant suburb for saying that things needed to change.[9] Meanwhile, he actively antagonized the lenders that served as the undercapitalized company's lifeline, by no-showing at meetings and failing to inform the lenders that he would instead be sailing around Lake Michigan. When executives came to him with product and quality problems, he would blame the messenger, screaming, "if you can't sell [these bikes], I'll find someone who can!" That arrogance manifested itself in a need to show everyone exactly who was boss. For example, Ed would often show up to meetings wearing a polo shirt when everyone else had been instructed to wear ties, and once forced the company's top fifty dealers to wait hungrily outside a banquet room because he insisted that he be the one to lead them into dinner.[10]

That arrogance led to a staggering set of blunders in international markets, such as the disastrous Hungarian plant that threw the bicycles out as soon as they finished putting them together. His misadventures with Taiwan-based Giant Manufacturing Corp.

demonstrate this hubris; only *after* entering into a disastrous out-sourcing agreement with the small company, Ed realized that Schwinn should have acquired or formed a joint venture with the company rather than provide them with the opportunity to become a formidable competitor. His offer to invest in Giant amused its executives, who no longer needed Schwinn's business, having used the huge Schwinn contract to grow its business exponentially. When Giant in turn offered to invest in Schwinn to save it, Ed's curt refusal insulted Giant managers, who would later take their vengeance in bankruptcy court as Schwinn's largest (and least sympathetic) creditor.

Perhaps no decision better demonstrated Ed's total disconnect with the company's culture and his brash, wholly unjustified confidence that everything a Schwinn touched would turn to gold as his assault on the company's decades-old Chicago plant. Rather than recognizing the workers there as the stewards of Schwinn's greatest asset—its reputation for quality—Ed resolved to break the union that had organized. After spending millions in legal fees in vain attempts to prevent the union's formation, Ed decided to invest tens of millions in a new plant in distant Greenville, Mississippi, a "right-to-work" state with weak union laws. The plant was a disaster from the beginning; no managers wanted to relocate there, and commuting required a flight from Chicago to Memphis and then a short commuter flight or a three-plus hour drive. The nonunion employees there, though cheaper than their UAW counterparts in Chicago, had none of the loyalty to the company or experience with manufacturing bicycles that had produced such high-quality products, and dealers loathed the new Greenville bikes, which arrived at dealerships with mismatched colors, missing parts, or requiring immediate repair. Ed cut off his own nose to spite his face in launching the Greenville plant, which never turned profitable and actually lost more than $30 million over ten years. He was right to consider a new plant, but he wouldn't listen to anyone regarding its location or design. In particular, everyone feared telling Ed that his brother was doing a poor job running it.

As these missteps collectively brought the company into the crisis phase, Ed demonstrated a mystifying arrogance that infuriated creditors and executives. The company's market share tumbled from 25 percent in the 1960s to 5 percent in the 1980s, largely lost to the BMX and mountain bikes at which the company had thumbed its nose. When Schwinn dealers informed executives that lighter-weight bikes were becoming popular, Schwinn responded: "Customers want to ride bikes we make, not carry them."

Ed refused to dilute the Schwinn family's ownership by raising outside capital. (See Box 3 for a set of common governance issues that arise during turnarounds of family businesses.) This left Schwinn entirely reliant on its lenders for working capital financing, ironically, the same banks that Ed enraged by showing up late or not at all to meetings intended to discuss the company's precarious financial situation. When lenders arrived for an early afternoon meeting only to hear from Ed's secretary that he had left for the day to sail the 80-foot junk boat he had imported from China around Lake Michigan, they considered that the final straw. Their pleas to Ed to accept an investment offer from the private equity arm of investment bank Donaldson Lufkin & Jenrette had fallen on deaf ears, and they quickly began sweeping all of the cash in Schwinn's accounts to reduce their exposure on Schwinn's loans. The ensuing liquidity crisis plunged Schwinn into bankruptcy court, where unsympathetic creditors forced the sale of the assets of the company, with the fourteen members of the Schwinn family trust receiving just $2.5 million for a business once worth more than $100 million.

Observers recognized Ed's arrogance and obliviousness as the primary driving forces behind the collapse of this American institution, but Ed continued to believe that he had done nothing wrong. "I run companies," he declared after moving to Wisconsin, jobless. "I'm looking for a company to run." In a move that surprised only Ed, no companies came calling in pursuit of his leadership, and he was last seen operating a small retail store in Geneva, Wisconsin, named the Cheese Box, offering "gift boxes of cheese and sausage for every occasion."

J. Crew

A better example of leadership comes from J. Crew,[11] which traces its origin back to a low-price women's clothing line founded by

Box 3: Governance and Leadership Issues in Family-Owned Businesses[12]

Schwinn's downfall can be attributed to many things, primarily a growing disconnect with consumer preferences for lighter mountain bikes, disastrous leadership from its CEO, and the refusal to raise outside financing that left it entirely dependent on its lenders for working capital. Its governance as a closely held family business also crippled the company, for it created a common power dynamic that undermines the board's ability to perform its duties of care and loyalty. While there are many well-run family-owned companies, the real test is what happens when one underperforms, particularly how it reacts to leadership issues. Other issues that family businesses face in addressing their governance include the following:

Insiders and Outsiders

In many family businesses, generations of inheritance and divorce lead to ownership becoming distributed across dozens of family members, both insiders who operate the company and outsiders who may work in another industry or not at all. Often, outsiders lack proximity to the company's business operations and resent what they perceive as the insiders' inflated salaries and lavish perks. Meanwhile, insiders often gripe about disbursing dividends to outsiders, particularly when the company has a down year and requires additional liquidity but outsiders have become accustomed to a certain level of income and think their dividend should be no smaller than the prior year.

Retaining Non-Family Talent

Family businesses often struggle to attract quality turnaround managers from outside the family if they are reluctant to offer a package with a competitive level of equity participation. Even if families are willing to offer such market rate terms—or if they are creative enough to synthesize them with some sort of phantom stock or warrant position—they may not be able to convince outside managers that they have the necessary checks and balances in the organization.

Credibility with Lenders

Every workout lender has a dozen or more nightmare stories about working with a family business where decisions were made in the best interest of the family, not the business. This has made many lenders wary of extending the same credit to a family-owned business in a turnaround that they might offer to a public company in a similar financial position. To combat this bias, turnaround managers must gain real power in the organization and convince the lender that they will have the ability to make real changes. Lenders often demand personal guarantees of company debt from family members.

Fractured Shareholder Base

After just one or two generations, families will have grown exponentially faster than the businesses they own, so a company entirely owned by a patriarch founder can have dozens of shareholders just two generations later. Some of those shareholders will work in the company, while others will not, and depending on how many offspring each child of the founder had, some of those shareholders will have two or three times as large a share as others and very different liquidity needs. These diverse shareholder bases can make it difficult to reach consensus on important issues, such as whether to fire the CEO (particularly if he is a relative) or whether to pursue a sale of the company or inject more money to fund a turnaround plan. Sometimes trust documents state who will be the CEO. For example, Ed Schwinn was the only possible candidate because his grandfather's trust agreement said the CEO must be the "first born of the generation"—just like the king/queen of England.

Lack of Foresight

The informal governance present in many family businesses can exacerbate crises and hamper a turnaround plan. For example, founders often simply divide shares equally among offspring, without enacting buyout provisions or tagalong rights to protect less involved shareholders. Family businesses also frequently lack adequate succession planning, which can prompt a crisis in the event of the unexpected passing of a family member active in

(Continued)

Box 3: (Continued)

management. As struggling companies often take a heavy toll on managers' home lives, the divorce of a family member executive can also paralyze a family business, particularly when both husband and wife (and possibly sons and daughters as well) hold managerial roles in the company. In such cases, boards and management teams can fragment, thus leading to decisions made out of spite or based on sides taken in a family dispute that has spilled over into the business arena.

Fairness

Like Orwell's *Animal Farm,* employees at family businesses may all be equal, but some (family members) may be "more equal" than others. Any inequality with respect to salaries, vacation, dress code, attendance, working hours, or expense accounts will inspire resentment among nonfamily members and undermine the critical message in a turnaround that everyone is in it together. This can prove especially troublesome when underqualified family members are promoted over more experienced employees, making it difficult to retain the high-quality employees who become critical to implementing a turnaround.

Record Keeping

Some family businesses have been doing business with suppliers or customers for decades, and their contracts may be entirely verbal in nature. Although they may be enforceable in court, this makes it difficult to determine their assignability or rejectability in event of a bankruptcy filing or change of control. Transfers of shares between family members are also rarely well-documented, which in a sale could require expensive legal fees to reverse transactions or create adequate documentation.

Organizational Chart Irrelevance

Turnaround managers working with family businesses can find that the decision-making power in a company does not follow any traditional organizational chart. The "favorite grandson" of a patriarchal founder can wield disproportionate power despite being a junior executive with limited experience, or the wife of a deceased founder can be pulling strings behind the scenes despite having never held an official position in the company. As in all businesses, identifying the key thought leaders and influencers is critical to the turnaround manager, but in a family business, those are more likely not to correspond to organizational charts.

Downsizing Difficulty

When positions must be eliminated, turnaround managers can struggle to convince the board of a family business that some of those laid off should be family members. In addition, companies can expose themselves to potential liability acts if severance packages offered to laid-off family members are substantially more generous than those offered to other employees.

Trends

There is an old expression, "rags to riches to rags in three generations." This reflects the frequent observation that the third generation of a family-controlled company is the one that destroys it. There are interesting reasons for this, but many countries have a similar expression.

the Cinadar Family and sold through in-home trunk shows. They later developed a mail order business and the founder's daughter created the vision for a new brand in 1983, inspired by the preppy look of Boston collegiate rowers, which she named J. Crew. The catalog was launched shortly thereafter and featured classic American men's and women's wear designed to mirror the Ralph Lauren look at a lower price point. The catalog grew to $100 million by 1988. In the early 1990s, J. Crew expanded into the retail business to reach consumers who preferred to shop in stores. Texas Pacific Group (TPG) purchased a majority interest in J. Crew for $560 million. The brand began to stray by targeting younger consumers and attempting to be more trend-forward and cheap instead of offering classic merchandise. This shift led to heavy discounting, overaggressive store expansion, and finally, by 2002, J. Crew was in violation of bond covenants and at a substantial risk of default. Meanwhile, the company had gone through five CEOs under TPG's ownership.

In January 2003, Mickey Drexler was named CEO. Known as the "Merchant Prince," he had spent his entire life in the fashion industry. When Drexler was CEO for Gap the company grew from $400 million to $14 billion in sales, but then he was criticized for his overaggressive store expansion and strategy, and he left. He turned down a multimillion dollar severance package from Gap because of a noncompete clause and joined J. Crew as CEO. Drexler invested $10 million in the company and was given a 22 percent equity share. Drexler faced payables that were already stretched to almost forty-five days and suppliers threatening to shut them off. The company had a Z-score that predicted that bankruptcy may be on the horizon. The company also suffered from high employee turnover. Drexler worked quickly to turn the company around. When he first got there, he made all of his senior staff interview for their jobs.

He axed entire product collections when necessary. At a product presentation in his first meeting with his key staff, he asked them to "throw everything on the floor you don't love." The head of the women's line found herself jettisoning half of the product line created under the previous management team. Stating that "everything and anything is under attack," he created a turnaround plan that effectively addressed and improved J. Crew's strategic position, financial condition, and operations. From a strategic perspective, he recognized that the root cause of the problems was J. Crew's loss of its brand reputation, which stemmed from plummeting product quality, so he immediately began repositioning J. Crew as an upscale retailer offering luxury for less. More important, the renewed focus on quality enabled J. Crew to tap into a new market. Drexler recognized that the retail industry consisted mostly of price players and luxury players, with much less competition filling the space between the two. To deliver on the value proposition, Drexler focused on improving quality, fit, design, color, style, and fabrication. He banned the J. Crew name or logo from the outside of all garments, arguing that the upscale consumer he was targeting did not want to advertise brands on their clothes. He pushed his team to focus on the details of a garment, such as the lining or the trim. Drexler had inherited old inventory and poorly designed clothes for the Christmas selling season and decided to take the financial hits immediately because he needed to generate cash immediately. First, he focused on inventory reduction. He ordered steep discounts on old merchandise in order to liquidate the extensive inventory, some of which was up to five years old. He also cancelled already placed orders for goods that he found unappealing to prevent a further buildup. For select items, he created a sense of scarcity to reinforce the image of luxury and to better manage the inventories, effectively training consumers to purchase products early rather than waiting for sales because there was a higher probability products would sell out. To make sure there was not a buildup of unwanted inventory, he also instituted a policy whereby sales were final. Moving upscale also required improving customer service. Leading by example, Drexler continues to insist on personally reviewing and addressing customer complaints, and can be seen at headquarters making late-night phone calls to anguished customers. Drexler had no qualms about walking into stores and quizzing strangers, both clerks and customers, about their likes and dislikes. He has also shifted inventory from stores with disappointing sales to those that were thriving, and made further operational changes such as relaunching Crew Cuts, a children's line.

Drexler entered the $45 billion wedding industry in 2005 after a telephone operator for J. Crew's catalog business told him that women were buying simple sundresses in more than one color to use as bridesmaid dresses. With that information, Drexler knew customers wanted bridal dresses and was willing to experiment to see if it worked. This reinforced J. Crew's new upscale image, as they used the same satin that Vera Wang and Chanel frequently used even though J. Crew's were to cost $1,800 against Vera Wang's $5,000. He closed approximately 70 percent of the company's factories and began to use manufacturers that had been producing goods for such high-end designers such as Prada, Coach, and Oscar de la Renta. Next he closed unproductive stores and slowed new store growth. The reduction in store count and store size reinforced the higher-quality, more upscale image of the new J. Crew. He even got involved in the paint scheme of each retail store and focused on introducing hip music with the belief that customers who enjoy the overall shopping experience more would stay in the store longer and ultimately buy more. It is interesting to note that Drexler's micromanaging style may have been a weakness during the latter stages of his tenure at the much larger Gap because the company had grown too large for his personal supervision of small details. This leadership style, however, proved to be a strength at the much smaller $800 million J. Crew. During the turnaround, Drexler insisted on interviewing every employee, choosing models for the catalogs, and reviewing customer complaints. He still visits retail locations, chooses window displays, and challenges store employees on clothing selection and layout. He would often fiddle with clothes on the racks and move displays during store visits. He was able to recruit an experienced and deep management team from leading retailers, such as Gap, Saks, Coach, and Ralph Lauren. After three years with Drexler at the helm, J. Crew had a successful IPO. Earnings before interest and taxes swung from a loss to a margin that was the highest for any specialty retailer. While the company was losing money, it was not yet late in the crisis phase when Drexler assumed control, and thus he was able to focus his turnaround efforts on the strategic side of the business. TPG used the IPO to fully divest its stake, leaving Drexler as one of the largest shareholders in the company. Drexler has made the first family, the Obamas, his fans. All four wore the brand during their inauguration festivities. When Drexler took up the reins in 2003, J. Crew had $609 million in debt and 196 stores. Today, it has 121 stores, less than $50 million in debt, and $298 million cash on hand. Drexler says he hates "loser talk." To him that means saying "it can't be done."

Apple, Inc.

It is often assumed that the founder and entrepreneur cannot run a company once it gets bigger, particularly if it goes public. Steve Jobs, one of the founders of Apple, was brought back to save the company he founded. He was brought in when Apple went from market leadership and product technical quality to struggling to continue with a viable product line. In particular, Microsoft's Windows 95 and the extremely aggressive marketing campaign behind it substantially hurt Apple's sales and performance. There were a series of poorly performing CEOs, including Gilbert Amelio, who became CEO in 1996. Within eighteen months Apple had lost a net $1.6 billion and revenues were falling at the rate equal to 27 percent per year in the first quarter of 1997 alone. Amelio was a severe cost cutter, reducing all employment by over one-third and cutting back on all efforts at innovation. An article in *Newsweek* in late July 1997 summed up the market sentiment: "talk about fiddling while Rome burns. As Apple Computer laid off workers and hemorrhaged money, how did chief executive Gilbert F. Amelio spend his days? Discussing upgrades to his personal jet and planning his new executive offices. At a company renowned for its populist egalitarianism, that was a public relations blunder of the first order. It cemented his reputation as arrogant, isolated and out of touch—everything Apple didn't want to be." As former Apple executive and founder of Be Software Jean-Louis Gassée said in 1997, "Apple doesn't need a CEO; they need a messiah."[13] Through the acquisition of a company he had founded, NeXT, Steve Jobs was brought back as the company's muse, creating a positive change in the product mix and marketing at Apple. The strategic decision that Jobs made that was very important and controversial at the time was to continue in both the hardware and software industries. Nearly everyone who was a so-called expert in the industry said Apple should be broken up and the software pieces sold or spun off. Jobs, however, saw those two competencies as central to maintaining Apple's niche status as a PC company. He eliminated products he considered to be peripheral to Apple's core focus and terminated relationships with clone manufacturers, viewing them as a competitive threat and dilutive to Apple's own cause. These netted $400 million and returned Apple to its core competency of convenient consumer technology. Jobs and his team moved forward to "fire" many of their previous resellers and distributors, who they viewed as uncommitted to promoting Apple. Instead, they opened their own retail operations, initially through a "store-within-a-store" strategy inside Best Buy and Comp USA stores, and later as their successful own independent retail operation. Of course, developing and releasing the iMac, the Power Book, the iPhone, the iPod, and the iPad under his guidance certainly helped. As explained in the Introduction, much of this success stemmed from the leadership that the company's founder provided during a period of crisis—leadership that comes from the same kind of entrepreneurial energy that first brought the company to prominence.

Leadership in Crisis: A Case Study

In December of 2000, the board of directors of diversified food equipment manufacturer Middleby Corporation had finally grown tired of CEO David Riley's underperformance. Middleby developed and manufactured equipment for cooking and food preparation in restaurants, including fast food chains and other institutional food processing operations. The company had spent almost a decade expanding its product line without regard for margin attractiveness or strategic fit. They had a staggering 10,000 product lines, thinking they had to be a one-stop shop for commercial kitchen equipment. An ill-timed two million share repurchase during an industrywide slowdown in sales, expensive failures in enterprise resource planning (ERP) system implementations, and an oil-less fryer that didn't work after four years of R&D efforts had left the company with a share price at an all-time low and in violation of covenants on its $20 million, multicurrency, revolving credit line and $15 million senior unsecured note.

Rather than sit idly by, however, the board acted swiftly and decisively, dismissing Riley and promoting Selim Bassoul, the president of the company's Southbend division, to lead Middleby's restructuring as its COO and later as CEO. As a show of good faith to all the stakeholders, Bassoul mortgaged his house to buy the company's stock.[14]

Bassoul had demonstrated a capacity for crisis leadership at Southbend, where he became legendary for charismatic displays and unorthodox motivational techniques, such as the time he persuaded ten employees to volunteer their free time on nights and weekends to paint the 130,000 square-foot factory in exchange for an extravagant dinner and night on the town with him. At Middleby headquarters, Bassoul resorted to outlandish employee appreciation tactics such as dropping bonus checks from airplanes or distributing sales executives' bonuses from a rented armored truck, and organizing impromptu staff dinners. These personal connections with the employees he was trying to lead through a turnaround helped him clarify changing individual roles and improve company morale.

Bassoul met with Middleby's customers, as well as customers of his competitors. He learned what they didn't like about Middleby's products, quality, and customer service and learned what they wanted. He met with lenders to sell his ideas and buy time.

While winning over the key stakeholders in the organization, Bassoul conducted the analysis necessary to determine the appropriate turnaround strategy, which he called a five-point strategic plan focused on

- Rationalizing Middleby's business model by shedding business lines (such as mixers, serving stations, refrigeration units, and cabinets) that did not fit the new strategic vision of a company focused on its core competency of higher-margin cooking and warming products
- Diversifying and strengthening the customer base by extending a "no-quibble" return policy to restore a quality reputation and adding prisons, nursing homes, and educational institutions as customers, which are more recession resistant
- Creating a global brand by expanding offerings to include specialized products for global growth markets such as samosa fryers and tandoori ovens for Indian customers
- Creating a culture of innovation by re-investing in R&D so that Middleby could bring three new products to market every year
- Improving employee morale and accountability by cutting the number of layers of management from seven to three

Bassoul's overwhelming success at Middleby stems directly from his display of the three critical traits of turnaround managers. He demonstrated courage throughout the process by facing up to many stockholders who didn't want change, expecting the markets would improve; he showed decisiveness in his many rapid decisions, such as his discontinuation of 5,000 products that shrank top-line sales but restored the company to profitability. It was his credibility and honesty that got lenders, customers, suppliers, and employees to be willing to follow and support his many changes.

Perhaps his most courageous move came in the midst of the turnaround, when he convinced the board to bid for and purchase Blodgett, the market leader in convection ovens and char broilers. The Maytag subsidiary had 25 percent greater annual revenues than all of Middleby, making post-merger integration a daunting task, but Bassoul's due diligence convinced him that Middleby could cut costs through scale efficiencies to justify the acquisition.

Although impressed with Bassoul's early leadership, shareholders and the board did not expect such an aggressive proposal from their new CEO, having only just grown comfortable with the new, leaner Middleby. The company's credit ratings had yet to recover fully, and many felt that the company should simply weather the economic downturn and strengthen its balance sheet. Memories of a time before Bassoul's tenure also resurfaced. In 1989, Middleby had acquired Hussman Corp.'s foodservice equipment business, a disastrous purchase that had caused four years of litigation and management distraction. With the new millennium came hope that the company would avoid similar mistakes; many thought that acquiring a company with greater annual revenues than Middleby would represent a significant risk to those hopes.

Armed with meticulous due diligence research, Bassoul swayed the board to his point of view on Blodgett by leveraging the credibility with the board that he had developed both at Southbend and in leading the first steps of the Middleby turnaround. "I felt hesitant at first," admitted board member John Miller III, "but this was the guy, if anybody, that could make it happen." Impressed with Bassoul's courage and tenacity, the board voted unanimously to approve the merger, and that summer Middleby agreed to acquire Blodgett for $74 million in cash and $21 million in high-yield subordinated notes. Even after credit markets softened in the wake of September 11, 2001, Bassoul persisted, finally persuading Bank of America (the lead lender on the deal) of the transaction's merits, thus allowing the merger to close in December.

The purchase of Blodgett not only diversified Middleby's product portfolio but also allowed it to forge relationships with important new client accounts such as Yum! Brands, owner of Pizza Hut, Kentucky Fried Chicken, Long John Silver's, and Taco Bell. Customers had historically rated the Blodgett equipment as outstanding but lacking in customer service, so Bassoul paid customers personal visits and extended them Middleby's "no-quibble" warranty protection and reputation for service. Diligent post-merger integration efforts proved successful, with increased customer retention and repeat orders allowing the company to achieve almost all of the cost savings and streamlining opportunities it had identified during due diligence within just nine months.

Bassoul deserves praise for the courage, decisiveness, and credibility he displayed in leading Middleby through a crisis, but the company's board deserves credit as well for recognizing and responding to a crisis before it deepened further. Middleby's prior CEO had led them to the brink of the crisis phase, but the board made the difficult decision to change the company's leadership before it could slide further. It is no coincidence that Bassoul's plan then proved so successful, for had the company slid further down the organizational distress curve, it doubtlessly would have proven more difficult for Bassoul to hire and retain high-potential employees, provide a clear mandate for change, and inspire confidence in employees that his plan would work. His efforts show that the "ready-fire-aim" approach can unite employees behind a strong strategic vision to start and maintain the turnaround. It is often best to get everyone aligned behind a common goal even if that vision later changes in the face of new information such as an acquisition or other opportunity. Bassoul's efforts to flatten Middleby's organizational structure, tie compensation to performance, and unite employees behind common cause improved morale and enabled the company's impressive operational improvements. Under Bassoul's leadership, Middleby's stock rose 1,600 percent from its low when he took over, and the company was recognized by *BusinessWeek* as one of the 100 Hot Growth Companies of 2007 and by *Forbes* as one of America's Best Small Companies. Bassoul's purchase of Middleby stock was a great investment, as was Middleby's investment in him.

Conclusion

Leadership is the critical ingredient that makes it possible to execute a well-conceived turnaround plan. Even the most cleverly designed plan will fail if managers lack the credibility to convince their charges to pull together, the courage to make unpopular decisions, the decisiveness needed to forge ahead in times of uncertainty and rapidly approaching deadlines, and the willingness to communicate both good and bad information. In the next chapter, we examine the thirteen-week cash flow model, which serves as the backbone for financial decision making in a turnaround.

Chapter Four

Cash Not GAAP

Cineplex Odeon's founder was famous for many things: inventing the multitheater concept, creating the paper popcorn container, and using a holiday weekend to barbwire the entrances of his competitor's headquarters building. He also legitimately used a change in accounting assumptions to turn an operating loss of $45 million into a reported $40 million in profit, even though the company was bleeding cash.

You may have heard catchphrases like "cash is king" and nodded intuitively while wondering exactly what that means. In a turnaround situation, it means that cash flow is the *only* measure of financial performance that matters. It seems simple, but to the average chief financial officer, who has spent his life training to master the intricacies of generally accepted accounting principles (GAAP) as determined in the United States by the Financial Accounting Standards Board (FASB), it seems like a confusingly rudimentary tool that ignores all of the complicated accrual methods that previously seemed critical to representing a company's financial performance accurately. In this chapter, we examine why the 13-Week Cash Flow Model[1] differs from GAAP analysis, and how it should be used as a diagnostic and performance measurement tool in a turnaround.

Fair warning: Although the concept is easier to master than the over 10,000 pages of GAAP rules and guidelines, this subject is more technical in nature than our other chapters. Consultants who specialize in turnarounds can almost do these in their sleep. The first time is the toughest.

GAAP's Shortcomings

An example given earlier was how the truck stop company, Flying J, was shocked when they ran out of cash for payroll even though they appeared profitable under GAAP. By contrast, Lehman Brothers intentionally took advantage of how GAAP accounting rules worked when they used repurchase agreements or "repos."[2] Repos are a way for companies such as investment banks to get additional financing. Assets are transferred on the books to another party, who gets cash in exchange by agreeing to transfer back the assets in the future and repay the money. Lehman then got creative and booked the incoming cash as sales, which made them look more profitable. The cash went out to pay huge salaries, bonuses, and other liabilities. This was allowed under GAAP rules, even though Lehman remained obliged to repay cash to repurchase the assets at some later date. At present, no one knows how many other firms use this technique, but it helped push Lehman toward its eventual liquidation. Cash flow forecasting would mean that the repayment, which includes interest, would show as an outflow in the model, treated as a debt payment.

GAAP arose out of an understandable desire to look at the bigger picture of a company's financial performance by separating the recognition of revenue from the actual collection of cash, and to come up with a common numerical language to review financial performance. In most normal circumstances, this makes a great deal of sense; for example, if a company bills its clients for $100 million of goods that cost it $80 million to produce, but as of December 31 (or any other date representing the company's accounting year end) has only actually collected $50 million from its customers, it would be unreasonable to deduce that the company had a terrible year because it "lost" $30 million. If the same company collected the outstanding balance of $50 million during the first quarter of the following year while only billing $10 million, it would be silly to determine that the company had earned $50 million of profit on just $10 million of sales in the quarter. To address these questions regarding the timing of revenues and expenses, GAAP uses the accrual method, which essentially produces a "smoothing" effect wherein revenue is recognized not when it actually arrives in the company's bank accounts but rather when a credit sale is made, or a contract is completed, or some milestone (often a percentage of a long project being completed) is achieved.

Though sometimes useful in looking at a stable company's overall financial health (although even then, it permits such flexibility in terms of the assumptions used that "creative" managers can still distort a company's true health even while complying with GAAP's rules), GAAP becomes completely and totally irrelevant in a turnaround situation. First, GAAP is designed as a numerical language to keep score, an entirely backward-looking measure of a company's performance. Using it to make decisions about a company going forward is like driving a car relying only on the rearview mirror. Second, more important, the only thing that matters is the actual cash flows coming in and out of a company. Following GAAP principles, one might look at the next financial quarter (roughly 13 weeks), see that the company expected to make a profit overall, and assume that all is well. However, if one conducts a rigorous analysis plotting out exactly when cash will arrive in the bank account from customers and leave to pay suppliers, the very same company could be projected to run a negative cash balance for much of the quarter, potentially triggering a shutdown and liquidation. GAAP uses so many smoothing techniques, it's like saying you can't drown in a lake that *averages* four feet deep.

As turnaround consultant Alan Handley summarizes the problem succinctly,

> I'm a CPA by background, and it's like a scarlet letter I have to wear; I have to say I'm a CPA. I hate it because CPAs tend to focus on these conventions that were set up for one purpose, but they get away from the truth of the real business. People focus on net income; I could care less about net income. You tell me what net income number you want and I can get it by manipulating the assumptions like depreciation, or when we recognize revenue, and so on. Construction is the worst, too, because construction accounting is basically cost plus margin, so the more I spend in a quarter, the more "net income" I generate even though I won't get paid until the project reaches completion points. It's kind of a game, so I can generate whatever net income I want. If you actually rely on GAAP, it just destroys the underlying rationale of the 13-week cash flow, just by definition.

In reality, managing to true cash is alien to most managers because

- Almost all companies manage using some form of GAAP or IAS (International Accounting Standards)
- Wall Street measures companies' performance on so-called "earnings," not cash, all measured by GAAP/IAS
- Incentive programs focus on GAAP earnings, not cash
- Managers use profit and loss statement (P&L) items to prepare budgets according to GAAP and are measured against same
- GAAP accounting allows ways to, for example,
  - Book sales well before (or whether) cash is received
  - Capitalize and thus spread out P&L effect of capital expenditures, maintenance items, R&D, acquisition costs, and so forth
  - Not show effect of payment of debt
- Companies use a shortcut to calculate/forecast cash flow by
  - Calculating P&L
  - Adding back depreciation
  - Subtracting capital expenditures
  - Perhaps adjusting for changes in working capital
  - And then completely missing the *timing* of cash flows

Note: GAAP should not be confused with Gaap, the character in demonology study who is a prince in hell and can make men insensible and invisible. According to some authors, Gaap can make men ignorant.[3]

The 13-Week Cash Flow Model

To address GAAP's shortcomings, turnaround practitioners use the 13-Week Cash Flow Model, which comprehensively maps out the company's cash inflows and outflows on a week-by-week basis. The model rolls forward every week to maintain a consistent 13 weeks' (one financial quarter) worth of liquidity forecasting, which allows for ongoing measurement of the model's accuracy, critical given the "garbage in, garbage out" tendencies of all financial models, whose conclusions rely so heavily on their assumptions. The 13-Week Cash Flow Model (hereafter, 13WCFM, or simply "the model") ignores GAAP, EBITDA, or any other conventional accrual and smoothing methods of financial reporting, and instead focuses only on actual cash receipts and disbursements.

The model generally includes three distinct sections, each with its own spreadsheet: a page for anticipated cash receipts, a page for anticipated disbursements, and a page that aggregates the two to determine the company's debt capacity and availability going forward. After each week of the turnaround process, managers should reconcile the model against the company's actual bank receipts to measure its accuracy. This reconciliation (and any discrepancies it reveals) is one of the few metrics available for lenders and other external constituents to measure the ability of management to forecast near-term financial performance accurately. As such, the model has several applications in addition to its use as an internal forecasting mechanism. 13-Week Cash Flow Models are normally included as part of a debtor-in-possession (DIP) financing agreement, which provides companies with the capital necessary to fund a turnaround plan while operating in Chapter 11. (See Chapter Six for additional details on DIP financing.) Lenders will not even consider offering bankruptcy financing to a company whose management team has not produced a credible 13WCFM, and they will typically construct negative covenants into the financing agreement that require compliance with the agreed upon model's forecasts. Lenders will often require a 13WCFM for a company in the crisis phase to force them to be sure they don't run out of cash.

In constructing each section of the model, a manager must disregard all accrual and matching conventions, which can flummox classically trained CPAs. For example, if the company makes a normal sale on credit in week 2 of the model, it is not recorded directly on the 13WCFM in week 2 as GAAP accounting would dictate. Instead, we should look at the buying customer's historical tendencies (do they pay within the first ten days in order to take a 2 percent discount, or do they stretch their payables out past 30 days?) and make a reasonable assumption that the trend will continue, and plug the anticipated date of the cash's arrival

obj
cashflow
↓
cashout

recognize
cost

into the model accordingly. Similarly, if a company records the transfer of finished goods inventory into its COGS because a sale was made, this would not appear anywhere on the 13WCFM, for it is simply an accounting convention to determine how profitable that sale was under GAAP. The only transactions we would enter on the model would entail an actual cash receipt or disbursement, such as the purchase of inventory, which we would record as of the transaction's date. One common mistake is overlooking the capitalized accounts on the balance sheet that results from the principle of matching that is prevalent in accrual accounting. For example, repairs to property, plants, and equipment are often capitalized as assets on the balance sheet, which distorts their true effect on the company's cash flow; rather than recording such transactions as increases in asset balances, companies in a turn-around must recognize them on the 13WCFM as the outflows of cash that they are, when they are paid for. Similarly, customer deposits on yet-to-be-delivered orders are frequently recorded as liabilities, when in fact these are cash-positive transactions for which the fulfillment of the liability requires no or little (in the case of shipping expenses) cash outflow.

All of the balance sheet items developed on an accrual basis— such as accrued expenses, deferred expenses, and prepaid assets— must therefore be ignored, except to the extent that they involve a change in the company's cash balance. For example, the individual components of accrued payroll taxes or interest expense that one knows with certainty will involve an outflow during the next 13 weeks will be recorded, but one should never add expenditures related to booking the future obligation of the company to pay an amount that does not occur in the 13-week period.

Remember that the 13WCFM also disregards anything—assets or liabilities—that will not convert to a cash event as part of the company's operations over the relevant time period. Leasehold assets and intangibles, for example, have no place in the model, and so one should never worry about conducting impairment analyses or verifying the appropriate time period over which to depreciate or amortize assets. However, additions to PP&E that will require cash expenditures, or sale of existing PP&E that will result in cash inflows, are obviously entered into the model.

Relying on GAAP has brought down many companies, even when they weren't trying to hide something. For example, Itel Corporation was created to buy and lease expensive IBM mainframe computers. Itel paid large bonuses to salesmen, so when leases were signed they rang a large ship's bell hanging from the high ceiling of their lavish offices. The loud multiple rings made everyone in the office smile. They set records at the time by how short a time it took a startup to reach $1 billion in booked sales in 1980.[4] They used the model to acquire and lease other products such as railcars and intermodel containers. By measuring revenues and profits according to GAAP, they had a great lifestyle: sporty company cars, drinking fountains with Perrier water, annual week-long company cruises, flying 1,200 employees to Acapulco for a week, and other heavy spending.[5] Meanwhile, everyone ignored the easy "outs" in the leases, particularly for the high-priced mainframes; if a new model of mainframe was introduced, customers could walk away from the lease of the old model and purchase or lease the newer model from another provider. The development of new, faster computers was predictable, and sure enough, customers were returning equipment Itel had financed heavily with debt. In addition, Itel had booked as current income their predicted residual or future resale value of the equipment as it would come off lease. Because of the new models of machines, the actual resale value of the old ones plummeted. Itel received as cash substantially less than it had booked as revenue under GAAP. By 1987, Itel's revenues shrunk to $210 million and its debt had swelled to $1.3 billion. It declared bankruptcy.

For the purposes of illustrating the 13WCFM, I have included screenshots of various tabs in a version of the model built for one of Handley's clients, a manufacturer we have disguised as "Wolverine Tooling." As the model available on this book's Web site displays, Wolverine got into trouble when its gross margins and sales both fell so precipitously that they could no longer cover for the company's lax A/R collection policies. Table 4.1 shows the P&L statement for Wolverine, as well as its balance sheet. The rest of this chapter highlights ways to use those data to help construct the 13WCFM shown at the end of the chapter.

Table 4.1. Wolverine Tooling Company Balance Sheet

| | Fiscal Year End December 31 | | | |
| | $000s | | | |
	2007	2008	2009	2010
Assets				
Cash	1,000	1,000	1,000	1,000
Accounts receivable, net	15,000	17,500	20,000	26,000
Inventory, net	39,000	42,500	45,000	30,850
Prepaid expenses	5,000	5,000	5,000	5,000
Total current assets	60,000	66,000	71,000	62,850
PPE	172,500	175,000	177,500	180,000
Accumulated depreciation	(7,000)	(14,000)	(21,000)	(28,000)
PPE, net	165,500	161,000	156,500	152,000
Total assets	225,500	227,000	227,500	214,850
Liabilities and shareholders' equity				
Accounts payable	4,000	5,000	5,000	8,575
Accrued expenses	2,000	3,000	4,000	2,000
Current portion of LT debt	1,000	1,000	1,000	1,000

Line of credit	12,225	11,980	13,020	15,795
Total current liabilities	19,225	20,980	23,020	27,370
LT debt	30,000	29,000	28,000	27,000
Paid in capital	175,000	175,000	175,000	175,000
Retained earnings	1,275	2,020	1,480	(14,520)
Total equity	176,275	177,020	176,480	160,480
Total liabilities and shareholders' equity	225,500	227,000	227,500	214,850
Check		—	—	—
DPO = (Avg. AP / COGS) * 365	18.22	17.34	19.16	28.07
DSO = (Avg. AR / sales) * 365	54.41	49.23	63.36	82.52
Inventory turns = COGS / avg. inventory	2.58	3.05	2.56	3.73
Fixed charge ratio	1.44	1.26	0.89	(2.30)
Interest coverage ratio	2.70	1.99	0.57	(11.80)
Debt / EBITDA	2.89	3.06	3.63	(3.48)

(Continued)

Table 4.1. (Continued)

Wolverine Tooling Company Income Statement	Fiscal Year End December 31 $000s									
	Actual 2007	Actual 2008	Actual 2009	Actual 2010	Projected					
					1/31/11	2/28/11	3/31/11	4/30/11	5/31/11	6/30/11
Sales	$100,625	$129,750	$115,210	$115,000	$10,063	$10,063	$10,063	$10,063	$10,063	$10,063
COGS	80,125	105,258	95,250	111,500	8,553	8,553	8,553	8,553	8,553	8,553
	79.6%	81.1%	82.7%	97.0%	85.0%	85.0%	85.0%	85.0%	85.0%	85.0%
Gross margin	20,500	24,492	19,960	3,500	1,509	1,509	1,509	1,509	1,509	1,509
Percentage	20.37%	18.88%	17.32%	3.04%	15.00%	15.00%	15.00%	15.00%	15.00%	15.00%
SG&A	10,125	15,000	12,250	11,250	$805	$805	$805	$805	$805	$805
	10.06%	11.56%	10.63%	9.78%	8.00%	8.00%	8.00%	8.00%	8.00%	8.00%
EBITDA	10,375	9,492	7,710	(7,750)	704	704	704	704	704	704

Percentage	10.3%	7.3%	6.7%	-6.7%	7.0%	7.0%	7.0%	7.0%	7.0%	7.0%
Depreciation	7,000	7,000	7,000	7,000	583	583	583	583	583	583
EBIT	3,375	2,492	710	(14,750)	121	121	121	121	121	121
Other income (expense)	(1,250)	(1,250)	(1,250)	(1,250)	(5,104)	(104)	(104)	(104)	(104)	(104)
Net income before taxes	2,125	1,242	(540)	(16,000)	(4,983)	17	17	17	17	17
Provision for income taxes	(850)	(497)	—	—	—	(7)	(7)	(7)	(7)	(7)
Net income	$1,275	$745	$(540)	$(16,000)	$(4,983)	$10	$10	$10	$10	$10
	1.27%	0.57%	-0.47%	-13.91%	-49.52%	0.10%	0.10%	0.10%	0.10%	0.10%

Constructing a 13WCFM

The construction of a solid 13-Week Cash Flow Model begins with the systematic deconstruction of the balance sheet, specifically through the analysis of working capital accounts to determine when they will convert to cash events. Naturally, the sooner one can convert inventory and accounts receivable into cash inflows, the better, while the opposite is true for the conversion of accounts payable and accrued expenses into cash outflows.

In analyzing accounts receivable, managers should review the aging of various accounts, which will often require an examination of the invoices sent on each account to "unwind" those book-entry receivables. It is important to pay attention to the terms of each agreement; many large retailers are notorious for agreeing to 2–10 net 30 terms (a 2 percent discount if paid in the first 10 days, otherwise due within 30 days of receipt) and then paying sometime between 45 and 60 days and *still taking the 2 percent discount.* If one is willing to confront a good customer, it may refund the ill-gotten 2 percent, but until then, they will be happy to take a discount while stretching the supplier's cash to the breaking point.

Managers should exclude receivables amounts whose collection seems unlikely, such as those that have aged beyond 90 days, are subject to customer disputes regarding quality or warranty policies, or have been billed to customers who appear to be troubled themselves or who have filed bankruptcy. After disregarding these customer balances, managers should determine receivables dilution, or the extent to which customers take discounts on their bills because of damaged crates, mismarked goods, or other claims.

Throughout the receivables analysis process, mangers should remain conservative with regard to expected collection dates. Common errors include ignoring dilution and relying on aged accounts, whose collection probability is highly unpredictable. Meanwhile, managers should evaluate the company's in-house receivables function to determine whether it needs improvement in order to increase the velocity of the cash conversion cycle. When he lectures in my class, Handley often tells the tale of an unnamed A/R team with which he worked as a bank-inserted CRO:

You sometimes work with these small company A/R teams, or maybe a company so small that it's just a comptroller, and they're not making a big salary but they're actually the most important persons at the company, because *they're the ones who get the cash flow*. You would be *amazed* at the change in behavior you can produce when you offer people a $25 Starbucks card for whoever collects the most in a given week or month. Give them a $50 Starbucks card? Let me tell you, they'll be calling accounts they didn't even remember they had, just to win that coffee.[6]

In Table 4.2, you will find an example of how one would convert a company's accounts receivable into a 13WCFM.

Here, we see that the company has $6.833 million in receivables that are older than 90 days. We should not expect to receive any of these, so in the income statement we would be likely to book an uncollectible A/R reserve in that amount, but this figure should appear nowhere on the 13WCFM. Instead, we are focused entirely on the receivables we still expect to collect, and we must make a reasonable assumption about how many days it will take us to collect them. In this case, if we assume that we can collect receivables within 60 days, and that for the sake of conservatism,

Table 4.2. Wolverine Tool Company A/R Aging as of December 31, 2010 (in thousands of dollars)

	Days Outstanding				
	0–30	31–60	61–90	>90	Total
Home Depot	3,667	4,000	—	2,733	10,400
Lowes	2,750	3,000	—	2,050	7,800
Caterpillar	1,833	2,000	—	1,367	5,200
Jonny Construction Company	458	500	—	342	1,300
We Must Protect This House Builders	458	500	—	342	1,300
Total AR	9,167	10,000	—	6,833	26,000
	35.26%	38.46%	0.00%	26.28%	100.00%

all of the receivables between 31 and 60 days old are as "fresh" as possible (that is, they are only 31 days old), that means it will take 29 days to collect the $10,000 in receivables in the second column above. Again, for the sake of conservatism, we will round that 29 days (4.14 weeks) up to five weeks, suggesting that the $10,000 in cash will arrive during week 6. Some readers might wonder why we would be so conservative in rolling that entire sum—some portion of which in all likelihood is already older than 31 days—into week 6 instead of distributing it evenly across several weeks. It should be noted that we have simplified the model here, showing the receivables collected at monthly intervals. In reality, they would be put into the actual week each receivable is expected to arrive as cash. The concepts, however, are the same. It still pays to assume cash will arrive later than hoped. According to Handley, "It goes to credibility—if you have a lot of errors in your 13-Week Cash Flow Model, it turns into a feeding frenzy. If the team can't put together a good model, people ask, well, what else can't they do? Maybe they're just not the team to get this company back on track, so it's scrutinized pretty heavily."

These entries into the 13WCFM's receipts tab translate as demonstrated in Figure 4.1; note how receivables older than 90 days are disregarded entirely.

In summary, one should deconstruct the existing balance sheet for accounts receivable by

- Reviewing agings (and more likely invoices) to "unwind" receivables
- Paying very careful attention to terms
- Excluding amounts that are not probable of collection (those older than 90 days, those with customer disputes, credit memos, or from apparently troubled customers, etc.)
- Determining dilution (when a customer refuses to pay the full invoiced amount)

During this exercise, one must evaluate exactly how well the A/R function is operating and whether additional attention in this area could increase the velocity of the cash conversion cycle. It is important to be conservative, as it helps no one to be overly aggressive with the assumed timing of cash receipts. Common

Figure 4.1. Accounts Receivable Aging Translated into 13WCFM

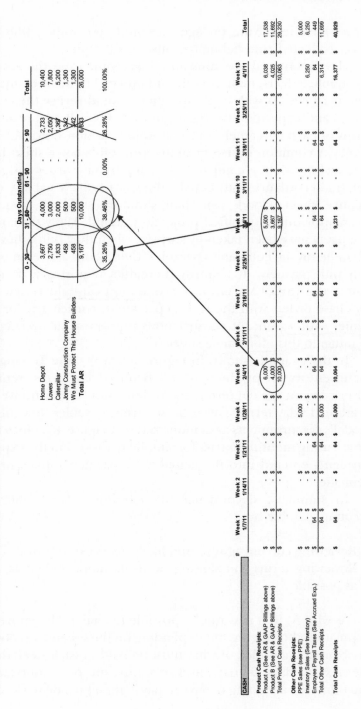

errors include relying on aged accounts receivable, which are never collected, and failing to consider dilution.

Having entered the appropriate amounts from the accounts receivable ledgers, managers should proceed to the accounts payable balances. As with A/R, managers should review the current agings and expected invoices to unwind the A/P, and review the terms of each agreement to see how best to slow down A/P payments. A common oversight stems from off-balance sheet liabilities, such as when a company issues a purchase order for goods, but (in accordance with GAAP) does not book a liability on its balance sheet. Goods can then show up suddenly, requiring payment within a specified projection period. Many turnaround managers have been taken by surprise when they think they have a handle on the company's payables, then goods arrive unexpectedly with payment due shortly thereafter, requiring a recalculation of the 13WCFM. As a result, one must carefully review open purchase orders with the A/P department, particularly for companies with significant construction in progress or R&D activity to mitigate this off-balance sheet risk.

In the example shown in Figure 4.2, Wolverine Tooling pays for inventory on products A and B on 60-day terms, rent and advertising on five-day terms, and utilities and administrative overhead on 15-day terms. Given those terms, payables flow into the model's disbursements as demonstrated in Figure 4.2. Once again we are using monthly entries for simplicity's sake, but the expected payments entered into the actual week payments *would* have to be made.

In summary, deconstruct the existing balance sheet for accounts payable by

- Reviewing current agings (and likely invoices) to "unwind" A/P
- Reviewing terms and slowing down payment of A/P as much as possible

As with A/R, it may not be possible to analyze the entire A/P population thoroughly, but depending on the system, it *is* possible to obtain a good idea of what must be paid in each week during the next 30 days, 60 days, and so on. Again, be conservative; if you think you are going to have to pay it, then include it. Common

Figure 4.2. Accounts Payable Aging Translated into 13WCFM

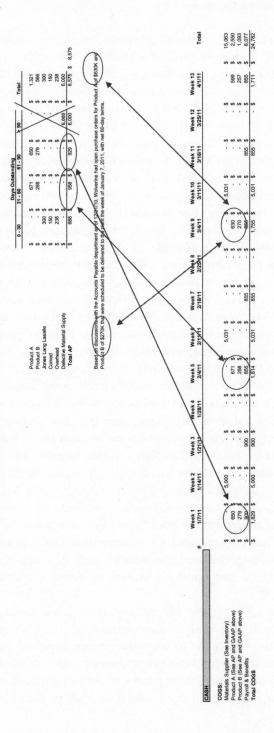

errors stem from off-balance sheet liabilities, such as goods for which the company has issued a purchase order, which do not require the company to book a liability under GAAP. The goods then show up at the company's front door, making payment due within the 13WCFM's projection period or even arriving with terms set at cash on delivery (COD). It is therefore critical to review open purchase orders with the A/P department when constructing a 13WCFM to ensure that management is aware of these looming cash disbursements. Companies that have significant construction-in-progress or research and development activity merit especially close review of off-balance sheet risks.

Inventory represents the third major component of working capital, and as such it must be integrated into the 13WCFM by reviewing the company's production schedule to determine how much inventory is scheduled to be consumed during the 13-week projection period and cash needed to buy new raw materials. It is important to scrutinize the company's claimed inventory balances; companies in a turnaround have likely responded to their distress by liquidating inventory as much as possible to free up cash. As a result, whatever inventory is still left over is often obsolete or otherwise unsalable, significantly reducing its potential to drive cash receipts. Companies often don't like to sell inventory below book value, as GAAP requires them to show a write-off and a loss, even though it is really a positive cash flow; in a turnaround, they must be disabused of this notion. In addition, special attention should be paid to work-in-progress, or WIP; as traditional borrowing agreements ascribe no value to WIP (that is, WIP does not increase the borrowing base), a more rapid conversion of WIP to finished inventory should become a priority. This will ease liquidity both by increasing any borrowing cushion with its lenders (by increasing finished inventory) and through the short-term restriction of raw good purchases to those critically needed to finish WIP.

Once an accurate inventory balance has been determined, managers should analyze the company's historical seasonal inventory buildup patterns to identify the appropriate maximum and minimum levels for inventory. Proper analysis of the timing of expected orders and their payment terms can then lead to significant improvements in the company's cash position, as many companies fail to manage inventory aggressively enough. In addition to relying on obsolete or slow-moving inventory to determine the timing of purchases, errors in this stage of the analysis include the failure to consider inventory that is in transit, having been shipped Freight on Board as of arrival at the company's property (FOB); in such a situation, the title to those inventory assets has not yet transferred to the company, thus preventing it from becoming visible in GAAP financials, but it will soon show up on the door and require cash outlays during the projection period.

Assuming Wolverine Tooling plans to maintain approximately four months of inventory, make new purchases when ending inventory balance drops below $30 million, and set inventory terms of FOB destination at seven days, and goods are usually delivered within seven days of the order, the company's cash disbursements for inventory purchases are as summarized in Figure 4.3.

In summary, to deconstruct the existing balance sheet for inventory,

- Review production schedule to determine how much inventory is scheduled to be consumed during the projection period
- Determine minimum/maximum levels for inventory
- Establish timing of orders, terms of order (COD, CIA, Net 30, etc.) for new inventory purchases
- Review obsolete and slow-moving inventory reserve

This analysis can often lead to significant improvements in cash position if company is not managing inventory aggressively if inventory is sold. Common errors are

- Failure to consider inventory in transit shipped FOB destination (not visible in financials as title hasn't transferred but is going to show up on your doorstep during projection period)
- Reliance upon obsolete or slow-moving inventory in determining inventory purchases

Another example: Once upon a time there was a publisher of children's books. Its list included the popular *Ask Isaac* series, written by scientist Isaac Asimov. Books were sold by commission-based employees who would call school librarians and public

Figure 4.3. Inventory Purchases as Reconciled with 13WCFM

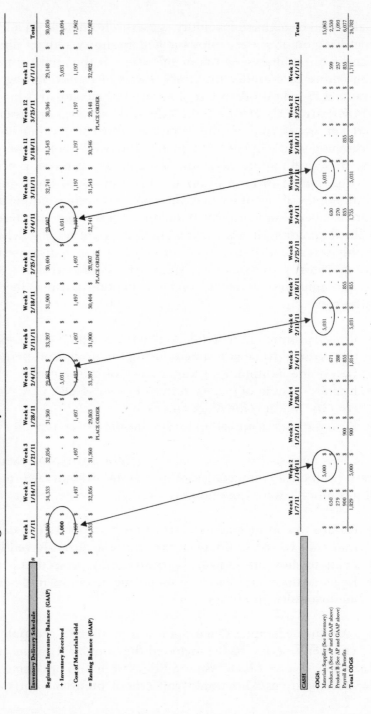

libraries to sell boxes of an assortment of books. They were sold on the basis that the customers had 60 days to review the books and return any they didn't want. Under GAAP, the sale was shown the day they shipped. Meanwhile, customers would return boxes of books, not pay, and leave the publisher's warehouse employees busy sorting the books, checking for damage, and putting each in its proper place back in the inventory. The publisher also paid for the freight to send the books as well as return them. Cash was going out to print and manufacture the books, pay for shipping, warehousing, SG&A (selling, general, and administrative expenses), and so forth. For the books that were kept, many libraries traditionally paid very late. Thus, the company bled cash but showed a profit almost up until the time it declared bankruptcy.

With the major working capital items out of the way, managers can then focus on smaller but still important accounts such as accrued expenses and liabilities, payroll and related taxes, property and sales taxes, professional fees (including, occasionally, an outside turnaround consultant's retainer), rent expenses, and interest expenses. Commonly overlooked items include other assets such as prepaid insurance expenses and additions to PP&E, which require cash payments that are amortized under GAAP.

Upon reconciling all relevant balance sheet accounts to the 13WCFM, managers should then review the income statement activity for cash disbursements that were not recorded through accounts payable, such as payroll expense, sales commissions, and contractually obligated bonuses. This should complete the simple unwinding of existing accounts that fills out the first month or two of the 13-Week Cash Flow Model, bringing the manager to the most challenging part of the model-building process: the subjective forecasting of future receipts based on historical A/R terms and dilution. This is as much art as science, for these forecasts must take into account historical trends, seasonality, potentially aggressive price negotiation from customers who feel they can exploit the company's weakness, and even details as granular as scheduled holidays that will cut a week's comparable sales by some 20 percent because purchasers won't be in the office. Because of the uncertain accuracy of these forecasts, managers should continually review and revise the model as they enter the second and third months of the projection period to ensure that they are not making faulty assumptions.

In the example of Figure 4.4, the 13WCFM makes the conservative assumption that the projected sales of $10.063 million in the month of January are all collected on the company's standard 60-day schedule, indicating that cash should become available in the week of April 1. Again, these would normally be spread into each actual week expected.

Managers will also have to make assumptions regarding disbursements to fill out the latter half of the initial 13WCFM. Managers should use some conservative take on historical performance for inventory turns to determine how long inventory will sit before being converted to a sale, while taking care to account for seasonality and production breaks, such as an extended plant closure for maintenance or during the December holiday period. For A/P expenses, managers can typically model assumptions based on the prior month's activity for routine, fixed expenditures such as utilities or rent payments, while more variable components must be linked to the factors that drive them. For example, SG&A expenses such as sales commissions are tied to sales, so the same assumptions regarding top line sales should drive the forecasts of those disbursements. In this step, common errors include overlooking nonrecurring expenses stemming from the company's financial distress, such as cure payments to lenders, retainers for attorneys, consultants, appraisers, and other professionals, and even bankruptcy filing fees. Most other expenditures should be relatively routine and predictable timing, such as payroll, taxes, debt service, and so on.

In the disbursements example in Figure 4.5, the expenses of $599,000 and $257,000 related to Products A and B are assumed to have been paid exactly 60 days after ordering; rent and advertising are paid five days later, and utilities and overhead are paid 15 days later.

The manager should now have completed the cash and debt roll-forward analysis, which draws information from the receipts and disbursement tabs to determine when the company will need cash. In Wolverine's case, the quarter will be a profitable one, but a properly completed 13-Week Cash Flow Model (shown in Table 4.3) would reveal that without significant cutbacks in expenses,

Figure 4.4. An Example of Projecting Forecasted Sales into Receipts

GAAP - Billings	Actual			Projected					
	10/31/10	11/30/10	12/31/10	1/31/11	2/28/11	3/31/11	4/30/11	5/31/11	6/30/11
Total Sales	$ 9,583	$ 10,000	$ 9,167	10,063	10,063	10,063	10,063	10,063	10,063
Product A	$ 5,750	$ 6,000	$ 5,500	$ 6,038	$ 6,038	$ 6,038	$ 6,038	$ 6,038	$ 6,038
%	60.00%	60.00%	60.00%	60.00%	60.00%	60.00%	60.00%	60.00%	60.00%
Product B	$ 3,833	$ 4,000	$ 3,667	$ 4,025	$ 4,025	$ 4,025	$ 4,025	$ 4,025	$ 4,025
%	40.00%	40.00%	40.00%	40.00%	40.00%	40.00%	40.00%	40.00%	40.00%
Total Sales	$ 9,583	$ 10,000	$ 9,167	$ 10,063	$ 10,063	$ 10,063	$ 10,063	$ 10,063	$ 10,063
Collection Assumption (Days)	12/30/10	1/29/11	3/1/11	4/1/11	4/29/11	5/30/11	6/29/11	7/30/11	8/29/11

Actuals

CASH	Week 1 1/7/11	Week 2 1/14/11	Week 3 1/21/11	Week 4 1/28/11	Week 5 2/4/11	Week 6 2/11/11	Week 7 2/18/11	Week 8 2/25/11	Week 9 3/4/11	Week 10 3/11/11	Week 11 3/18/11	Week 12 3/25/11	Week 13 4/1/11	Total
Product Cash Receipts														
Product A (See AR & GAAP Billings above)	$ 5,750	$ -	$ -	$ -	$ 6,000	$ -	$ -	$ -	$ 5,500	$ -	$ -	$ -	$ 6,038	$ 23,288
Product B (See AR & GAAP Billings above)	$ 3,833	$ -	$ -	$ -	$ 4,000	$ -	$ -	$ -	$ 3,667	$ -	$ -	$ -	$ 4,025	15,525
Total Product Cash Receipts	$ 9,583	$ -	$ -	$ -	$ 10,000	$ -	$ -	$ -	$ 9,167	$ -	$ -	$ -	$ 10,063	$ 38,813

Figure 4.5. Projecting Disbursements

GAAP	Actual			Projected					
	10/31/10	11/30/10	12/31/10	1/31/11	2/28/11	3/31/11	4/30/11	5/31/11	6/30/11
COGS	$ 9,292	$ 9,584	$ 9,000	$ 8,553	$ 8,553	$ 8,553	$ 8,553	$ 8,553	$ 8,553
SGA	$ 938	$ 938	$ 938	$ 805	$ 805	$ 805	$ 805	$ 805	$ 805
	$ 10,229	$ 10,522	$ 9,938	$ 9,358	$ 9,358	$ 9,358	$ 9,358	$ 9,358	$ 9,358
COGS:									
DM: Cost of Materials	$ 6,504	$ 6,709	$ 6,300	$ 5,987	$ 5,987	$ 5,987	$ 5,987	$ 5,987	$ 5,987
DM: Product A	$ 650	$ 671	$ 630	$ 599	$ 599	$ 599	$ 599	$ 599	$ 599
DM: Product B	$ 279	$ 288	$ 270	$ 257	$ 257	$ 257	$ 257	$ 257	$ 257
DL: Payroll & Benefits	$ 1,858	$ 1,917	$ 1,800	$ 1,711	$ 1,711	$ 1,711	$ 1,711	$ 1,711	$ 1,711
Total COGS	$ 9,292	$ 9,584	$ 9,000	$ 8,553	$ 8,553	$ 8,553	$ 8,553	$ 8,553	$ 8,553
SG&A:									
Rent	$ 300	$ 300	$ 300	$ 300	$ 300	$ 300	$ 300	$ 300	$ 300
Utilities	$ 150	$ 150	$ 150	$ 150	$ 150	$ 150	$ 150	$ 150	$ 150
Advertising	$ 250	$ 250	$ 250	$ 250	$ 250	$ 250	$ 250	$ 250	$ 250
Overhead	$ 238	$ 238	$ 238	$ 105	$ 105	$ 105	$ 105	$ 105	$ 105
Total SG&A	$ 938	$ 938	$ 938	$ 805	$ 805	$ 805	$ 805	$ 805	$ 805
Total Expenses	$ 10,229	$ 10,522	$ 9,938	$ 9,358	$ 9,358	$ 9,358	$ 9,358	$ 9,358	$ 9,358

Actuals

CASH #	Week 1 1/7/11	Week 2 1/14/11	Week 3 1/21/11	Week 4 1/28/11	Week 5 2/4/11	Week 6 2/11/11	Week 7 2/18/11	Week 8 2/25/11	Week 9 3/4/11	Week 10 3/11/11	Week 11 3/18/11	Week 12 3/25/11	Week 13 4/1/11	Total
COGS:														
Materials Supplier (See Inventory)	$ -	$ 5,000	$ -	$ -	$ -	$ 5,031	$ -	$ -	$ 630	$ 5,031	$ -	$ -	$ -	$ 15,063
Product A (See AP and GAAP above)	$ 650	$ -	$ -	$ -	$ 671	$ -	$ -	$ -	$ -	$ -	$ -	$ -	$ 599	$ 2,550
Product B (See AP and GAAP above)	$ 279	$ -	$ -	$ -	$ 288	$ -	$ -	$ -	$ 270	$ -	$ -	$ -	$ 257	$ 1,093
Payroll & Benefits	$ 900	$ -	$ 900	$ -	$ 855	$ -	$ 855	$ -	$ 855	$ -	$ 855	$ -	$ 855	$ 6,077
Total COGS	$ 1,829	$ 5,000	$ 900	$ -	$ 1,814	$ 5,031	$ 855	$ -	$ 1,755	$ 5,031	$ 855	$ -	$ 1,711	$ 24,782
SG&A:														
Rent (see AP and above)	$ 300	$ -	$ -	$ -	$ -	$ 300	$ -	$ -	$ -	$ 300	$ -	$ -	$ -	$ 900
Utilities (see AP and above)	$ -	$ -	$ 150	$ -	$ -	$ -	$ 150	$ -	$ -	$ -	$ 150	$ -	$ -	$ 450
Advertising (see AP and above)	$ 250	$ -	$ -	$ -	$ -	$ 250	$ -	$ -	$ 100	$ 250	$ -	$ -	$ -	$ 850
Overhead (see AP and above)	$ -	$ -	$ 238	$ -	$ -	$ -	$ 105	$ -	$ -	$ -	$ 105	$ -	$ -	$ 448
Total SG&A	$ 550	$ -	$ 388	$ -	$ -	$ 550	$ 255	$ -	$ 100	$ 550	$ 255	$ -	$ -	$ 2,648

the company would hit a negative cash balance in week 3, which would potentially force the company to shut down. Focusing entirely on EBITDA would have proven disastrous, as the forecast would fail to recognize the impending liquidity crisis. EBITDA analysis of these same numbers shows that a quarterly profit of over $2 million would be received. Even if broken down by month, serious losses don't show up under GAAP until late in the period, after the company would run out of cash earlier.

Once completed, the 13WCFM does not exist in a vacuum but instead should be subject to constant review and revision as new transactions take place and new information comes to light. Managers should also refuse to take the assumptions as givens; while Wolverine might be able to remain solvent with 60-day A/R collection periods, it obviously would be in far better shape with 50-day or even 40-day periods. As mentioned in the Introduction, managers should benchmark against competitors in the industry and against their own historical trends to determine what a "best-practices" collection policy might look like, and see how that would impact the conclusions of the 13WCFM.

Conclusion

The 13-Week Cash Flow Model is the most widely recognized tool of an experienced turnaround practitioner, and it can provide a much-needed dose of reality to incumbent management teams in denial or accustomed to masking the company's struggles with accrual accounting chicanery. In implementing a turnaround plan, just as much credibility is lost from producing an inaccurate 13WCFM as is gained from producing an effective one. In a period of constrained liquidity, managers must stay on top of the 13WCFM every day, ensuring that its projections contain a sufficient buffer to account for inevitable errors in forecasting. The discovery of any inaccuracy requires immediate recalculation, and if it is sufficiently severe, early disclosure to stakeholders who depend on it, such as lenders, a bankruptcy judge, a trustee, or a receiver. Just one week into the projection period, managers should begin constructing projections for week 14, so that the company retains a full fiscal quarter of visibility into its liquidity situation.

Table 4.3. Wolverine Tooling 13-Week Cash Flow Model Detail

	Week 1 1/7/11	Week 2 1/14/11	Week 3 1/21/11	Week 4 1/28/11	Week 5 2/4/11	Week 6 2/11/11
Opening Cash Balance	**1,000**	**1,000**	**1,000**	**1,000**	**1,000**	**1,000**
Cash Inflows:						
Product A	5,750	—	—	—	6,000	—
Product B	3,833	—	—	—	4,000	—
Other Cash Receipts	64	—	64	5,000	64	—
Total Cash Inflows (A)	**9,647**	**—**	**64**	**5,000**	**10,064**	**—**
Cash Outflows:						
Inventory Purchases	—	5,000	—	—	—	5,031
AP: Product A	650	—	—	—	671	—
AP: Product B	279	—	—	—	288	—
Payroll & Benefits	900	—	900	—	855	—
Rent	300	—	—	—	—	300
Utilities	150	—	150	—	—	—
Advertising	250	—	—	—	—	250
Administrative Overhead	238	—	238	—	—	—
Payroll Taxes	—	—	—	—	—	—
Insurance/Workers Compensation	500	—	—	—	—	—
Total Direct & Indirect Job Outflows	3,267	5,000	1,288	—	1,814	5,581
Capital Expenditures	1,000	—	—	—	—	—
Total Cash Outflows (B)	**4,267**	**5,000**	**1,288**	**—**	**1,814**	**5,581**
Cash Surplus/ (Deficit) (A-B)	**5,381**	**(5,000)**	**(1,223)**	**5,000**	**8,250**	**(5,581)**
Financing:						
Beginning Revolver	15,795	10,414	15,414	16,637	11,637	3,387
Cash Need	—	5,000	1,223	—	—	5,581
Paydown	5,381	—	—	5,000	8,250	—
Ending Revolver	10,414	15,414	16,637	11,637	3,387	8,968
Total Commitment	$25,000	$25,000	$25,000	$25,000	$25,000	$25,000
Cushion	$14,586	$9,586	$8,363	$13,363	$21,613	$16,032
		Low Cushion				
Ending Cash Balance	**1,000**	**1,000**	**1,000**	**1,000**	**1,000**	**1,000**

Week 7 2/18/11	Week 8 2/25/11	Week 9 3/4/11	Week 10 3/11/11	Week 11 3/18/11	Week 12 3/25/11	Week 13 4/1/11	Total
1,000	**1,000**	**1,000**	**1,000**	**1,000**	**1,000**	**1,000**	**1,000**
—	—	5,500	—	—	—	6,038	23,288
—	—	3,667	—	—	—	4,025	15,525
64	—	64	—	64	—	6,314	11,699
64	**—**	**9,231**	**—**	**64**	**—**	**16,377**	**50,512**
—	—	—	5,031	—	—	—	15,063
—	—	630	—	—	—	599	2,550
—	—	270	—	—	—	257	1,093
855	—	855	—	855	—	855	6,077
—	—	—	300	—	—	—	900
150	—	—	—	150	—	—	600
—	—	100	250	—	—	—	850
105	—	—	—	105	—	—	685
—	—	—	—	—	—	834	834
—	—	—	—	—	—	500	1,000
1,110	—	1,855	5,581	1,110	—	3,045	29,651
—	—	1,000	—	—	—	—	2,000
1,110	**—**	**2,855**	**5,581**	**1,110**	**—**	**3,045**	**31,651**
(1,046)	**—**	**6,376**	**(5,581)**	**(1,046)**	**—**	**13,332**	**18,861**
8,968	10,014	10,014	3,638	9,220	10,266	10,266	15,795
1,046	—	—	5,581	1,046	—	—	19,478
—	—	6,376	—	—	—	13,332	38,339
10,014	10,014	3,638	9,220	10,266	10,266	(3,066)	(3,066)
$25,000	$25,000	$25,000	$25,000	$25,000	$25,000	$25,000	$25,000
$14,986	$14,986	$21,362	$15,780	$14,734	$14,734	$28,066	$28,066
1,000	**1,000**	**1,000**	**1,000**	**1,000**	**1,000**	**1,000**	**1,000**

It should be noted that this technique is sometimes used as a daily cash flow model, or even extended to cover a full year of forecasting. Thirteen weeks (or a quarter of a year) is simply the time horizon used most frequently.

Finally, how does an executive solve the dilemma of properly managing his company focusing on cash flow, but have investors and government agencies talking in GAAP? The answer:

- Manage to cash, *but . . .*
- Report in GAAP/IAS

Chapter Five

Downsizing Is a Tool, Not a Goal

Too often, executives today feel they must have a corporate goal to downsize. In fact, Wall Street sometimes rewards a downsizing announcement with a jump in stock price. The executive him- or herself is almost always given a larger bonus by the board of directors for making such tough and difficult decisions, which may make them not so tough or so difficult. As we'll see later, they are probably foolish! In talking with various CEOs, I often hear they do it because Wall Street analysts expect that behavior. However, does simply ordering an 8 percent or 15 percent across-the-board cut in headcount show real leadership or decision-making abilities? No. In this chapter, we examine the pros and cons of downsizing, the issues that should be considered first, and the real effects on corporate performance.

Managers have too often seen layoffs as a panacea for deeper underlying problems, and therefore make one of the most common mistakes in a turnaround; they fail to reexamine their strategy and core competency and then reengineer the company's processes before identifying which costs and people to cut. How does a company know how far to cut, who best to cut, or which product lines or services would be most harmed by cuts if they didn't first examine their strategy, based on what the customers want? Once that is known, downsizing becomes one of the tools to implement the changes needed.

The 13-Week Cash Flow Model discussed in Chapter Four will drive much of the decision-making in a late-stage turnaround, for it presents an exhaustive analysis of the company's sources and uses of cash over the near term. A frequent—but by no means invariable—conclusion that managers make from the 13-Week model's findings is that the company must reduce its cash burn in order to buy itself time, and given the significant percentage of corporate expenses that payroll represents, a common response is to consider layoffs, downsizing, right-sizing, reductions in force, headcount reductions, or any other number of euphemisms designed to soften the fact that people will be getting fired.

Business Process Reengineering

In the context of a turnaround, business process reengineering (or BPR) essentially represents the operational leg of the turn-around tripod. If we conceptualize our strategic elements as iden-tifying the "what"—the customer segment(s) we want to address and the products or services we want to offer them—then reen-gineering examines how we should provide those products to those customers. As explained in Chapter Two, strategy generally must come first in a turnaround; reengineering determines the changes made to the ongoing operations of the business to make them more efficient, identifying the resources needed to support them while eliminating any processes and people that do not contribute to customer value.

Depending on which articles you read, business process reen-gineering is responsible for quantum gains of 30 percent to a tenfold improvement in performance. BPR is credited with Wal-Mart's reduction of its restocking time from six weeks to thirty-six hours, HP assembling server computers in four minutes, and even a surge in sales at Taco Bell.[1] Because of misuse, the term reengi-neering has fallen out of favor. For convenience, we'll use it here, but it is now known by many names, including change manage-ment and business process redesign.

Reengineering originated as the brainchild of former MIT professor Michael Hammer and management consultant James Champy, who together authored *Reengineering the Corporation* in 1990. Its concept of starting from scratch with a metaphorical "clean sheet of paper" to make fundamental redesigns of a busi-ness's processes quickly became a buzzword in the 1990s. Hammer and Champy's theories centered on the shortcomings inherent in the division of labor into specialized functions, which began with one man drawing out the wire to make a pin, another to straighten it, and so on, rather than having one man make the pin start-to-finish,[2] and ultimately evolved into the separate functional departments of marketing, engineering, and so forth that we see at the modern corporation. They argued that this functional specialization had led to a proliferation of bureaucracy that increasingly fragmented work processes to the point that much of the "work" being done served no actual purpose to the company's customers. In response, they postulated that companies should not undertake the Total Quality Management (TQM) approach advocated by W. Edwards Deming, which advocated constant, gradual improvements, but rather should undertake rapid, revolutionary change all at once. Processes and tasks should be eliminated rather than automated wherever possible.

Hammer and Champy established three main principles for those wishing to reengineer their companies.[3] First, one must reject the status quo entirely and "reengineer" the business from scratch in an effort to reach its absolute maximum efficient form. The rationale behind this "clean sheet of paper" approach is that many of the work processes at companies both large and small add no value to the customer, and therefore should be discarded entirely rather than improved. Second, this imagining of the ideal company should start from the end of the flowchart—that is, from the customer's perspective—and only focus on adding to this clean sheet of paper the company's actions that somehow provide value to the customer, either by higher quality, more features, lower prices, quicker delivery, greater variety, superior service, or any other metric that customers actually care about . . . and are willing to pay for! Finally, having identified these value-adding activities, management should organize the company not around roles—such as finance, marketing, and manufacturing—but rather around the processes that add that value. For example, in many companies, simply making a sale requires activities across several functional departments: the sales department has to pitch to the client and then quote them a price; that price may need to be approved by an executive, with oversight by legal to make sure that the contract is to their liking. The customer derives no benefit from this specialization, and in fact, will be likely to find the inherent delays as the document gets shuttled from one department to the next—often for several iterations—frustrating and bewildering. Reengineering this process means creating cross-functional teams who are familiar with tasks necessary to the process to prevent delays and disruptions that create negative customer value. "You no longer have a file folder as the repository of data, passed between workers like a baton," Hammer explained, "You've got the capability of different people sharing tasks or performing multiple tasks at once."[4]

One highly successful example of reengineering in a turnaround comes from Caterpillar, the previously mentioned global manufacturer of earthmoving and construction support equipment. After a spike in international competition nearly bankrupted the company in the early 1980s, causing losses of $1 million a day, CEO George Schaefer led a radical process that fundamentally reengineered the company, finding its hierarchical, siloed organizational model badly misaligned with its customers' needs. Each functional general office (GO) of marketing, finance, pricing, manufacturing, and so forth had become its own fiefdom, with a painfully slow filter of information up and down each silo and little cooperation across them, yielding products that cost too much to produce. If, for example, a salesperson needed a minor design or price change to meet competition, months could pass before a decision was made, and the sale was lost. Despite facing inertial resistance and pressure to make across-the-board cuts, Schaefer created an internal team of "breakthrough thinkers" who could truly take a fresh look at the business from scratch, allowing them to break free of the status quo and imagine the company's processes as they should be to meet customers' needs. The resultant decentralized organization that emerged from the reengineering was implemented all at once. The GOs disappeared overnight with everyone assigned to a business unit and accountability moved downward along with decision-making authority. All units were now measured on profits and return on assets, thus losing the excuse of blaming headquarters. They sped the flow of information significantly, allowing Caterpillar to do a far better job of remaining responsive to changing customer demands.[5] Caterpillar is an example of a successful turnaround through reengineering.

Another large organization used volunteers to reengineer a small part of its processes before doing cutbacks. For an organization the size of the one in question, a staff of seventeen managing purchasing approvals didn't seem unreasonable, until you reflect that all they did was approve every purchase. The actual purchasing process from approved vendors occurred elsewhere; these seventeen people literally sat in their offices and filled out approval forms for every requested item in the organization, from expensive items all the way down to pencils and the cups in the cafeteria, with multiple layers of approval necessary within the department itself. Not surprising, the sheer number of requests for minute items overwhelmed the system, bogging it down to the point that requests for something as simple as a replacement water cooler took up to six months; people joked that the people in approvals must write very, very slowly. The reengineering team realized that the approval system in no way required such manpower, so they set a dollar amount hurdle at which a request would require approval and determined what sign-offs were needed that affected the approval of vendors. They trimmed the staff to six while reassigning the other eleven employees to areas where the organization actually needed resources, thereby significantly cutting all response times. No doubt remembering similar log jams where they worked, my students always chuckle when I identify the organization in question as none other than our own Northwestern University.

Because of a shift in power from manufacturer to their retail customers, Pillsbury knew it had to change its strategy and decided to reengineer the company.[6] It was an early-stage fix so they had time to do it right. They correctly identified that there was a tension between a cost-reduction focus and radical redesign of core processes to get the job done right. They understood that companies must eliminate or outsource functions that don't provide differentiation valuable to customers. They determined how to eliminate unprofitable products and shorten product development times and overhaul their supply chain to meet customer needs. The Pillsbury study showed $300 million in expected savings from the complete overhaul. Shortly after the study was completed, however, Pillsbury acquired Pet Foods and senior managers' attention was diverted. The seventy-five people from the reengineering team, without top management approval, launched divisional changes anyway, achieving $50 million per year in savings, with faster response times from suppliers and quicker replenishment to customers.[7] They proved reengineering works at divisional levels.

As with any management technique that comes to enjoy widespread popularity, reengineering has its share of critics. Supporters of more gradual approaches such as TQM (Total Quality Management) find its outright rejection of the status quo alarming and reactionary, arguing that one risks throwing the baby out with the bathwater. As I explain in my classes, I feel that such gradual improvement can only work in a non-turnaround situation where the processes are reasonably well run, or at worst, a company still in the blinded phase, when the time pressure is less critical, and a company can accept incremental change. Any further down the organizational distress curve, however, and a company simply will not have the time for anything less than radical changes, even if decided at a ready-fire-aim pace. Once the BPR has been implemented, TQM should be used to perfect the process, fine-tuning and updating the process over time.

The greatest criticism of reengineering stems, unfortunately, from its misuse by cost-focused managers all too eager to swing the axe: it became synonymous with layoffs and downsizing. As I have explained, however, this need not be the case. Reengineering should be the step taken before downsizing to determine whether layoffs are actually necessary in the first place. It is truly remarkable how many times I have seen successful turnaround professionals enter a company facing a real crisis, and upon reengineering the company's operations determine that there was an opportunity to *grow* out of the problem, eliminating the need for layoffs entirely or at the very least mitigating the size of the necessary cuts. Reengineering can also identify situations in which a department needs significant reductions but that additional resources will be needed in other areas, so turnaround managers can simply re-assign those employees to new roles rather than laying them off. Unfortunately, reengineering became such a powerful buzz-word in the early 1990s that it became ubiquitous before everyone claiming to practice it fully understood what it meant, and far too many people began to identify it with cuts, having heard some variation of "I'm sorry, we're reengineering, so you're out."

In short, reengineering should not be synonymous with layoffs, but rather, it is the analytical process through which one must go in order to determine whether layoffs are necessary, and if so, where and in what numbers. Where complete reengineering of a company is impractical, a Six-Sigma approach is a frequently used tool to examine a specific department or set of processes.

Today, Six Sigma analytical methods are applied to the reduction of any kind of subjective errors or elimination of duplication. It requires one to define a process where there are poor results, taking measurements to determine current performance, analyzing the information to find where things are going wrong, improving the process to eliminate errors, and adding controls to keep it from happening again.[8] Jack Welch and his successor at GE, Jeff Imelt, spent up to $600 million a year mostly for almost two thousand Six Sigma experts, known as "black belts," to bring about $10 billion in savings.[9] Companies used the technique to reduce factory inventories, to discover double handling of doctors' insurance claims, and to improve throughput in accounts payable departments. If this process precedes downsizing, it, too, can determine the best and perhaps only places to cut staff.

Downsizing: Pros and Cons

Even if a company has first addressed its strategy, and then reengineered its business processes, layoffs are often considered as a default option. The thinking is simple: we have to cut costs, so heads must roll. A study by Professor Paul Wertheim of Pepperdine University determined that of the stocks of companies announcing major layoffs, almost 40 percent outperformed their peers immediately following the announcement.[10] Typically, Wall Street analysts applaud such a move as "necessary cost-cutting" and an example of "belt-tightening to run leaner," often rewarding these companies with a ratings upgrade. However, the same study found that more than 60 percent took an immediate hit on the price of their stock. More important, within three years following the announcement, two-thirds of that 40 percent who got an initial bump in price significantly *underperformed* their peers. Why? I maintain that the kneejerk reaction to enact layoffs without deter-mining how they fit into strategy fails to consider the complex implications that layoffs entail, as managers become enamored with the primary upside of reduced costs while ignoring their many downsides. These other advantages and disadvantages are listed next. Even when in a crisis and into ready-fire-aim mode, they must be considered.

Advantages to Downsizing

- *Cost savings* on salaries and benefits can be significant, although they are frequently overestimated.
- Layoffs can also help you *get rid of underperformers*, if you have documented their performance and can't make better use of whatever talent or knowledge they have.
- *Increased productivity* can result if you have actually identified underperformers or those who remain committed to the status quo and eliminated them.
- Layoffs can *reduce decision time significantly*, resulting in a faster, more agile company, particularly if the layoffs eliminate layers of middle management through which information must diffuse. As pointed out in Chapter Three, Bassoul's turnaround at Middleby made the company significantly less bureaucratic by reducing the layers between himself and line-level employ-ees from seven to three, leaving the company less hierarchical and more able to respond quickly. Caterpillar accomplished the same thing through their reorganization, as discussed previously.
- Layoffs *signal to employees the seriousness of the company's situa-tion*, which can reduce internal resistance to the turnaround effort.
- The combination of the previous two benefits can *break barriers to change*, convincing potential opposition within the organiza-tion to let go of the status quo and support the turnaround plan.
- Layoffs also generally earn *approval from banks and investors*, who tend to perceive the executive ordering the turnaround as having greater credibility for having made a difficult decision.

Disadvantages to Downsizing

Ironically, one major downside to layoffs is actually near-term _increased costs_ stemming from severance costs, which can accelerate payments at first, resulting in an actually _worse_ cash position than would have occurred in the absence of layoffs. It's critical to factor in both savings on payroll and any accelerated severance payments when building a 13-Week Cash Flow Model. These costs are increased if a company's mass layoffs or plant closing fall under the Worker Adjustment and Retraining Notification (WARN) Act of 1988, which covers employers with more than 100 employees who have worked more than six out of the past twelve months and work more than twenty hours per week. The law has both federal and state versions, and employers must comply with both on any occasion that layoffs result in more than ninety-nine lost jobs or more than 499 lost jobs if the number represents less than 33 percent of the employees at the single employment site. In Illinois, for example, the number of lost jobs that triggers the act is only seventy-five, and each state has a slightly different version. Most require that employers enacting a mass layoff meeting those conditions must give their employees sixty days notice before the layoff, and failing to do so would trigger sixty days of paid wages for the employee. In fact, some courts have found that controlling shareholders of a company violating the act—and not simply the company itself—may be held personally liable for any violation of the WARN Act.[11] This book is not intended as a legal treatise, but rather as a guide to signal when you should contact an attorney, and any time a company thinks it is even close to triggering WARN Act protection is unquestionably such a time. (See Box 4 for other legal issues to keep in mind during a downsizing.)

Other than situations involving the WARN Act, companies should remember that their obligations to employees do not arise from a federal or state legal duty but are rather contractual in nature. Any documentation relating to a company's severance policy, either in an employment agreement, or an employee handbook, or on a company's corporate intranet or human resources Web site, such as "one month of severance per year of service,"

Box 4: Other Legal Issues in Announcing Layoffs

In a downturn, many companies will try to avoid layoffs by taking other cost reduction measures, such as announcing hiring freezes, curtailing travel budgets, and deferring bonuses. However, one popular technique that has gotten several companies in hot water is a substitution with temporary workers or "independent contractors."

Companies would generally prefer to pay all of their workers as independent contractors rather than as employees, for it greatly reduces the cost of payroll and benefits for those workers while making it significantly easier to terminate them. Companies paying independent contractors do not need to provide medical benefits, and they shift the cost of monitoring the independent contractor's income for taxation purposes onto state and federal governments. A "tax gap" therefore results when companies pay employees as independent contractors, created by those who do not file, who underreport income, or who underpay their tax liability.

Spurred by this tax gap, governments have begun cracking down on the misclassification of workers as independent contractors rather than as employees. This has been especially prevalent in the IT field, where large projects require a rapid buildup in human resources. In 2000, Microsoft settled a lawsuit for $97 million for misclassifying workers who had been with the company as far back as 1987 as temporary workers. Time Warner later settled a similar suit concerning so-called "perma-temps" for $5.5 million.

The IRS and labor agencies have also begun cracking down on troubled companies attempting to misclassify workers as salaried employees in order to avoid paying them overtime. A full exploration of either of these issues is beyond the scope of this book—the IRS has established a twenty-prong test to determine whether a temporary worker should actually be an employee, for example—but these are important issues that managers should contemplate with the help of trained legal and accounting advisors before making downsizing decisions regarding temporary employees and independent contractors.

can be considered a contractual obligation to make those stipulated severance payments to employees.

Perhaps the greatest disadvantage of layoffs is that the employer runs the *risk of employees filing lawsuits*. I tell the students in my class—as well as the clients I represent who are contemplating layoffs—to *assume* that they *will* be sued under various state and federal discrimination laws following any layoffs, and the only hope is to consult legal counsel in order to reduce the likelihood of losing. Invariably, layoffs are likely to involve the termination of employees falling into several protected classes, typically age, gender, race, and national origin. The best way to avoid lawsuits from employees claiming they were terminated because of their membership in a protected class is to have a clear, justifiable rationale for the layoffs. One very effective defense is if the terminated employee in the protected class worked at a plant that was entirely closed, or in a division that was shut down completely; that makes it very difficult to prove that the dismissal had anything to do with membership in a protected class. Another defense is a track record of poor performance reviews on the terminated employee, but it is important that these be formally documented, not conducted in a perfunctory or largely ceremonial manner, with evidence showing that reviews were taken seriously in the organization, ideally so seriously that other poor performers had been let go in the past. Performance reviews also cannot be pretextual; it is very difficult to justify poor reviews as the reason for dismissal if the employee received no such reviews for years, then received an impromptu negative review on Thursday before receiving her termination on Friday. General Electric serves as the industry standard in this regard, as their rigorous 360-degree review process provides significant documentation where Jack Welch's created goal of cutting the bottom 10 percent of employees every year establishes an organizationwide imperative for the evaluation and pruning of underperformers.

Even if an employer protects itself by preparing all of these defenses and complying with the necessary regulations, it must still make it clear to all remaining employees that responses to reference checks from firms interested in hiring the laid-off employees should consist only of positions held and dates of service: the HR equivalent of name, rank, and serial number, and nothing else. In one turnaround I executed, we had to lay off an underperforming worker who was part of the protected age group at age sixty. His underperformance was well documented through a series of performance reviews, which made us comfortable that we would be safe against any alleged age discrimination. Of course, a few weeks after his dismissal, a hiring firm called the company for references, but knowing that HR or any executive might acknowledge that he was dismissed for cause, the terminated employee had listed the direct phone number of his former supervisor as a reference. Although a poor employee, this worker had been known as a pleasant enough person, and so not wanting to hurt his colleague of so many years, the supervisor tried to do him a favor and protect him.

"Oh, no," he fibbed. "He was fine, we just had to let him go because of his age." We were sued, quickly settled, and cut the terminated employee a check for his *full* asking price within the hour, knowing that a losing case like that one wasn't even worth any legal bills.

Layoffs also cause the *loss of expertise or institutional memory*, which can be carried away by the terminated employees. In one noted turnaround, a steel mill decided that given the anticipated downturn in demand for steel, it would no longer need the 1,150 accountants it had on staff, so it cut the department 20 percent across the board. The cost savings were significant . . . until the company realized that among those departed were the only ones who knew how to close the company's monthly and quarterly books. Other examples include the dumbing down of newspapers by cutting the best senior reporters and increasing the number of color pictures.

That steel mill example also demonstrates the disadvantage of potential *later rehiring costs*. Companies sometimes lay off workers, only to realize later that either they overreacted by cutting too close to the bone or that they had reduced capacity just in front of a cyclical rebound. Either way, they find themselves understaffed, and often need to rehire the workers they laid off. As you might expect, ham-fisted attempts to hire those employees back at their old salaries with their severance packages returned do not prove terribly successful, so frequently they must hire ex-employees back as consultants while *still making severance payments*.

In the case of this steel mill, the rehired accountants enjoyed a nearly 200 percent income increase while receiving a month's salary for every year they had been at the company. For those with three decades of tenure, it amounted to nearly a 500 percent raise.

After layoffs, the survivors frequently display a _loss of trust_ in management. If the announcement remained shrouded in mystery even though everyone knew of the company's turmoil, workers may lose faith in the openness of management's communication style. They may begin to question management's commitment to workers if the entire executive team stays, or even worse, receives record bonuses, as AT&T CEO Robert Allen did in 1995 after announcing 18,000 involuntary layoffs. Perhaps most corrosive to morale is the perception that management caused the layoffs through their own ineptitude; many survivors of the layoffs will think that the management team got the company into this mess, yet the punishment is being meted out among the rank-and-file, a perception that discourages them from following management direction in the future.

Companies also suffer from _increased risk aversion_ among surviving employees, who know the axe has fallen and always suspect that it could again. In an atmosphere of suspicion and fear, no one wants to stand out in any way, whether for something as important as proposing a new idea that could flop (what if it doesn't work?) or as trivial as asking coworkers out to lunch (why does he have so much time on his hands that he can spend an hour away from the office?). The natural inclination to fade into the wallpaper and avoid notice is absolutely corrosive to team morale, and inhibits the kind of bold action necessary to save a company in distress.

The potential for _sabotage_ persists anytime layoffs are announced. At a Chicago-based candy maker, we knew we would have to initiate a plant shutdown that would trigger the WARN Act's notification standards; that is, we had to give employees sixty days' notice. However, a previous shutdown notification had prompted one of the employees to sabotage one of the assembly lines, so we were reluctant to run the risk of further such problems. At most businesses, the economic costs of sabotage are limited to any destroyed inventory or plant equipment, but at a food company the effects can be disastrous, as they can trigger FDA inspections that destroy the public's faith in the safety of the company's products. After weighing these options, we finally decided to give the required WARN notice and simply close the plant in sixty days while paying employees their wages. "Stay bonuses" were added to encourage everyone to make sure the plant ran well until it shut down. If the plant shut down early for any reason, no bonus would be paid.

Overloaded survivors can reduce a company's effectiveness post-layoffs, as they struggle to fill the roles left behind by their departed coworkers. The math is simple; unless there was already a great deal of slack in the system or there is a highly effective reengineering plan, a 20 percent cut in manpower means that the survivors must now do 25 percent more work, leading to burnout.

All of these factors tend to drive *low morale* following layoffs, as survivors wonder whether there will be another wave. Employees still at the company tend to mourn for their terminated coworkers and feel a sense of "survivor's guilt." They may spend more time sharpening up their résumés than performing actual work, as they have grown to feel more like independent contractors that the company views simply like cogs in a machine, assets to be stripped out when the opportunity arises. Moreover, the combination of poor morale, overloaded survivors, and the loss of institutional knowledge can cripple the effectiveness of outward-facing functions such as customer service. This in turn increases customer turnover, thus creating a vicious cycle of further downward pressure on both sales and morale.

There have been instances where those laid off are "happier" than those left behind in a very low morale environment. One study of layoffs at Boeing found that the "victims of Boeing layoffs were less depressed and drank less than those who remained,"[12] during the period 1996 to 2006 when the company laid off tens of thousands of employees. The survivors kept seeing more and more parts outsourced and friends downsized even as they "re-proved, re-auditioned, and repositioned"[13] themselves as their bosses demanded. Résumés were honed on company time.

One friend, a senior manager at another company, was under constant stress as he saw the downsizing occurring all around him. Then his wife brought him an unusual gift: the front panel of an office hallway cabinet that once held a fire extinguisher. It had a newly painted red metal frame and a glass front. Hanging from the bottom was a small metal hammer. A sign on the front said, "In case of emergency break glass." He had it mounted on the wall of his office. It had a picture of him taken at a company event to show through the glass. Behind the picture, however, he kept an updated copy of his résumé, always at the ready. That knowledge took some of the edge off his stress.

By contrast, companies that manage to avoid layoffs enjoy several advantages, first and foremost among them the worker loyalty it engenders. Companies such as Southwest Airlines built a remarkable culture of allegiance and trust by not once making layoffs in its nearly four decades of operations. Even in the wake of September 11, when every major airline announced significant layoffs and several filed for bankruptcy protection, Southwest stuck to its no-layoffs policy, cutting costs by delaying orders for new planes, cancelling renovations at headquarters, and halting route expansions.[14] Other companies have similarly avoided having to lower the axe by announcing hiring freezes, delaying raises and bonuses, cutting overtime or reducing the number of shifts at a plant, redeploying workers, offering early retirement, and cutting training, marketing, and travel expenses. (It's worth pointing out that Chainsaw Al undertook very similar cost-cutting measures at Scott Paper, but he did so *in addition* to staggering layoffs, rather than in place of them.) Not only does this engender incredible employee loyalty for Southwest—particularly in an industry where rancorous labor relations have become the norm—but it also positioned the company to take market share from understaffed competitors once demand rebounded. Finally, companies that avoid resorting to layoffs also enjoy an edge in recruiting talented employees, buoyed by the reputational effects of having done right by their existing employees.

To avoid the problems of mass layoffs, an unusual example of such creative avoidance of layoffs came from France Télécom, whose legacy employment contracts from its prior days as a nationalized company left it with tens of thousands of employees who were technically still civil servants with guaranteed jobs for life. After going on an acquisition binge during the go-go days of the dot-com boom, the company found itself mired with $89 billion in debt, unable to make the layoffs necessary to cut costs and return to profitability. Employees could be dismissed only if they stole something. Instead, the company solicited voluntary departures from any employees who wanted to become an entrepreneur, hired a team of investment bankers and consultants in offices all over France to train these employees and hone their business plans, and seeded the approved business plans with the necessary startup capital to launch the new businesses. Beginning in late 2005, France Télécom funded thousands of small businesses, from pizzerias and sports bars to scuba diving shops, even a magician. The company even paid for one employee to take classes in winemaking and advanced him the funds necessary, including for the purchase of a tractor, to start producing his own brand of champagne. Each business plan was vetted by an internal team, with a 90 percent approval rate, and employees had the option of returning to their jobs after three years if the fledgling businesses proved unsuccessful.[15]

The France Télécom example may have little direct relevance to any business not so terribly constrained by draconian labor laws that prevent the dismissal of employees. (Efforts to loosen these labor protections in 2006 were met with widespread rioting and protests, and later layoffs caused dozens of suicides, which led to the resignation of the executive in charge of the layoffs.[16]) However, it does demonstrate the creative lengths to which a company can go in its effort to avoid layoffs, and in the process winning the loyalty of its employees. Perhaps more instructive is the example of Beth Israel Deaconess Medical Center in Boston, which found itself facing a significant reduction in state funding in the wake of the recent economic downturn. The hospital's financial hardship threatened its longstanding policy of admitting and treating anyone who could make it through the front door, a mission statement that exacerbated its financial struggles when other hospitals began forwarding clearly indigent and uninsured patients to Beth Israel to protect their own margins. CEO Paul Levy held a meeting of the hospital's higher wage earners—nurses, technicians, and physicians—and explained that the consulting firm the hospital hired had told him he would have to lay off the bottom 10 percent of workers, low-wage jobs that entailed replacing sheets, polishing the floors, and delivering food. Arguing that most of those employees were barely making it as is, many of them first-generation immigrants working second and even third jobs, he asked the assembled throng to make sacrifices in order to save their lower-paid coworkers.

Applause broke out. Soon Levy began receiving more than a hundred e-mails per hour from employees, volunteering to forego pay raises and making suggestions on how to cut costs without laying off workers.[17] While Beth Israel's nonprofit culture made such cuts palatable where they might not be at for-profit organizations, it goes to show that very often employees will band together and actually grow closer if a company can avoid layoffs, whereas they can instead become disaffected and morose if a company cannot.

Family businesses offer a slightly different variation on this question of intracompany dynamics governing the appropriate strategy when a layoff appears necessary. Rivalries among siblings, different sides of the family, or different generations can come boiling to the surface in times of crisis, paralyzing a turnaround effort or even influencing opinions on where layoffs are necessary in order to settle old family scores. Alternatively, loyalty to family members may tempt managers to avoid needed cost-cutting, to the extent that it could constitute a breach of fiduciary duty to creditors and the entity itself when the family business enters the zone of insolvency. As explained in Box 3 in Chapter Three, a turnaround manager must remain aware of such subtle dynamics that can undermine effective governance and decision making— particularly when a family member will be one of the downsized employees—in turning around family businesses.

Short-Term Versus Long-Term Strategy

An important issue in downsizing is weighing short-term strategy against long-term. When Robert Nardelli took over as CEO and chairman of Home Depot in 2001 he chose the former. Founded in 1979, Home Depot went through rapid growth with a strategy of low prices and hiring customer-friendly, experienced trade people for every department, reaching $40 billion in sales by the year 2000. Growth slowed and earnings fell 20 percent in the fourth quarter of 2001 partly caused by the economic environment at the time. Nardelli came in and slashed costs. In particular, he drove down payroll as a percentage of sales by cutting back on store personnel and replacing full-time employees with part-timers. While this gave a short-term boost to earnings, it alienated a loyal customer base as the company became known for terrible customer service and untrained associates. Turnover rates were much higher for the part-time associates. Similarly, his price increases on many products helped in the short run but drove customers to competitors. Nardelli was able to decrease cost of goods sold by his $1.1 billion decision to create a centralized purchasing and inventory control system, replacing the systems used by each of the store managers. Again, there were short-term gains, but it took the store managers' knowledge of their local markets too far from the equation. These and other measures were part of his attempt to create a disciplined group of employees who followed his orders, driving out any entrepreneurial thinking. Although Nardelli came up with good ideas, such as trying to attract more female customers, his implementation approaches always alienated others, especially the previously frequent customers to the stores.

Coupled with a massive acquisition binge and hasty entrance into multiple new business lines, these issues meant that Nardelli took the company away from its core competency of providing knowledgeable personnel and competitive products to customers. Home Depot's stock during his tenure first increased, then underperformed, dropping by nearly 30 percent while the S&P 500 increased by 12.8 percent and close competitor Lowes' stock outperformed the S&P by nearly 150 percent. Nardelli left after six years at the company, was paid over $300 million over that time, and received a $215 million severance package. The board had given him a contract that focused on short-term results and guarantees to entice him to join the company. His successor brought back knowledgeable personnel and improved customer service.

Reversal of Fortunes

As Home Depot shows, disastrous downsizing can be reversed over time, even if the losses it created cannot. There are a few other examples.

From humble beginnings in 1914 as a bus company set up to transport workers to iron ore mines in Minnesota with only eight buses, Greyhound grew into an American icon with almost 5,000 stations and 10,000 employees.[18] They changed their strategy and ownership multiple times along the way, acquiring companies in meatpacking, soap manufacturing, money order services, bus manufacturing, and even airline leasing. Along the way, Greyhound went through three different kinds of failed turnarounds under three CEOs. In the late 1980s, the then CEO provoked a heated union strike that ended in the company filing bankruptcy. Frank Schmieder, a former investment banker, was the new CEO when the company emerged from bankruptcy in October of 1991 as a public company. He knew aggressive cost-cutting would impress Wall Street's securities analysts, despite his limited experience in the transportation industry. He operated for the next three years under the mode of managing Wall Street expectations, focusing on short-haul trips that forced long-haul passengers to change buses multiple times. Multiple rounds of layoffs reduced costs, and the company offered deep promotional discounts for advanced fares.

While the workforce continued to shrink, causing Wall Street to heap praise on the company, the management team did not cut back on their own executive perks, including newly remodeled offices, first-class travel, season tickets to professional sports teams, and annual executive retreats for managers and their wives at the luxurious Greenbrier Resort. As a result of cutbacks in people, ticket offices, buses, and maintenance facilities, customer relations soured and remaining employees felt alienated. Ridership began to slide in 1992 as customers felt the impact of the bare bones strategy with fewer routes, older buses, and more transfers. Management blamed the decrease in ridership on increased pressure from airlines. Employee turnover at terminals reached 100 percent annually and experienced regional managers were being fired and replaced by part-time workers. A well-touted new computerized reservation system was launched without being properly tested in an effort to meet the timeline of the rollout promised to Wall Street analysts. The computer and toll-free service numbers soon became overwhelmed and the whole system shut down. Over 80 percent of those who made advance, no-money-down reservations were no-shows, but cash-paying walkup customers could not buy a seat because the system indicated the buses were full. In addition, management sold a meaningful number of their own shares of Greyhound stock before any performance warnings were given to the Wall Street analysts. With the company being on the verge of bankruptcy only three years after exiting the courts, Schmieder resigned due to pressure from shareholders.

The next CEO, Craig Lentzch, decided that the company had to go back to basics. First, he secured an out-of-court refinancing to prevent the company from having to file for bankruptcy again. His strategy was to rebuild again to an inexpensive nationwide network and focus on increasing revenues and ridership by improving customer service. He also partnered with the competition, including regional bus service operators and Amtrak, for potential synergies and began new strategic initiatives to benefit from changing demographics of its target market. The long-haul routes were initiated again, but for the higher-traffic areas only. Greyhound added more departures for high traffic routes, such as New York to Boston, and introduced brand-name chains into concession options at stations. Service was further improved by establishing priority seating for long-haul passengers and hiring people trained for better handling of customer calls. Lentzch paid careful attention to employee relations, including updating driving, hiring, and training programs and proactively initiating the negotiation of union contracts over a year before expiration. Believing the markets along the U.S./Mexico border were significant growth opportunities, management invested $2.5 million in a joint venture in Mexico to provide through bus service on selected routes. In the United States people take less than 2 percent of long distance trips by bus compared with 98 percent in Mexico, where buses are the primary mode of transportation. He even attracted more leisure passengers by initiating bus routes along special destinations such as casinos, airports, and train stations. His B to B diversification focused on express package shipping between rural and urban areas. The new buses he ordered gave a roomier, more comfortable seat, which also had lower maintenance costs, and added lower steps to accommodate senior citizens. Lentzch transformed a nearly insolvent company into a stable, growing business by focusing on strategy, finances, and operations, not by starting with cutbacks of people but rather by determining the number and skills of employees needed based on the new strategy initiatives that first focused on individual and business customers' needs. Lentzch could never make up the losses caused by his predecessor, but he brought profits and morale back.

Managing Morale During Layoffs

Sometimes, layoffs will prove inevitable even after a company revamps its strategy and reengineers its business processes, but even then, a management team must understand that there are right and wrong ways to proceed with a layoff so as to minimize (not eliminate) its effect on employee morale. In an excellent article in the *MIT Sloan Management Review*, Karen Mishra, Gretchen Spreitzer, and Aneil Mishra explain that clear communication is critical to preserving employees' feelings of trust toward the company and empowering them to perform their jobs.[19] They explain, as I have written above, that layoffs should be seen as a last resort, with a penultimate option to offer early retirement with a reasonable severance package so that headcount reductions can result from voluntary departures. Although this does make the company seem less heartless, it also runs the risk of losing the most qualified personnel, who may jump at the opportunity, secure in the knowledge that they will have no trouble finding other employment while pocketing a nice severance package. One of my colleagues, Professor John Ward, is very popular among students. We tried to lure him away from another university for years, until it ran into severe financial difficulties stemming from a slowdown in Medicaid payments to its hospital system and medical school. Unable to terminate professors with tenure, it offered a generous buyout package for any tenured professor who would leave voluntarily. Naturally, professors who lacked faith in their ability to find tenure elsewhere refused the offer, while the strongest professors there—such as Ward—took the buyout and had an offer for tenure from a competitor university within a matter of days. His situation demonstrates that even nonprofit organizations are not immune to the adverse selection that can happen when a company offers a blanket voluntary early retirement; very rarely do the "bad apples" leave rather than the most valuable employees.

I once served on a conference panel with a veteran executive of AT&T who opined that they had gone through six rounds of layoffs during his tenure, and in his opinion, they had fouled up every one of them. In one example, they had offered the same voluntary retirement packages across the board, but the highest percentage of acceptance was in the sales department. Many of the company's top corporate salesmen took the buyout and immediately jumped to a competitor, using their strong customer relationships to steal away corporate business from AT&T. The use of a noncompete agreement can mitigate this risk, but only slightly, as such agreements are notoriously difficult to enforce, particularly in certain states. Reasoning that you cannot prevent someone from earning a living, most courts are reluctant to enforce noncompetes unless they are significantly restricted in the scope of competitive activity prohibited, the geographic region in which it is active, and the time frame (generally six or twelve months is about the maximum most courts will enforce). One exception to this reluctance to enforce such agreements is in acquisition agreements; if you purchase a business and part of the deal structure provides for a noncompete from the selling shareholders, courts will reason that you provided consideration in exchange for a bar on competition during some reasonable time frame.

If involuntary dismissals are in fact necessary, a rigorous reengineering process should reveal this, as well as where those layoffs should be concentrated. Executives frequently look at the bottom line and declare "we need 15 percent across-the-board cuts," but in considering whom to lay off, I preach equity, rather than equality. Simply taking some arbitrary percentage needed to return to stop the bleeding and spreading it equally across all departments may seem fair and democratic—"we all have to share the burden"—but it is also lazy and ill-advised. A successful reengineering will invariably reveal that some departments are overstaffed by three times that amount, while others may actually need additional resources to implement any strategy.

There is some question as to how transparent the planning process should be before announcing a layoff; in order to avoid potential sabotage, paranoia, or "working to rule" (a situation where a union intentionally begins slowing down work according to legacy union contracts that specify obsolete rules or rates of speed), I recommend keeping the process as quiet as possible. If employees know that layoffs are coming, companies often see a spike in worker's compensation claims, as employees attempt to avoid the ax by going on disability leave.

Upon announcing necessary layoffs, it is absolutely critical that a sound reengineering process has identified how many are necessary. In general, one should err on the side of caution and cut further than may be necessary; turnaround plans always take longer and cost more than one expects, and so it is better to cut a bit closer to the bone than was absolutely necessary. Naturally, this is tempered by the risk of cutting too far and having to rehire employees as expensive consultants, as mentioned previously, but the countervailing risk is even greater. Successive waves of layoffs give employees the perception that the company is in a death spiral, and that they could be next at any given moment. This effect is heightened any time management makes the well-intentioned but ill-advised decision to appoint one executive to announce the layoffs at a series of facilities one-by-one, as one major investment bank did in the aftermath of the dot-com bust. After traveling down the West Coast and gutting, in succession, the Seattle, San Francisco, Menlo Park, and Los Angeles offices, he became known as "Dr. Death," and bankers spent more time e-mailing wild speculation about his next destination than on conducting actual work.

To avoid the corrosive effect on morale that multiple waves of layoffs cause, turnaround managers should "measure twice and cut once." This becomes a huge credibility test for the team running the turnaround: by putting a stake in the ground and assuring the survivors of the layoff that there will be no more layoffs, they earn credibility only so far as they keep their promise. Making such a declaration and then going back on one's word inspires a lack of confidence among the workforce and further depresses morale.

In order to dampen the psychological blow that layoffs will represent, managers should furthermore identify all the constituents affected by the announcement. This includes not only the laid-off workers and the survivors and their unions, but also the community in which the business operates, relevant government agencies, and the local press. With careful planning, one can mitigate the company's loss of goodwill by demonstrating that it has made a good-faith effort to reduce the impact the layoffs make on each stakeholder. For example, companies can earn credibility by inviting other local employers to interview the affected workers or seeking to secure funds under the Job Training and Partnership Act to ease their transition to new positions. If the turnaround plan makes a facility redundant or unnecessary, it can be donated to a local economic development agency or other nonprofit organization, thus demonstrating a commitment to community. Companies can even offer to make higher-than-stipulated payments to local governments to help them survive a precipitous drop in tax revenues due to the shutdown of a plant.

When it comes time to announce the layoffs, management must display honesty and compassion. It is absolutely critical that employees hear about the layoffs not from the media but from management itself. This has grown increasingly difficult in a world of twenty-four-hour communication, as the ease of spreading information through social networks such as Twitter means that companies should assume that if one employee has heard the rumor, every employee has heard it, even in sprawling companies that operate across several continents. As a result, the company's media relations department—if it exists—should attempt to stay ahead of the story by preparing a simultaneous mass dissemination strategy. In its 1999 bankruptcy filing, Purina Mills used an overnight delivery service to ship 10,000 video copies of the CEO's message about the company's planned restructuring, and conducted town hall meetings where employees could ask the CEO questions and have their concerns addressed, which preceded one-on-one managerial discussions with the employees terminated.

Compare Purina's approach with that of Julian Day, who terminated 400 Radio Shack employees with an e-mail that read: "The workforce reduction notification is currently in progress; unfortunately, your position is one that has been eliminated."[20] The e-mail further notified recipients that they had thirty minutes to pack up their desks and say goodbye to coworkers before they were escorted off the premises. The resultant media storm demonstrates how simply taking the time to notify affected employees in person makes a huge difference in how the layoff is perceived both inside and outside the company.

Instead, managers should speak honestly with employees about why the layoffs were necessary. While terminated employees can grow hostile, I have found that sometimes it helps to express genuine regret about the situation and explain that sometimes it is necessary to cut 20 percent of the jobs at a company in order to save the other 80 percent. If the terminated employee then argues that he or she should not have been among those laid off, it helps to have documented performance reviews justifying why they were chosen, or some other ironclad reason such as the entire department or division being let go.

Contrary to popular opinion, Fridays—particularly those before a long weekend—are not a good time to announce layoffs, as it prevents employees from getting their questions answered. It is far better to announce the layoffs earlier in the week, and then offer those employees the day off; productivity almost always plummets on the day of the announcement, so employees appreciate the chance to go home and notify their families of the news.

After announcing layoffs, companies should follow the general rule mentioned in Chapter Three that it is almost impossible to overcommunicate in a turnaround. This prevents myths—such as rumors of new waves of layoffs—from disseminating through the company, hampering morale. To the extent the company has any resources to help laid-off workers find new employment, it should do so, as in the example of BankBoston offering to pay laid-off workers' salaries for six months if they took a position in public service.[21] Management should also follow through on making any subsequent announcements on time and as planned, not a day early and not a day late. After announcing a layoff, all eyes will be on management, as survivors make up their minds whether to trust the managers who have laid off so many of their coworkers, so every day is an exercise in regaining lost trust and building incremental credibility.

Companies should also be careful to manage their news flow around the time of layoffs. Although Wall Street analysts sometimes dismiss CEOs taking a $1 salary during periods of distress as an empty gesture, employees can respond well to the belief that those at the top of the organization are sharing in the pain. On the other end of the spectrum, management should be very careful about announcing CEO management bonuses or stock grants until well after any turnaround has proven successful, or they risk facing the kind of hostility that prompted workers at a Caterpillar plant in Grenoble, France, to hold four managers hostage following a layoff announcement. During the twenty-four hours of confinement, workers subjected them to "a night of pounding revolutionary rock music and shouted threats" while barraging their cell phones with threatening calls and texts.[22] Only intervention by French President Nicolas Sarkozy ended the stalemate, which represented the fourth time in just thirty days that French workers had resorted to such "bossnappings." France Télécom finally worked with the national government to encourage employees to become true civil servants. They created a program to redeploy employees to public-sector job openings at city halls, hospitals, and schools. France Télécom paid the salaries of employees who switched for the first four months and even paid the difference in pay for up to a year.[23] Many who switched felt they were more satisfied by their new vocations.

It is amazing how fast news travels. When an internal e-mail at a Chicago law firm where I officed part time announced cutbacks on people and that there would be no more free coffee, it made it to the newspapers and on-line chat boards in minutes. That weekend we had a dinner party at our house and all the guests brought me instant coffee as a gift.

The Xerox Turnaround: Credibility Changes Everything

In the late 1990s, Xerox Corporation was bleeding cash, with inventory levels climbing far faster than sales, and remained solvent only with repeated new debt financings.[24] Management focused first on lowering expenses by consolidating its four geographically oriented customer administration centers into three. However, this hasty maneuver actually increased costs while eroding customer goodwill, because in the rush to cut costs by consolidating the centers that handled billings and collections, Xerox customers suffered major delays, lost orders, billing errors, and unreturned customer phone calls. Put on the defensive,

Xerox's sales teams had no choice but to focus on damage control rather than on generating new sales.

Other strategic errors during this same time included a reorganization of the Xerox worldwide sales force that shifted nearly half of the company's sales team from a geographic orientation to an industry focus. This might have worked had the company bothered to train its sales reps for their new roles. With sales reps lacking both geographical connections to their customers and the product expertise necessary to make up for their distance from customers, sales plummeted, prompting another Xerox response in the form of sharp price cuts. Just as Dick Brown's overly aggressive bidding policies at EDS tied the company into the NMCI debacle, Xerox's price cuts left the company trapped in massive unprofitable contracts. The company reached full-on crisis mode when it recorded a billion dollar foreign currency loss. The Securities and Exchange Commission would later determine that between 1997 and 2000, Xerox defrauded investors by using a series of undisclosed accounting actions as a way to meet or exceed Wall Street's expectations. Needless to say, credit markets dried up as far as Xerox was concerned, and the company could no longer turn to its lenders for additional capital.

Meanwhile, the company's plummeting stock price (which fell by more than 95 percent from the beginning of 1999 to the end of 2000) had pushed morale to new depths, made worse by wave after wave of layoffs. Nine thousand employees were let go in April 1998, followed by 5,200 more in April 2000. Smaller waves of 100 here, 200 there occurred periodically through late 2000, followed by 4,000 layoffs in January 2001 and 11,000 more in October. Each successive wave depressed morale further, until one analyst noted morale was "down in the dirt."[25] Employees began trading Dilbert cartoons lampooning the cuts, and gallows humor dominated the company's atmosphere.

The board named Anne Mulcahy president and chief operating officer to turn the company around, later promoting her to CEO in 2001. Mulcahy considered filing the company into bankruptcy—which would have allowed the company to relieve its staggering debt burden, protect the company from potential litigation, and buy the company some time to execute its turnaround—but decided that a filing would do irreparable damage to Xerox's brand, supplier relationships, and consumer perceptions. In addition, bankruptcy would grant creditors significantly more control over the company's strategy and operations, damage its supplier relationships, compel customers to find alternate suppliers due to the uncertainty about Xerox's future, incur exorbitant professional fees, and potentially wipe out shareholder equity entirely.

Mulcahy instead focused on executing a three-pronged turnaround. Worried that Xerox would not be able to fill orders, many clients had begun limiting their business with the company. Along with severe customer service issues, this required that Mulcahy meet directly with key customers to get their input on strategic decisions. Mulcahy's leadership team engaged in a reengineering process to identify exactly what added value to each one of Xerox's most important customers. She met with customers to demonstrate that Xerox valued them, to convince them of Xerox's solid future, and to reassure them that service problems were being addressed.

Discussions with clients served as the foundation for her decisions on strategy and reengineering effort, which concluded that Xerox needed to continue bringing new and innovative products to the market. Against the advice of so-called experts, who insisted that Xerox continue to slash the R&D budget, Mulcahy identified R&D as a critical value that Xerox provided to customers, and pushed spending in the area to 6 percent of revenues. This proved key to restoring Xerox's image as an innovation leader and reestablishing the company's competitive position in the rapidly changing document-processing market. Xerox strategically transitioned from the dated light-lens equipment market to newer digital products and became competitive in the color market, with the objective to develop technology that produced color printouts and copies quickly at a reduced cost. Mulcahy's team developed strategies to market competitive products to three key markets: the production market, large office market, and the services market.

This sound turnaround plan immediately provided Mulcahy with the credibility needed to pull together a fragmented, depressed employee base. She announced one final round of layoffs upon being promoted to CEO, and stuck by that decision throughout the rest of the turnaround process. Her decision to exit the small and home business markets eliminated approximately 1,200 positions across two entire divisions, which, as already mentioned, makes discrimination lawsuits more difficult to pursue and is understandable to all concerned.

In addition to the production-level employees in these two divisions, Mulcahy focused her one and only round of layoffs on middle management by stripping out Xerox's matrix-style management structure. This reduced the number of hierarchical layers between her and the production floor, resulting in a leaner, more nimble Xerox with reduced decision time. To improve performance and ensure that the sales force could better meet customer needs, Mulcahy took actions to clarify accountability, and she enhanced salaries and incentives for remaining sales reps.

Perhaps most important, Mulcahy remained open in her communications with employees at all levels to minimize fears about job security, and kept her promise to make only one round of layoffs. In order to avoid losing that credibility with further cuts, no cow was considered sacred, with once lavish lunches replaced by tuna fish sandwiches, employees crowded in two-to-a-cubicle, and travel and training expenditures slashed.[26] Day by day, employees who had grown increasingly suspicious of upper management began to have faith that the ship had been righted, and that Mulcahy was making the hard decisions in a fair and honest manner.

The resultant boost in morale became obvious to outsiders, as Xerox widened its distribution channels by expanding its network of agents, resellers, and retailers, which allowed the company to respond to customer requests quickly and made products more easily available in the market. In turn, the expansion helped restore customer confidence at a time when service capabilities had become increasingly important.

Xerox's turnaround plan slashed operating expenses by $1.7 billion by reducing redundant layers of management, consolidating operations that had previously run in a siloed environment, trimming administrative costs, and tightly managing discretionary spending. The company achieved additional cost reductions by outsourcing the manufacture of products for the office market to an electronics manufacturing services company, which included the sale of several plants to this provider and the transfer of Xerox employees running those operations. In addition, Mulcahy resolved customer billing and order processing problems by creating a venture with a GE Capital unit to manage financing, administration, order processing, billing, and collections.

All these moves required multiparty cooperation, which allowed Xerox to avoid filing for bankruptcy. Unlike some CEOs who remain isolated from customers and the everyday workers in their organizations, Mulcahy made a point of continually speaking with customers and employees regarding their needs and incorporating their input to drive the development of a new strategic vision. In addition to visiting various Xerox facilities, Mulcahy instituted roundtable discussions and town hall meetings where workers could discuss the obstacles they faced in changing Xerox for the better. Mulcahy delivered bad news personally, making sure that employees understood that difficult choices were necessary to save the company and its remaining jobs. Mulcahy launched an aggressive turnaround plan that returned Xerox to full-year profitability by the end of 2002, along with happier customers and employees, a decreased debt load, and a revitalized investment program in research and development. Much of this success stemmed from her ability to inspire confidence in an employee base badly battered by wave after wave of layoffs, and earn back their trust.

Conclusion

In conclusion, I have always maintained that downsizing is a *tool*, not a goal; if cuts are necessary, then they are necessary, and while painful, it is far better to save 70 percent of the company's jobs by sacrificing 30 percent than to let the entire company liquidate. However, managers too often begin to think of downsizing as the end rather than a means to it. Very often significant cuts are not necessary and can be minimized by re-assigning workers to new functional areas or product lines that need additional help. Identifying these opportunities, however, requires a sound analysis that starts with a clean sheet of paper and focuses on the things a company does that actually add value to customers.

If, upon conducting a business process reengineering, Six Sigma, or any other customer-focused analysis, it becomes clear that cuts are necessary, management should take care to do everything possible to minimize the damage they do by considering a variety of stakeholders and thinking creatively about how to mitigate the effect on terminated employees. A company's treatment of the departed employees gets back immediately to survivors, and they will largely form their opinions about current management based on how they feel their coworkers have been treated and how the layoff announcement was handled. In the next chapter, we examine what happens when even layoffs cannot keep a company solvent and it is forced to file for protection under the U.S. bankruptcy code.

Chapter Six

The Bankruptcy Process as Sword and Shield

I often start a certain lecture by asking, "What do the following have in common?" I then go through a list that includes Kim Bassinger, Tia Carrere, Anna Nicole Smith, Vail Ski Resort, Elite Modeling (agent to many super models), Corelco Pictures (made many successful Rambo and Schwarzenegger movies), Willy Nelson, Sharper Image, and singing groups Run-DMC and TLC. As I go through these and then add Linens 'n Things, United Airlines, and other major corporations, the audience gasps when they realize that they all went through bankruptcy. Some used it as a sword to sever unprofitable contracts, others used it as a shield to get out from under a pile of debt that was due.

It is important to understand at least the basic concepts of bankruptcy in order to be successful in any turnaround or refinancing. Even just the threat of it affects late phase turnarounds. The Absolute Priority Rule discussed below affects refinancing negotiations in any phase of the crisis curve as well.

The word *bankruptcy* actually comes from the combination of the Latin words *bancus* ("bench") and *ruptus* ("broken"). Its origin lies in the history of the Roman market, where merchants conducted all business at a bench in the public square. If he could not pay his debts, the centurions would proceed to his bench and—with great fanfare and ceremony—shatter it as a signal to the world that one should no longer do business with him.

The American Bankruptcy Code is far more forgiving, and the process of declaring bankruptcy entails little of the shame, stigmatization, or violence against furniture that it did in ancient Rome. Until other countries recently began to imitate it, the U.S. Code stood out from much of the rest of the world by demonstrating a commitment to a "fresh start" wherein debtors could work out the best possible arrangement with creditors, pay back as much as possible, and then emerge with a clean financial bill of health. It was not always thus; the country's legacy of English common law had it following the tradition of debtor's prisons, and it took a revolution and new legislation over the next two centuries to break free of these moribund traditions.

The young country's Congress passed its first attempts at a more forgiving bankruptcy law in part because Robert Morris had been jailed for failing to pay his debts. A fierce patriot, key architect of the nascent American financial system, namesake for two private colleges, and one of only two people to sign the Declaration of Independence, the Articles of Confederation, *and* the U.S. Constitution, Morris had pledged everything he owned to help fund the Continental Army during the Revolutionary War. When these debts—and subsequent business misadventures—left him incapable of paying his debts, his many supporters in Congress began to question the wisdom of a system that assumed that the best way to get an overextended man to resolve his debts was to throw him into prison until he found a way to pay.

The debate over how America should treat its debtors—both individuals and corporations—raged for nearly a century, until the growth of the railroad industry gave it a push in the right direction. At the time, companies that went bankrupt had their assets taken by creditors. Railroads, however, required previously unheard-of sums of money to build, which generally required that they be financed by bond issues, secured by the actual assets of the company: railroad tracks laid out across North America. After buying a very small piece of the financing, an investor had claim to a tiny portion of the actual track on the ground. Naturally, this created great difficulties when a railroad became insolvent, as one small investor could threaten to hold out on any agreement and instead seize his tiny share of the track, thereby rendering the rest of the railroad essentially worthless and taking away a key benefit to the citizenry. As a result, courts allowed greater lenience to railroads, allowing them to continue operation while bondholders swapped their debt securities for equity. Courts also gave suppliers to the railroads a priority claim against the new entity in order to encourage them to continue supplying during the reorganization process, even while forbidding other corporations from reorganizing. Out of these legal innovations, the American Bankruptcy Code slowly emerged, most notably the section dealing with corporate reorganizations: Chapter 11.

Since then, the code has developed to handle far more sophisticated bankruptcies. A combination of large pay hikes to its pilots (who were all shareholders due to a previous restructuring), a slowdown in business, the events of September 11, and skyrocketing oil prices led to United Airlines filing for bankruptcy in 2002. They used the bankruptcy process to negotiate cuts in costs with suppliers, contractors, and employees. The mechanics, pilots, and flight attendants were all forced to take pay cuts and change work rules. The company also used the bankruptcy to cancel its pension plan for all current and retired employees, the largest such default in corporate history. United emerged from bankruptcy in 2006, paying $296 million in attorney and consulting fees to its professionals and all of the committees' professionals.

The U.S. Bankruptcy Code

When the phrase "Chapter 11" is used, it refers to a certain part of the U.S. Bankruptcy Code as passed by Congress and updated occasionally. It should be noted that bankruptcy can only be handled by federal courts because Article 1 section 8 of the U.S. Constitution gives Congress the exclusive power to establish bankruptcy laws.

The U.S. Bankruptcy Code actually consists of nine chapters, with some numbers "saved" for another day. The first three (Chapters 1, 3, and 5) deal with general provisions, bankruptcy case administration, and the relationships between creditors, debtors, and the estate, respectively. These three chapters apply to both individual and corporate bankruptcies. Chapter 7 deals with liquidations, which can occur both for companies deciding to dissolve and for individuals selling off most or all of their possessions to satisfy creditors. Chapter 9 covers the adjustment of the debts of a municipality, while Chapter 12 is tailored to the unique economic situations faced by family farmers or family fishermen. Chapter 13 covers most personal bankruptcies for those individuals who have regular income to pay off some debts. Chapter 15 is the newest chapter, and represents the United States' adoption of the United Nations' Model Law on Cross-Border Insolvency. This newest chapter was considered necessary given the increasingly global implications of corporate bankruptcies with supply chain partners, creditors, customers, shareholders, and employees spread across many different international jurisdictions. That leaves only the focus of this chapter, to highlight Chapter 11, which deals with corporate reorganizations.[1]

The goal of Chapter 11 is to maximize the value of the distressed firm's assets, either through a reorganization plan approved by the bankruptcy court, through a sale of all or part of the company, or through a liquidation; that is, sometimes a company files for Chapter 11 protection with the assumption that it will reorganize or sell itself as a going concern, but finds such alternatives unfeasible and converts to a Chapter 7 liquidation. This goal of maximizing asset value is required as a way to be fair to creditors, then following the Bankruptcy Code's strict delineation of how those assets are to be distributed during the resolution of the case. Known as the Absolute Priority Rule, it explains in exactly what order stakeholders are to be paid. Essentially, it is a food chain that determines which classes of stakeholders get to eat, and in what amounts. Sometimes a company will find itself insolvent under state law without filing a federal bankruptcy petition; every state has a version of this food chain as well, some of which differ slightly but for the most part mimic the priority of claims established in the Code. (See Box 5 regarding the state law approach to insolvency.) Every country has their own version of this food chain as well, as I explain in the next chapter; many have increasingly come to emulate the U.S. Code.

The power of the Absolute Priority Rule stems from the fact that it lays out a specific order of each class of claimants, and stipulates that until the first (highest-ranked) class of claimants is paid in full, the second-highest class cannot receive anything;

Box 5: State Laws

State Laws involving insolvent companies typically cover other ways to liquidate a company rather than reorganize. The two most popular are the following.

Assignment for the Benefit of Creditors

Here, all the assets of a company are assigned to an independent fiduciary or *assignee*. The assignee's job is to gather and sell all the assets usually at some form of auction. He or she then takes the proceeds and distributes them to the creditors, usually according to a list under state law, similar to the Absolute Priority Rule. This process is used for liquidation and is usually much cheaper than bankruptcy and often with less publicity. The biggest drawbacks, however, are that the officers and directors of the company are still vulnerable to lawsuits, and other types of lawsuits are not stopped in the absence of an automatic stay. Also, the title to the assets may not be delivered free and clear of all liens, which can be done in bankruptcy.

Foreclosure

Foreclosure by creditors is covered by Article 9 of the Uniform Commercial Code, where the secured creditor(s) will conduct a foreclosure sale. This is often used for a relatively quick sale of a business's assets. It has risk for the secured party if the sale doesn't occur as part of a public auction to ensure that market value is received or junior creditors will object.

There are other lesser-used alternatives and ways under state law to avoid liquidation, such as through a contractual workout with key creditors, a sale of the company approved by creditors, and so on.

---

until the second-highest class is paid in full, the third-highest class cannot receive anything; and so on. In practice, it does not always work out precisely that way, for a variety of reasons we examine in more detail later, but most notably because the parties negotiate and reach a consensus how best to split the prize.

The Absolute Priority Rule

In the United States, the Absolute Priority Rule establishes the priority of claimants as follows, with the top of the food chain listed first:

1. Secured claims
2. Super-priority claims
3. Administrative claims
4. Unsecured claims with priority
5. Subordinated claims
6. Equity interests

The key is that, unless the first class of claims is paid in full, the classes below it are not entitled to anything. Each class in turn must be paid before those below it can receive anything. Each of those claimants has numerous subcategories as well, but I only highlight the key factors of each one:

Secured claims are those debts where the creditor—generally a bank or other lender—has an enforceable lien on a particular piece of property (the collateral) owned by the debtor. It is highly desirable to have such a lien, because secured claims are paid first, and under the Absolute Priority Rule, must be paid in full before any other claims can be paid at all. In order for the creditor's lien to be enforceable (and therefore to be considered a secured claim), the creditor must "perfect" the lien by providing both attachment and notice. Attachment creates the enforceable security interest through the contractual exchange of consideration (e.g., a loan from a bank) in exchange for a security interest in a specific piece of collateral to which the debtor has ownership rights; a company cannot grant a bank a lien on the Brooklyn Bridge, for example. So-called "revolving" liens are permissible, such as a lien that attaches to all of a debtor's inventory, both at the time of the contract's signing and that inventory acquired thereafter. A creditor then perfects the lien by providing notice to the rest of the world that she holds a lien on the specific collateral, thereby preventing other parties from thinking that the collateral was unencumbered. People often think that such notice must require sprawling documents cloaked in legalese, but in fact, there is simply a one-page Uniform Commercial Code (UCC) document that must be filled out and filed with the state's Secretary of State Office, which today can be done via the Internet. The trick is to get legal advice as to which state. Real estate liens are only slightly trickier, as they require the filing of a mortgage in the county where the piece of real estate sits.[2]

Secured creditors should note two other concerns regarding their claims. First, failure to perfect the lien will prevent it from being honored as a secured claim, thus dropping the creditor's claim down into the much lower-ranked class of unsecured claimants. Timing is also important; if two creditors hold liens on the same piece of collateral, the first to perfect is the first in right to that collateral. Second, a creditor's claim is only secured to the extent that the value of the collateral is greater than or equal to the amount of a claim; any deficit will be converted to a general unsecured claim. For example, if a bank lends $10 million to a company and perfects its lien on the collateral, but then the value of the collateral falls to $7 million, the bank's claim will be bifurcated into a secured claim in the amount of $7 million and an unsecured claim in the amount of $3 million. As a result, asset-backed lenders must diligently monitor the value of the collateral underlying their claims to ensure that they do not find themselves undersecured.

Super-priority claims consist of any loans the company takes out while in bankruptcy, which are known as debtor-in-possession (DIP) loans. _Debtor-in-possession_ is a term used when the company is still operating, with some form of management still running it. Because suppliers will generally put companies in bankruptcy on Cash in Advance or Cash on Delivery, debtors often face a significant cash crunch on a bankruptcy filing, requiring the raising of DIP financing to fund its operations during the reorganization process. (See Box 6 for more information on DIP financing.)

Administrative claims consist of any professional fees paid to attorneys, accountants, investment bankers, valuation experts, or other service providers, as well as any amounts owed to suppliers who provide goods or services after the filing. Again, this elevation of post-petition claims encourages suppliers to do business with a bankrupt company by ironically making it less risky to supply a

Box 6: DIP Financing

The mere existence of DIP financing seems to surprise even some reasonably sophisticated executives, who wonder why in the world a bank would ever lend to a company already in bankruptcy. One critical reason is that though such loans are super-priority claims as a matter of law, a debtor who can demonstrate that financing was only available from the DIP lender can often convince a court to grant the DIP lender a lien that has priority over the existing (i.e., prebankruptcy) secured lenders' claims, moving the DIP lender to the very top of the food chain. Such liens are called "priming" liens, and DIP lenders will often insist on a priming lien on the debtor's inventory and receivables regardless of whether a prebankruptcy creditor already has a lien on them, a second lien (right below prebankruptcy secured creditors) on other encumbered property, and a first-priority lien on any unencumbered property. In order to receive such a priming lien, however, a DIP lender must receive the consent of the secured creditors. Occasionally, prebankruptcy lenders whose collateral consists of the inventory and receivables will consent to the priming in exchange for a second lien on unencumbered assets (behind the DIP lender), knowing that the company will go into liquidation (and therefore destroy the value of their collateral) if a DIP lender does not inject the necessary capital to maintain the company as a going concern. If the secured creditors still object to being primed, a court can still grant a priming lien if it finds that the secured creditors have adequate protection, either by receiving some portion of the DIP loan to pay down their pre-petition claims or because the value of their collateral exceeds the amount of their claim to allow the DIP lender to receive a priming lien on the surplus without unduly impairing the secured creditor. That will invariably lead to a battle of the experts, with the existing secured creditors arguing that the collateral is not of sufficient value to provide them the adequate protection necessary to justify a priming lien. Creditors holding liens on isolated assets—one overseas manufacturing facility, for example—will often object to being primed on those remote assets, but if the rest of the collateral is sufficient, the DIP lender may allow those lenders to avoid being primed. Whether through priming or otherwise, the

(Continued)

Box 6: (Continued)

key is for the DIP lender to feel there is sufficient collateral to protect the loan.

The elevation of those loans to a higher priority is a critical justification for making such loans, as it ironically makes lending to a bankrupt company safer than lending to the same company prebankruptcy when it was ostensibly healthy. Priority, however, is but one part of the picture, with the other part being fees. DIP lending can bring with it some of the most lender-friendly terms available in the world. In addition to massive fees and very high interest rates, DIP lenders often receive authorization from the federal bankruptcy judge that if the debtor fails to meet the projections in its 13-Week Cash Flow Model, the DIP lender can foreclose immediately and seize assets with a clear title, without having to go through any lengthy lawsuit or foreclosure process.

Typically, the existing senior lender is first in line to become the DIP lender, and unless they demand totally outrageous terms, the bankruptcy court will agree to let them extend the DIP financing. For example, a lender might offer to roll its existing debt into the new DIP loan, in exchange for an increased interest rate and perhaps 500 basis points as an upfront fee. Such lenders will also request a stipulation from the bankruptcy court that all of their liens have been perfected and above challenge, that the bank and its officers and directors cannot be sued for any act that occurred before the bankruptcy filing, such as for accepting preference payments. This is known as a "defensive" DIP (as opposed to an "offensive" or "new money" DIP), and has caused a great deal of controversy when one existing secured lender uses a priming lien to vault ahead of other secured lenders (referred to as "rolling up" pre-petition debt into post-petition debt). If other creditors object, courts have looked to determine how much of the new DIP loan is actually used to fund operations as opposed to paying down the pre-petition debt, and how necessary the DIP loan was; if there is significant new capital contributed to the company's operations and the need was high, courts will be more likely to allow such a roll-up.

The collapse of the DIP financing market during the recent credit crunch explains why so many companies that had filed for Chapter 11 with the intention of reorganizing ultimately had to convert to Chapter 7 liquidations. The preceding credit boom exacerbated these situations, because credit was so plentiful that companies such as Circuit City and Linens 'n Things borrowed liberally, leaving them without meaningful unencumbered assets to offer to DIP lenders (and in several cases with prefiling second- and even third-lien loans on existing assets). Finally, in the darkest days of the near economic implosion, assets became so difficult to value that even when a company had unencumbered assets or perhaps encumbered assets that might have a sufficient cushion to provide adequate protection to existing lenders, the valuation uncertainty dissuaded the few would-be DIP lenders from getting involved. Even for those companies who obtain it, DIP financing is expensive. Lyondell Chemical Company obtained an $8 billion loan while in bankruptcy, paying a 13 percent interest and a 7 percent fee late in 2008 when overall interest rates were very low.

company in bankruptcy than one that may appear healthy from the outside but is within months of filing. The payment of professional fees can prove exorbitantly expensive, particularly if the court decides to recognize more than one official committee, for the debtor must pay all of the professional fees of each official committee. For example, Kmart paid out $150 million in professional fees. (See Box 7 for more information on the formation of committees.) United Airlines paid out $335 million in fees to lawyers (some of whom billed more than $1,000 per hour) and to consultants. The Lehman Brothers case will go over $1 billion in fees.

Unsecured claims with priority include certain taxes owed, consumer deposits for goods yet to be delivered, and up to $14,000 per employee in owed salary, benefits, and bonus. Occasionally this will come up with an employee that is owed a performance or retirement bonus by a company that files for bankruptcy; the amount given priority is capped at $14,000, and any excess is bifurcated into the next lower class, general unsecured claims without priority. In individual bankruptcies, this used to include spousal and child support, but the 2005 changes to the Code made it impossible to discharge such debts.

Unsecured claims without priority come, for all intents and purposes, last; although there are lower classes of claimants, very rarely do they see any significant recovery. These so-called "great

---

Box 7: Committee Formation

Typically, the bankruptcy court will immediately appoint members to official committees, the most important of which tends to be the unsecured creditors' committee, for they are most frequently the first impaired class, or the "fulcrum security." However, the court may also approve other official committees—such as a secured creditors' committee, a bondholders' committee, an employees' or retirees' committee in a case with large pension obligations, or rarely an equity holders' committee when it seems as though there may be some residual equity value—that have the same power to hire professional service providers such as accountants and attorneys to advance the interests of the class as a whole. In such cases, several issues arise of which managers should be aware.

Committee Composition

The trustee will usually invite the largest twenty creditors listed on the petition to join the committee, and then pick up to eleven representatives depending on the size of the company. (This is the job of one of the trustees who are employees of the U.S. Justice Department, charged with overseeing bankruptcy cases to ensure fairness standards are followed in every case. These trustees are distinguished from an independent trustee, who is approved by the court to take over the management of a liquidating company or one which committed fraud.) The unsecured creditors' committee will be the first in line to challenge any reorganization plan advanced by management, and will be an important group from whom the debtor must seek approval to sell any assets outside the course of ordinary business. The committee does not have veto power, but courts will often listen to them because they represent key stakeholders. If you are ever asked to be on such a committee, do so; it will be very instructive and you will be part of some very interesting negotiations.

Professional Fees

Typically, the debtor must pay all professional fees for any official committee. Stakeholders can organize an unlimited number of

---

unofficial committees, but only those approved by the court as serving some valid purpose in the reorganization process receive this valuable reimbursement. As a result, the debtor will generally try to limit the number of official committees as much as possible to avoid paying four teams of attorneys instead of just three.

Cooperation Versus Collusion

Membership on such a committee does not preclude competitors from cooperating to produce the desired result in a reorganization. Collusion is perfectly acceptable with respect to sharing information on what the debtor offered one creditor in terms of an out-of-court restructuring, or what one creditor was told about the debtor's financial condition. Such collusion is acceptable, however, only so long as competitors do not discuss anything relating to pricing. I tell my students that if they are ever in such a situation—whether on a creditors' committee or simply at an industry trade show—where a competitor begins talking about pricing in the market, the only solution is to jump out of your chair and run screaming out the door with your fingers in your ears. It helps avoid jail time.

Hedge Funds on Committees

Hedge funds and other high-risk traders raise a number of issues on creditor committees, as their chase for higher returns prompted them to offer second-lien and even third-lien financing to companies during the credit boom, leaving them holding large positions in many bankruptcies today. The Code dictates that members of the creditors' committee hold a fiduciary duty to the group they represent, and—because they are privy to material, nonpublic information regarding the company's reorganization plan—their organizations may only continue to trade any publicly traded securities of the debtor if they can demonstrate strict "Chinese Walls" preventing the in-house passage of information from committee members to traders. As a result, many hedge funds have begun refusing invitations to join such official committees, sacrificing control over the process for the ability to continue trading in the debtor's securities.

unwashed" include all pre-petition debts owed to trade creditors and suppliers as well as any portion of an undercollateralized secured claim that has been bifurcated. On average, these claimants receive just pennies on the dollar, so there are always contentious battles fought in the name of climbing up the food chain, or alternatively, kicking someone else down it. In a rare case, Flying J, the truck stop company, had an unusual outcome; the unsecured creditors were paid in full because of a successful turnaround of the company by a new CEO and several subsidiaries were sold off in bankruptcy, so the original shareholders wound up with ownership of a midsized company with far less debt. By contrast, a more frequent outcome occurred for Breed Technologies, the primary manufacturer of automobile airbags and seat belts. The senior secured lenders received all of the stock of the reorganized company, with nothing left over for anyone else; over $1 billion owed to creditors was just wiped off the books.

Subordinated claims follow the general unsecured claims. Subordination can arise contractually when a lender agrees to be placed lower in the hierarchy than general unsecured claims in exchange for a higher interest rate or other favorable terms, or a bankruptcy judge might subordinate them to punish a lender with unclean hands, such as one who has committed fraud, breached a fiduciary duty, or meddled too much in the running of the company. This is known as "equitable subordination." Finally, any claims arising from a successful derivative shareholder suit (as mentioned in Chapter Three) would constitute a subordinated claim.

Preferred equity and *common equity* are the last two classes of claimants, respectively, and very rarely do they participate in any recovery in a Chapter 11 proceeding.

For larger companies each of these food chain categories has multiple subgroups, as the actual food chain of any group of creditors usually represents that company's capital structure. For example, there may be different bonds that were sold over the years and one would look to the bonds' legal documents to determine the priority among them.

The Absolute Priority Rule affects all negotiations in a turnaround situation, particularly once a covenant is breached, such as the covenants listed in Box 1 at the end of the Introduction.

This causes the breached party to negotiate the next steps the company must take to be in compliance again. When it becomes clear that not everyone on the list can be paid, that's when the fulcrum security begins to drive the process and perhaps push for bankruptcy to force the company to maximize its return. If for example there are sufficient funds to pay the secured lenders and holders of Bond A, but not pay Bond B in full, Bond B becomes the "fulcrum security." Whether the fulcrum security is a second-lien secured creditor, bondholders, or the general unsecured class, it is the center of most of the negotiations in any turn-arounds. The power brokers at any phase of a crisis are usually the secured lenders. They are the ones who have to be kept satisfied in any outcome.

Negotiations can take place at any level. For example, common equity holders are always last in line, and therefore cannot receive a penny until every other class of creditors (and preferred shareholders, if there are any) are made whole. This rarely occurs; if there are sufficient assets to make all the creditors whole, there is typically little incentive to file for bankruptcy protection. However, despite the fact that equity shareholders are usually "wiped out"—that is, they receive nothing—in a Chapter 11 reorganization, the shares of publicly traded companies who have filed for bankruptcy still trade, albeit at a very depressed price. Often, the speculators purchasing those potentially worthless shares are hoping that in order to get a plan of reorganization confirmed, creditors will throw some sops to those out-of-the-money parties below them, including shareholders. Although equity holders may not have a right to any such consideration (often provided in the form of some small share of the reorganized company's future equity value), they can threaten to "melt the ice cube": delay the process by filing appeal after appeal, which prolongs the bankruptcy and keeps the meter running on expensive attorneys, accountants, and advisors for all parties involved, slowly eroding the value of the estate that can be distributed to all stakeholders. That same type of threat is also used to extort additional value from senior lenders for second-lien holders or bondholders who hold no collateral. The main way to arrive at a plan that provides some value to classes that otherwise might receive nothing is through a "consensual plan," where the classes of creditors agree to a split that differs from the Absolute Priority Rule for business reasons.

The food chain guides all of the negotiations before and during a bankruptcy filing, for it determines who gets what in any recovery analysis. With that in mind, we now examine the pros and cons that affect any decision whether or not a company goes into bankruptcy. (Note that it can happen voluntarily or the company can be put in bankruptcy involuntarily, as described under The Bankruptcy Process, below).

Advantages to Bankruptcy

○ Bankruptcy *helps a company's immediate liquidity crisis* by granting it an automatic stay on the collection of debts. Though suppliers will generally respond by putting the company on CIA or COD terms, mitigating this effect, the ability to avoid payment of leases and other contracts while under bankruptcy protection is a powerful lever. Put differently, if a company *still* faces a cash crisis despite not having to pay its rent on real estate or leased equipment, a strong argument can be made that it should have filed a Chapter 7 liquidation instead of Chapter 11 reorganization.

○ In addition to alleviating the short-term cash crisis, the automatic stay also provides *protection from creditors and from most litigation,* with exceptions pertaining to certain tax liabilities and criminal actions. Officers and directors can often obtain releases from civil litigation as part of the reorganization plan.

○ As previously mentioned, a bankruptcy filing *forces creditors to the bargaining table,* thereby preventing them from overly aggressive negotiating tactics based on leverage they might gain from acting as a holdout to an out-of-court restructuring.

○ Similarly, the bankruptcy process *allows for a cram down of certain creditors,* particularly those who have threatened to "play terrorist" and attempt to submarine a reasonably fair plan of reorganization.

○ As the case of Winn-Dixie, discussed later in the chapter, demonstrates, the *discharge of debts* is a highly compelling advantage offered by bankruptcy. While out-of-court restructurings must rely on highly negotiated agreements with creditors and slow-moving divestments to rationalize upside-down balance sheets, the sheer power of the bankruptcy judge can wipe out an entire class of creditors in the time it takes for a gavel to hit a desk.

○ Bankruptcy can also offer *preferential tax treatment,* as the IRS will negotiate payment plans over seven years and the company usually does not have to show debt reduction as income.

○ *The rejection of executory contracts* makes it vastly less difficult for a company to reduce its exposure to prior poor decisions, either by escaping leases on unprofitable stores or plants or by exiting unprofitable contracts that force it to supply goods below market. Similarly, the ability to assume and assign such contracts to a third party for cash allows the debtor to monetize an asset that provides it with no value but could prove valuable to the third party.

These rejection or assumption decisions can lead to some interesting disputes, however, particularly when creditors are fighting to wrest control of a company from a recalcitrant management team. In the bankruptcy of a large Internet service provider that had expanded far too quickly to support its mounting debt obligations, creditors were furious to discover that the CEO had spent little time forging a credible turnaround plan and instead seemed only to care about whether he could convince them not to reject the licensing contract he had signed (which would cost the company more than $100 million) for the naming rights to the local NFL team's football arena. Even to bankruptcy attorneys, turnaround consultants, and workout lenders already accustomed to dealing with management teams in various stages of denial, his behavior was so bizarre that they began referring to it not as a Chapter 11 bankruptcy but rather as a Chapter 51: the CEO wasn't playing with a full deck.

○ Most of all, bankruptcy offers *a fresh start.* After the shock of the filing wears off, a successful reorganization and emergence from bankruptcy can improve employee morale and convince both customers and suppliers that the company is once again on the right track.

Disadvantages to Bankruptcy

○ Bankruptcy usually has a *negative impact on customers,* who take this very public declaration of the company's distress as a sign that perhaps they should shift their business to healthier competitors who can deliver product on time, honor warranty obligations, and provide post-sale service.

○ Similarly, *suppliers become suspicious* and tend to put the debtor on aggressive payment schedules such as COD or CIA, and may express reluctance to revert to more standard payment terms even after the debtor has successfully emerged from bankruptcy. This is true of small and large companies alike.

○ *Morale suffers* during a bankruptcy, as employees are typically aware only of the negative connotations of the process and none of its protections. Unless convinced by a strong, clear message from the top that the Bankruptcy Code will allow the company to emerge a stronger, more viable competitor, they often assume that bankruptcy is synonymous with liquidation and expect the worst.

○ Bankruptcy is *unfathomably expensive,* because the costs of arranging DIP financing and paying for accountants, valuation experts, and attorneys for both the company and all of its official committees add up very rapidly. Enron's bankruptcy resulted in professional fees of more than $750 million, while estimates for the fees from the recent Lehman Brothers and General Motors bankruptcies both topped $1 billion.[3] Small companies can also face costs that harm their chances of recovery.

○ The necessity of responding to every creditor's filed claim or disputative motion is *distracting to management,* at precisely the time when it must focus on executing a three-pronged turnaround. Instead, management attention and time can be frittered away on responding to lengthy inquests from expensive creditors' committee attorneys and others.

○ *Management's loss of control* is another drawback, as aggressive creditors who may not be nearly as knowledgeable about the company's business can take on disproportionate amounts of control, potentially sacrificing the company's long-term viability in exchange for a fast recovery on their claims.

○ *Reporting requirements increase* in bankruptcy, even over the more stringent reporting requirements established by Sarbanes-Oxley. This can exacerbate management distraction and present an additional cost to the debtor, which must devote resources to ensuring that monthly financial statements are filed in a timely manner with the court.

○ The *high failure rate* of bankruptcy is another disadvantage; fewer than 10 percent of companies in Chapter 11 successfully reorganize.[4] Obviously, this is due in part to a selection problem; typically, only companies late in the full-blown crisis phase file for bankruptcy, so a low success rate is to be expected.

○ Finally, *future claims are accelerated* in bankruptcy. A secured creditor's $10 million loan might have a maturity date some twenty years in the future, but when the debtor emerges from bankruptcy, that claim must be paid in some fashion. That acceleration of payments does not occur in an out-of-court restructuring.

Even a brand new operation can fail and the pros of bankruptcy outweigh the cons. The new Aladdin Hotel and Casino in Las Vegas, built on the site of the demolished old casino, was opened at a cost over $1 billion.[5] The facility included 2,600 hotel rooms, a casino, and a conference center. While the casino opened in August 2000, three months later Aladdin had a $73 million debt service payment due and only $10 million in cash, with a negative cash flow of over $11 million in four months. The owners bought some time by negotiating waivers on debt payments and added $33 million in new equity from one partner in order to keep Aladdin afloat. The project had gone wrong from the beginning. There were cost overruns in excess of $200 million and constant changes in the design from the size and position of the swimming pool to the façade of the building, to difficult access from main streets to the casino. It was a poor casino layout, there was no nightlife, there was no money for promotions, and the building was generally overstaffed. Just over a year after it opened, Aladdin had to file for bankruptcy. Management actions included obtaining $50 million debtor-in-possession financing, converting space to a 32,000-square-foot spa, creating a wedding chapel, increasing entertainment events, adding advertising promotional campaigns, and reducing labor and administrative costs by over $18 million. After getting the hotel turned around, over the next three years, with occupancy up to 90 percent and operating income swinging from a $34 million loss to a $55 million gain, the Aladdin Resort was eventually sold to Planet Hollywood for $90 million in equity and the assumption of $545 million in restructured debt. Aladdin management had made big strategic mistakes originally. They had misaligned their strategy, in that they claimed they had a focus on high rollers but could not offer the perks to attract high rollers to the casino. For example, there were no luxurious hotel suites. The Aladdin also had an average brand and should have targeted the average tourist. They also failed to react to the changing Vegas landscape. Experienced operators now built mega resorts with 3,500 rooms or more and offered high-end restaurants, shopping, entertainment, spas, and nightlife. These were needed to attract tourists who will stay in the hotel and spend money on resort premises. The Desert Passage Mall, which was right next door, could have easily been integrated into the design, but there was a rift between owners of the properties. Each of those mistakes was corrected through the bankruptcy process. Strategy changed, the operation problems were corrected, and the debt burden was lessened when creditors had to swap their debt for the equity.

The Bankruptcy Process

Companies can enter bankruptcy either voluntarily by filing a petition with the Bankruptcy Court, or involuntarily if at least three unsecured creditors with a total of at least $10,000 in undisputed claims file their own petition. (If a company has fewer than twelve creditors, any single creditor can file an involuntary petition.) While by no means unheard of, involuntary petitions occur less frequently than do voluntary petitions. The petition to file is a surprisingly simple form requiring only a brief description of the business, checked boxes indicating the approximate value of the company's assets and liabilities, and a list of its twenty largest creditors, which the court then notifies about the filing. Only companies that have a place of business or property located in the United States may be debtors in a U.S. bankruptcy case. The court test to determine insolvency is similar to the test for the zone of insolvency: an inability to pay debts as they come due, or an upside-down balance sheet where the market value of the company's assets is less than the market or book value of its liabilities.

For debtors, entering bankruptcy offers a number of immediate advantages, the first of which is time. Because the automatic stay provision of the U.S. Bankruptcy Code—explained in greater detail below—prevents creditors from seizing assets or demanding immediate payment, bankruptcy protection stops the bleeding, buying debtors time to reexamine their strategy, stabilize their operations, value the business, examine options for divestiture, and raise capital: essentially, to execute all three legs of the turnaround tripod. It also provides them with a singular platform from which they can address the varying interests of their diverse stakeholder base. In particular, this can be helpful because it puts all creditors of similar classes on equal footing, rather than making the debtor feel compelled to pay first those who push the hardest. The Code's numerous protections, summarized above, allow for the opportunity to reorganize the business more drastically and with fewer punitive measures than would be possible outside of the bankruptcy process. Finally, a bankruptcy filing forces dissenting creditors to the table. Whereas a reorganization negotiated out-of-court can frequently suffer from one dissenting creditor threatening to block a plan from receiving consensus, the Code provides for a variety of ways to prevent such holdouts from enriching themselves unfairly with threats of rejecting any agreement.

Though the automatic stay provision prevents creditors from demanding immediate payment or seizing any collateral upon which they have a lien, creditors also benefit from the bankruptcy process by gaining significant control over the company's management team. The filing of a bankruptcy petition frequently acts as a wakeup call to previously obstinate management teams, and if it does not, the Code provides creditors with the opportunity to question management under oath and even demand their replacement. Those frustrated with the actions of other creditors—whether of the same class of claims or otherwise—will also value the Code's ability to force a settlement among dissenting creditors. Finally, creditors will enjoy the benefits of the Code's protective measures, which provide them with various protections to ensure that they are treated fairly and the value of their collateral is not jeopardized unnecessarily.

The first thing that happens when a bankruptcy court approves a petition for bankruptcy is that the court imposes an automatic stay on creditors that prevents them from demanding payment or seizing their collateral. This prevents a run on the debtor's assets, thus giving the company time to formulate a coherent plan of reorganization. It also halts any lawsuits or judgments against the company, which explains why so many manufacturers of asbestos-related products filed for bankruptcy protection to escape the massive liabilities they incurred in losing toxic tort litigation. Over thirty companies, including Owens Corning and Armstrong, filed for bankruptcy protection from hundreds of thousands of lawsuits for alleged asbestos exposure.

To compensate secured lenders for their loss of the ability to seize their collateral, the court often grants such complaining creditors some form of adequate protection, which could come in the form of additional liens or cash payments from the debtor. The value of such adequate protection will depend on the creditors' negotiating power, which is highly correlated with how critical their collateral is to the company's ongoing operations. Certain creditors may be eligible for relief from this automatic stay—allowing them to seize their collateral—if the court finds that the debtor has no equity in the collateral and that the collateral is not necessary for an effective reorganization. Alternatively, a court could find that there is cause for relief from the automatic stay, such as a lack of adequate protection.

Landlords or secured creditors collateralized by buildings frequently object that they lack adequate protection when a company has declared bankruptcy and wants to continue using the collateral facility but due to cash constraints have stopped paying for maintenance on the building. Such creditors will argue that without necessary maintenance, the value of the collateral will erode, requiring a formal adequate protection hearing before the court to determine what is necessary—cash payments, for example—to provide adequate protection rather than allow the creditor to seize the building. Real estate presents a reasonably simple challenge for the court, as it generally holds its value, but a more difficult challenge arises in the case of a leased fleet of trucks, heavy equipment, or aircraft, which require constant, costly maintenance. The adequate protection hearing will invariably involve a battle of the experts, so managers should always consult with legal counsel if they find themselves on either side of such a hearing.

The day after a company files, creditors can no longer pick up the phone and harass management in hopes of receiving payment, as that would violate the automatic stay and result in grave consequences, determined at the discretion of the presiding bankruptcy judge. Courts have held violating creditors in contempt of court, awarded debtors compensatory or even punitive damages, and forced creditors to reimburse the debtor's costs and expenses, such as legal fees. Once again, any creditor should be very careful about potential violations of the automatic stay, and should consult with legal counsel before taking any action that might constitute such a violation.

While the automatic stay is just that—automatic—many of the other protections of the bankruptcy code require that the debtor's attorneys file a flurry of so-called "first day motions" immediately upon commencement of the case. One of the most important such motions is a request for the use of cash collateral. Cash collateral consists of any cash, securities, deposit accounts, or other cash equivalents in the debtor's possession. Upon filing for bankruptcy, the debtor is prohibited from using any such cash collateral in the ordinary course of business without either the court's approval of that usage or the consent of every entity that has an interest in those assets. Frequently, asset-backed lenders will lend against a company's receivables, with the company's receivables base serving as the collateral for the secured loan. The moment a receivable gets converted to cash, however, the lender still has rights to the cash as part of its collateral, and will often object to the use (i.e., the spending) of that cash collateral. Without approval from that lender, the company must petition the court for permission to use cash collateral, which requires a cash collateral hearing that once again boils down into a battle of the experts arguing over what the collateral is actually worth. This happened in the case of J.A. Jones Construction, which went into bankruptcy with multibillion dollar embassies, dams, and other large construction projects unfinished. The company needed the progress payments from the government to pay the subcontractors to continue to work. The lenders said that was their cash collateral. In the end, the insurance companies wound up footing the bill. Savvy lenders should be careful to ensure that in such situations, every customer buying on credit is informed in no uncertain terms that they are to pay to a bank account under the lender's control. This avoids a situation where an unscrupulous management team could—at the risk of significant civil and criminal penalties—attempt to disguise the sources and uses of cash collateral from its creditors.

After the frequently nasty contentiousness of the adequate protection and cash collateral hearings, there is a slight lull in the action as various groups prepare for battle: unsecured creditors vs. secured creditors, secured creditors vs. other secured creditors, shareholders vs. the board of directors, and all of the creditors vs. the debtor. The debtor must file its statement of affairs and various schedules that detail the company's assets almost down to the number of light bulbs in storage closets, and committees begin to form. The debtor begins its monthly reporting to the court regarding its financial performance, with potentially drastic repercussions—such as the determination that its creditors no longer have adequate protection—if it fails to meet the projections of its 13-Week Cash Flow Model.

Creditors are often horrified to learn that interest stops accruing on any unsecured debt immediately upon the filing of a bankruptcy petition. In addition, any undercollateralized portion of a secured claim also stops accruing interest during the bankruptcy proceedings, so in our previous example where a claim in the amount of $10 million was secured by only $7 million, interest at the claim's contractually agreed-upon rate only accrues on the balance of $7 million. The $3 million becomes an unsecured claim. As an undersecured claim it does not accrue interest. This is especially painful during extended bankruptcy filings, some of which used to drag on for more than five years! Then-recent revisions Congress made to the Code make it difficult for a company to stay in past eighteen months.

Courts will be asked to examine a company's transaction history to determine whether it made any preference actions. In an effort to discourage the kind of aggressive debt collection activities that can force a company into bankruptcy, the Code allows the court to avoid and revoke any payments made within the ninety-day period prior to the bankruptcy filing. The theory behind this rule is that the company did not suddenly become insolvent on the day they filed for bankruptcy protection, but rather that it was a gradual process that took some time. The Code sets an (admittedly arbitrary) look back of ninety days prior to filing. A court revoking preference actions can infuriate suppliers, who suddenly find themselves asked to return a check to the bankrupt estate of a company that probably *still owes them money!* However, there are seven defenses to preference actions that can help creditors avoid having to return payments from the debtor; the most popular are the following.

The one used most often is to demonstrate that the payment happened in the "ordinary course of business," made on the same terms and conditions and within the same time frame as prior payments from the debtor. In bankruptcy, no good deed goes unpunished, and it may not pay to be nice. If a customer calls, explains that it is experiencing a slight cash crunch, and asks to pay within forty-five days rather than the usual thirty, if there is the slightest suspicion of impending bankruptcy one should refuse and make up some excuse along the lines of times being tough all over. It doesn't pay to be nice here, because allowing the customer an extra fifteen days—or even five days—eliminates the option of using the ordinary course of business defense to a preference action should they file within ninety days of the receipt of the payment. Of course, the customer might still fail to pay you within the normal thirty-day period with the same result, but the point is that one should never willingly grant permission to an act that would prohibit the use of the ordinary course of business defense.

One could grant the customer their extension and instead use the "new value defense" against preference actions, which requires that they prove that they supplied new goods or services to the debtor after the preference payment in question. If the value of these new goods or services provided exceeds the amount of the payment, there is no preference action; if not, they can be offset dollar-for-dollar to reduce the amount of the preference action. Furthermore, any payment made on the date specified per a certain contract may be exempt from avoidance as a preference payment. As usual, this is a simplification of the legal issues surrounding bankruptcies, and companies should consult legal counsel in the event that it receives notice from a court that it may have received a preference action.

This does not, however, mean that a company should not accept a payment simply because it expects that the supplier may be filing bankruptcy soon. *Always* accept the payment; it is far easier to negotiate from a position of strength (having cashed the check of a company that later files for bankruptcy) and make the debtor—or more accurately, its creditors—jump through the legal hoops necessary to prove a preference action and reclaim the payment. In almost every single situation I have seen, even if there are no defenses available to the company, its creditors will settle for a percentage of that preference action; it may be 80 percent or it may be 50 percent, depending on the parties' leverage and negotiation skill, but it is rarely 100 percent returned by creditors.

This ninety-day "look back" window for preference actions pertains only to company outsiders, however. On any payments to the insolvent company's insiders—including officers, directors, subsidiaries, or parent companies of the debtor—the court will look back a full year to determine preference actions. This can include retirement bonuses or retention bonuses, which have come under increased scrutiny in recent years. A preference can include granting a lien on assets of the company if not done when the goods first changed hands.

The court will also look back two years—and even more in the case of a violation of similar state law—to determine whether the debtor has committed a fraudulent conveyance. Such fraudulent conveyances can occur in a nonbankruptcy context as well, and involve the company in question engaging in any transaction (such as an asset sale or incurrence of debt) for "less than a reasonably equivalent value." Such actions can be avoided and reversed under the Code, although the lengthy look-back period—which can reach as much as ten years in the case of monies sent to certain trusts—makes actual reversal difficult and compels some reasonable settlement. The general test for a fraudulent conveyance is whether the price paid was equal to the fair market value of what was received by the debtor. This prevents an insolvent individual from selling a valuable asset such as a home, automobile, or even a whole company for a nominal sum to a relative or friend in order to shield it from creditors, with the expectation of buying it back once the creditor has settled for some greatly reduced repayment plan.

The best defense comes from proof that a professional advisor such as an investment banker signed off on the price received for the asset, provided a fairness opinion, or ran an efficient auction to determine the transaction's fair market value. Companies in distress that plan to sell assets to remain liquid must therefore be very careful to ensure that the price they receive will pass muster to bankruptcy court observers. In one noted case, the families controlling Cole Taylor Bank merged with Reliance Acceptance Group, Inc., a company focused on financing subprime car purchases. Years later, Reliance collapsed amid allegations of improper accounting standards, and filed for bankruptcy exactly one day before the fraudulent conveyance statute of limitations would expire on the sale of Cole Taylor Bank back to certain board members. The public shareholders filed a bevy of lawsuits against the Cole and Taylor families, ultimately forcing an expensive settlement on their fraudulent conveyance claim based on the fact that the bank had not received a formal fairness opinion on the sale of the bank.[6] The deal may have been at arm's length but it's tough to prove using hindsight.

While the court conducts these tests for any alleged preference actions or fraudulent conveyances, the company can begin operational changes by reexamining every executory contract to which it is a party, which in bankruptcy means any contract where both sides still have ongoing obligations to fulfill. The most common examples of such contracts are unexpired leases of equipment or real estate, long-term purchase agreements, service contracts, or insurance contracts. One of the Code's greatest powers offered to debtors is the ability to reject these contracts while under bankruptcy protection, allowing companies to escape from painfully unprofitable leases or supply contracts, almost without penalty. As we will see later in this chapter, supermarket chain Winn-Dixie used this aspect of the Code to escape from more than $100 million in annual payments on so-called "dark store" leases: leases on properties where the company had already closed the stores but from which they could not escape outside of bankruptcy. The penalty for such rejection is minimal; in the case of a rejected lease, the landlord receives a general unsecured claim for damages limited to the greater of one year's rent or 15 percent of the total rent remaining for the duration of the lease up to a maximum of three years. As general unsecured claims typically receive pennies on the dollar, this is a powerful way for the debtor to cut costs, one that is unavailable except while under bankruptcy protection. Fanny May Candy management made a major error when they went into Chapter 11, then failed to get out of about half of their store leases, which were losing significant cash. The CEO believed he could now turn them profitable. He failed and only nine months later went into bankruptcy again. Only this time the company was liquidated and its name was sold.

The ability to reject executory contracts should serve as notice to companies doing business with a troubled enterprise. In another example of no good deed going unpunished, landlords who agree to reduce the rent for a troubled tenant can find themselves doubly punished if the tenant then files for bankruptcy soon thereafter. If the tenant subsequently rejects the lease, the claim for damages that the landlord receives will be based upon the reduced rental rate, even if that rate was in effect for a short time.

The power of this clause was weakened significantly by the 2005 changes to the Code, termed the Bankruptcy Abuse Prevention and Consumer Protection Act (BAPCPA). Previously, companies could wait until the final day of their bankruptcy proceedings to declare whether they would assume or reject each contract. This provided companies—particularly those with many leases, such as retail chains—extraordinary negotiating leverage over landlords, as the threat of a rejection could compel stubborn landlords to negotiate more favorable lease terms; remember that all of the rent accruing during these sometimes lengthy bankruptcy proceedings would simply be converted to an unsecured claim, which might receive pennies on the dollar. After the passage of the BAPCPA, companies have only 120 days—which they may extend only once by 90 days with the court's approval—to identify which executory contracts they intend to reject. Seven months may seem like a long time, but in practice, companies with hundreds of leases signed over the course of a full commercial real estate cycle, on hundreds or even thousands of stores in dozens of states, with widely varying levels of profitability, face an incredibly complex data analysis task. Keep in mind that during those first 210 days, the company is trying to determine its refocused strategy, which may involve closing unprofitable stores, exiting unprofitable product lines, examining its entire supply chain, reengineering its operations, or abandoning unprofitable regions. Naturally, one might be inclined to hang on to any profitable stores, but management would have to conduct a sophisticated optimization analysis to determine whether that store would still be profitable if all the nearby stores were shut down, ostensibly reducing the return on local marketing dollars and increasing the cost of shipping if the regional distribution center was similarly closed. Or a store losing money could turn profitable under a new strategy. The point is, it often takes 120 days simply to gather the data necessary to *embark* upon these kinds of sophisticated analyses, leaving scant time to draw the appropriate conclusions and then hastily negotiate contracts with landlords before the window closes.

Companies in bankruptcy may also assume such executory contracts, and assign them. For example, a debtor may have a long-term agreement with a supplier dictating that the supplier sell the debtor a specified amount of raw sugar at a fixed cost. Since the signing of that contract, the debtor has filed for bankruptcy and determined that it plans to sell the division that requires raw sugar because that division no longer fits its revamped strategic vision. However, because the price of sugar has risen since the signing of the contract, that contract represents an asset of the debtor's estate; even though the debtor cannot benefit from the below-market price in the contract, *someone* can. As such, the debtor would choose to assume the contract, and then assign it to the highest bidder: presumably some other third party all too happy to buy sugar at an unusually low price. Another example is a retail chain with one or more long-term leases signed when rents were low; they often assume and assign them to another company and collect a fee. Landlords don't like this, because they'd like that additional rent.

Many companies hear that any contract can be rejected or assumed in bankruptcy and attempt to circumvent this by including a clause in any lease or long-term purchase agreement claiming that the contract is "void in the event of a declaration of bankruptcy by either party." This does not work, as the Code stipulates very clearly that parties cannot contract around bank-ruptcy law.

Other recent changes to the Code involve retention plans for employees. When Kmart filed for bankruptcy in 2002, manage-ment attempted to claim that the company's 280 highest-ranking executives all required retention bonuses because every one of them was needed to turn the company around; now companies must demonstrate that such executives have higher-paying job offers elsewhere in order to justify such payments. (Naturally, if the option is staying at a lower-paying job with an insolvent company or a more lucrative job at a healthy one, it's difficult to convince someone to stay without a retention bonus.)

Another important topic that every supplier should be aware of is that of "reclamation." Under another recent Code change, if you send goods to a company that declares bankruptcy within forty-five days of receipt, you can reclaim those goods in writing within twenty days. The customer has a few defenses, especially if they sold the goods or a bank lien attached, but you have a shot at getting them back or at least a higher priority claim.

Plan Confirmation

For the first 120 days of a Chapter 11 case, the company—which means its management—has the exclusive right to present a plan of reorganization, which they may extend with the court's approval by another ninety days. If they fail to present a plan during that time, or present one that fails to win approval, then other stake-holders have the right to present their own plans. When present-ing a plan, they must also produce a thick disclosure statement, not dissimilar to a "red herring" prospectus produced for an initial public offering or any other public securities offering. The plan must state how each class and subclass of creditors is to be paid, by what (cash, debt, stock, etc.), and the percentage recov-ery they can expect. (See Box 8 on the basics of plan confirma-tion.) The disclosure statement will discuss how the company got into trouble, how they plan to get out, how they will find the money necessary to pay back creditors, and the strategic, opera-tional, and financial changes necessary to make the company viable once again. Its most important determinations, however,

Box 8: Plan Confirmation

Unless the debtor is to be sold or liquidated, a plan of confirmation is necessary to emerge from bankruptcy protection. The debtor may file such a plan at any time but only enjoys the exclusive right to file a plan for 120 days—with the possibility of a ninety-day extension subject to court approval—and seek confirmation within 180 days. After the exclusivity period has expired or the debtor's plan fails to receive confirmation, any interested party may propose a plan.

Plans must designate the claims and interests by the various classes, demonstrate which classes are not impaired by the plan (that is, they are made whole by the plan), and show how the impaired classes are treated, with all members within each class treated equally. The plan must also provide some means of implementation; for example, the distribution of equity shares to junior claimants occurred through an initial public offering of the reorganized Winn-Dixie entity; other plans may need to show the source of funds when any cash is given to creditors.

The bankruptcy court grants great flexibility in the structuring of various plans, allowing them to impair various claims, provide for the rejection or assumption of executory contacts, dictate the sale or liquidation of specific assets or business units, and modify the rights of secured creditors. In fact, anything not specifically prohibited by the Bankruptcy Code is permissible in a plan, provided that it receives confirmation.

After the circulation of a disclosure statement that contains sufficient information to allow stakeholders to make an "informed and reasoned judgment" (e.g., an explanation of the plan, its various risk factors, and its proposed distribution to all interested parties), each class will vote. The plan can only receive confirmation if each class is either not impaired or votes to approve it, with a two-pronged test for approval: more than half of the claimants and two-thirds of the dollar value of the claims voting to confirm. At least one impaired class must approve the plan, excluding the votes of insiders such as officers and directors. Plan confirmation also requires that the court deem the plan feasible, with little likelihood of a subsequent reorganization necessary. Finally, all bankruptcy fees must be paid, as well as all administrative claims paid.

(Continued)

Box 8: (Continued)

If the plan fails to receive the votes necessary for confirmation from every voting class, the court can implement what is known as a "cram down," where one or more dissenting classes is "crammed down" over their objections. To receive court approval for a cram down, the plan's proponents must demonstrate that under the plan, each impaired creditor will receive *at least* as much value as they would under a Chapter 7 liquidation, which can lead to a battle of the experts regarding what a liquidation sale of the company's assets might fetch. (This requirement is necessary even in the absence of a cram down, but plans that fail to meet such a standard would rarely receive the votes necessary for confirmation.) Despite the cram down, the plan must still be "fair and equitable" to the dissenting impaired classes, and it cannot discriminate against them unfairly.

Upon plan confirmation and approval by the court, the debtor is bound and released, and the creditors are bound and barred. Essentially, this means that both parties are stuck with the plan's stipulations; for example, creditors cannot later attempt to recover even more value by reasserting their pre-petition claims against the debtor.

revolve around the post-emergence company's valuation and debt capacity, which in turn determine its post-bankruptcy capital structure; this process is where major battles often take place. It determines which creditors take what slices of the final pie.

In a highly simplified example with only three classes of claimants—secured, unsecured, and equity—an unprofitable company with $300 million in secured debt and $500 million in unsecured debt that files for bankruptcy might enact a three-pronged turnaround that convinces the judge that it will swing it from a money-losing proposition to one that produces $100 million in EBITDA, and that all it has to give to creditors is the equity in the company because there's no cash to pay the accelerated debt. Valuation experts might then convince the judge that such a company would be worth five times leading EBITDA for a total valuation of $500 million, and that such a company could support a 3:2 debt/equity ratio, resulting in a post-emergence company with $300 million of debt and $200 million of equity. In this example, the secured creditors (being owed $300 million) would receive all $300 million in debt, while the unsecured creditors (being owed $500 million) would receive 100 percent of the equity in the reorganized company for a total consideration of $200 million, leaving them with a 40 percent recovery, while the equity holders would receive nothing.

This admittedly simplified example of the recovery "waterfall" demonstrates the negotiation incentives each class of creditors faces in arguing how the emerging company should be valued. Regardless of the company's actual value, the secured creditors will be incented to argue for a very low valuation, probably one just below the amount of their outstanding claims. In the example above, if the secured creditors successfully convinced the bankruptcy judge that the company was only worth $300 million, they would receive 100 percent ownership of the company, irrespective of its capital structure upon emergence. (In this case, they would own $180 million in debt and $120 million in equity.) Unsecured creditors, by comparison, would be incentivized to argue for a more aggressive valuation, but still one that was right at or below the amount of their claims plus the secured claims. If they convinced the judge of an $800 million valuation with the same 3:2 debt/equity ratio, the unsecured creditors would hold 37.5 percent ($180 million) of the company's $480 million in debt (with the secured creditors holding the other 62.5 percent, or $300 million) and 100 percent of the company's $320 million in equity. Obviously, this is a significantly more lucrative recovery than the one that results from a $300 million valuation. However, the unsecured creditors would not want the valuation to creep much higher than the value of their outstanding claims plus those of the secured creditors, because at any higher amount, they must begin sharing with equity holders, who will naturally be incented to argue for the highest possible valuation they can suggest while keeping a straight face. The reason is simple: the higher the valuation (over the sum of the unsecured and secured creditors' claims), the higher the equity holders' share in the reorganized company. With a $1 billion valuation, equity holders would own 50 percent of the reorganized company's equity; with a $1.2 billion valuation, they would own 83.3 percent, and so on. Table 6.1 demonstrates how this waterfall works across varying valuations, and how the classes of claimants who sit lower on the food chain

Table 6.1. A Simplified Demonstration of the Reorganization Plan Waterfall

Valuation ($ millions)	Amount of Pre-Petition Claim	$200		$300		$400		$500		$600		$700	
		New Debt	New Equity	New Debt	New Equity	New Debt	New Equity	New Debt	New Equity	New Debt	New Equity	New Debt	New Equity
Amount of Pre-Petition Claim		$120	$80	$180	$120	$240	$160	$300	$200	$360	$240	$420	$280
Secured	$300	$120	$80	$180	$120	$240	$60	$300		$300		$300	
Unsecured	$500						$100		$200	$60	$240	$120	$280
Equity	N/A												

Valuation ($ millions)	Amount of Pre-Petition Claim	$800		$900		$1,000		$1,100		$1,200	
		New Debt	New Equity	New Debt	New Equity	New Debt	New Equity	New Debt	New Equity	New Debt	New Equity
Amount of Pre-Petition Claim		$480	$320	$540	$360	$600	$400	$660	$440	$720	$480
Secured	$300	$300		$300		$300		$300		$300	
Unsecured	$500	$180	$320	$240	$260	$300	$200	$360	$140	$420	$80
Equity	N/A				$100		$200		$300		$400

only begin to eat at higher valuations. Note that any increase in valuation between $300 million and $800 million goes entirely to the unsecured creditors, while any increase over $800 million goes entirely to equity holders.

In the example, the unsecured class of claimants is an impaired class at any valuation below $800 million, because they enjoy a less than 100 percent recovery. (By comparison, the secured class is impaired only at valuations below $300 million.) Note that these issues are the same for any size company. Just subtract zeros from these examples and the concepts are the same.

In order for a bankruptcy court to approve any plan of reorganization, allowing the debtor to emerge from bankruptcy, an impaired class of creditors needs to support the plan. Each class's approval is determined by a vote; in order to approve the plan, there is a two-pronged test for each class (and subclass): at least 50 percent of a class's constituents totaling at least two-thirds of the class's total dollar amount outstanding must vote to approve. Sometimes, an impaired class will object to the plan of reorganization, but courts have the power to overcome those objections with what is called a "cram down" if a number of tests are met, most notably a test determining that the proposed plan would still provide the objecting creditors with a greater recovery than they would receive in a liquidation. As such, some of the last things a judge examines in detail before approving a reorganization plan are the varying versions of liquidation analyses prepared by the various liquidation experts retained by the debtor and each class of creditor to ensure that the plan provides a greater recovery than a liquidation might.

In the meantime, there are frequently intercreditor battles brewing on the sidelines. If the plan is confirmed through a complex plan confirmation hearing that can take several days in court, the bankruptcy court can then allow the other intercreditor claims to be litigated. Many creditors will try to knock out other claims by arguing that another creditor has overstated its claim, presented an invalid claim, or failed to perfect a lien, thus making its claim unsecured rather than secured. In one turnaround where I acted as CEO, I recall my bewilderment at the fact that after months of acrimonious fighting with the company's creditors, I had finally brought everyone to agreement, only to find that they were now fighting among themselves to get larger shares of the reorganized company, while the company continued to pay their expensive legal bills! The way it works in bankruptcy court, they don't sue each other, they sue the bankruptcy estate; so I likened it to Creditor A trying to seek revenge on Creditor B by punching *me* in the face! Perhaps not surprising, my suggestion that everyone send their largest employee to a conference room— into which I would simply empty huge duffel bags of cash, and let them fight it out—fell on deaf ears. With the help of the company's CFO and our attorneys, we finally sorted out the intercreditor disputes and got the company back on the right track.

Cleanup on Aisle 11: Winn-Dixie's Bankruptcy Filing

By the turn of this millennium, publicly traded supermarket chain Winn-Dixie operated almost 1,200 stores across fourteen southeastern and midwestern U.S. states, and twelve in the Bahamas. The company's expansion through the 1990s mirrored a trend nationwide, as chains attempted to gain economies of scale and increase negotiating power with suppliers to counteract the industry's low margins.[7] During this time frame, Winn-Dixie faced increasing competitive pressure from Wal-Mart (now Walmart), whose scale and resultant buyer power allowed it to gain market share among cost-conscious, low-income customers, a problem exacerbated by the 20 percent wage advantage Wal-Mart enjoyed in a labor-intensive industry.[8] Winn-Dixie also faced increasing pressure on the high end of the market in the form of Publix, which differentiated itself not on price but on convenience and service quality, consistently receiving the highest customer satisfaction ratings of any American supermarket chain.

These competitive pressures led to declining profits and market share, prompting the Winn-Dixie board to appoint Al Rowland president and CEO in 1999. Rowland attempted to "right size" the company by consolidating and updating the company's stores, restructuring management, and eliminating underperforming products. Under Rowland's leadership, the company planned to exit its stores in Texas and Oklahoma, where competition with Wal-Mart was fiercest, and centralize its procurement. At the time, 90 percent of the company's procurement functions took place at the local or regional levels. This local focus had created strong relationships with local vendors and allowed stores to tailor their offerings to local clientele, but often put purchasing power in the hands of untrained, unsophisticated local managers who failed to coordinate their efforts with Winn-Dixie's marketing department.

The anticipated savings from Rowland's centralization efforts never materialized. Executive management failed to maintain its focus on restoring profitability in stores hurt most by competitive entry, instead diverting its attention to superfluous projects such as the launch of the Save-Rite warehouse stores division. Moreover, while centralization might have been a move in the right direction, management failed to execute it properly. For example, the Central Procurement Department (CPD) listed preselected products from which store managers must choose, but they had no power to control the dictated price or volume of those products. The disconnect led to stores having products with low demand forced upon them by headquarters, with margins declining due to the resultant spike in the wrong products in the wrong stores and manufacturing plants.[9] Rowland's tenure failed to bring about the desired turnaround, as morale began to plummet along with sales, so in early 2003, the board of directors ousted Rowland and promoted Frank Lazaran to CEO, previously the president of Safeway and Randall's Food Markets.

Lazaran immediately set about addressing Winn-Dixie's out-of-control cost structure by closing 135 stores, three of the company's fourteen distribution centers, and three of its fifteen manufacturing facilities. Even these cost-saving efforts did not come without a price, as the long-term leases remaining on the unprofitable stores resulted in a lease liability of $160.2 million being paid on closed stores per year. The complexity of the company's multi-tiered supply network, with multiple commodities and transportation modes, placed an even greater financial burden on the grocer. Finally, the closing of part of the manufacturing plants appeared insufficient, as Winn-Dixie continued to produce lower-quality products at a higher cost than what was available from outsourced vendors.

Though Lazaran managed to make some progress in slowing Winn-Dixie's cash burn and raised much-needed cash through

the sale of noncore assets, Winn-Dixie still held significant financial obligations related to store, distribution center, and plant
closings. Meanwhile, the company had done nothing to address
its increasingly undesirable positioning between Wal-Mart on the
low end of the market and Publix on the high end. Lazaran did
begin to address the company's aging stores, many of which had
received no capital investment for more than a decade. Although
the effort was unquestionably appropriate given the increasingly
dingy appearance of Winn-Dixie stores, the company lacked the
liquidity to carry it out on the grand scale necessary. By the end
of fiscal year 2004, the program had only launched in a third of
the company's stores.[10] Even then, it proved a costly endeavor,
costing some $75 million just as the company began struggling
to remain liquid. Ultimately, Lazaran's brief, eighteen-month
tenure as CEO brought about only a smaller, still struggling
Winn-Dixie. Now on their third attempt to find an executive who
could effect a successful turnaround, the board asked Lazaran
to step down and named Albertson's COO Peter Lynch as his
successor.[11]

Upon taking control of Winn-Dixie in December of 2004,
Lynch found an organization in shambles. Weakened relationships with suppliers at the end of fiscal year 2004 exacerbated the
company's growing cash crunch. Having witnessed Winn-Dixie's
eroding financial position (the company's shares had lost 85
percent of their value of the preceding six years and its credit
ratings were downgraded by both S&P and Moody), trade creditors began demanding shorter payment terms.[12] This reduction
in vendor and other credit by more than $130 million placed the
company in real danger of insolvency, with a correspondingly
negative perception of the company by consumers. As vendor
relationships turned sour, large vendors like Kraft, Proctor &
Gamble, and PepsiCo shifted payments for consumer promotions
at Winn-Dixie to better-performing retailers. To make matters worse,
vendors became unwilling to invest in test markets at Winn-Dixie
stores, thus limiting the introduction of new products and further
depressing consumer perceptions of the company. Finally, the
company's disastrously inaccurate forecasts of sales during the
2004 holiday season resulted in cash frozen in excess inventory,
forcing Winn-Dixie to increase its borrowings under its credit

agreement and further reducing liquidity.[13] In June 2004, Winn-Dixie entered into an agreement with its lenders to increase its existing senior secured revolving credit facility from $300 million to $600 million so as to mitigate the company's immediate liquidity needs. Trapped by noncancellable leases on dozens of under-performing stores, however, Winn-Dixie remained burdened by its high cost structure and had done little to improve its competitive position in the market.

During Lynch's first quarter as CEO, the company announced year-to-date losses of over $550 million. In the fall, Winn-Dixie violated the minimum fixed charge coverage covenant under the terms of its senior credit facility, preventing it from incurring additional indebtedness or issuing dividends until it climbed safely above the 2.25× minimum. The company found itself caught in a quandary; its stores had deteriorated to the point where customers were fleeing in droves to Wal-Mart or Publix, but it lacked the liquidity necessary to revamp them. The closure of unprofitable stores stemmed the bleeding slightly, but the company remained plagued by the $160 million ongoing "dark store" lease liabilities. A devastating piece by a local Jacksonville news station showed a customer returning goods purchased well after their stamped expiration dates. As the cameras continued to roll, Winn-Dixie employees were seen restocking the expired goods on the shelves.

Equity research analysts hammered the stock after a disastrous Q3 earnings call on Thursday, February 10, 2005, and vendors began refusing to extend credit to the embattled grocer. Fortunately, just days before the call, Lynch had hired restructuring consultants XRoads LLC to help the struggling grocer reexamine its operations and launch a successful turnaround effort. As the crisis reached a fever pitch over the weekend with vendors insisting on cash on delivery, turnaround leader Holly Etlin cut short a trip to Boston and flew immediately to Jacksonville to negotiate with merchants and assure that daily deliveries of perishables such as milk and eggs would continue. "I went with my winter clothes to Jacksonville, where it was 80 (degrees). I spent close to 100 percent of my time during those first days closeted with the merchants, talking to the major vendors . . . We were only going to pay them COD, and we wanted them to keep shipping.

That's how those first few days looked: classic complete hair on fire crisis management. It was truly amazing. I think I landed with three guys to begin with and by Saturday we had grown to ten."[14]

With Etlin's help, Winn-Dixie hastily prepared a Chapter 11 bankruptcy filing. Under bankruptcy protection, the company could continue to pay its merchants and keep the stores stocked during a critical holiday weekend while buying some time with its long-term creditors. Etlin's team immediately set about evaluating the performances and leases of every store in its portfolio. Bankruptcy protection allowed the company to reject executory contracts in the form of leases on any of its current stores, as well as all of the 150 stores that had already closed, thus ending the $3 million per week cash bleed on "dark store" leases. Winn-Dixie also received an automatic stay from recovery efforts of creditors, who were owed approximately $410 million in trade credit,[15] and halted various lawsuits pending at the time of filing.

Perhaps most important, the Blackstone Restructuring Group team led by Flip Huffard helped Winn-Dixie raise $800 million in the form of DIP financing through a bank group lead by Wachovia Bank, the agent of the pre-petition credit facility. The DIP allowed Winn-Dixie to refinance its existing credit facility and provided much-needed liquidity during the company's sudden cash crunch. With this cash in hand, Winn-Dixie finally gained sufficient breath-ing room to conduct a more thorough examination of its long-term capital requirements and strategic positioning in the highly competitive grocery industry.

This examination revealed problems that had long gone unnoticed under prior CEOs. Etlin's analysts determined that the vast majority of its profitable stores succeeded because they enjoyed either the #1 or #2 share in their markets, thus giving them pricing power and access to vendor promotions. Though Winn-Dixie still held such market shares in a number of attractive, high-growth markets in Florida and the Gulf states, its ill-advised expansion northward had led to the acquisition of stores as low as fifth or sixth share in markets such as Ohio. Almost without exception, such stores lacked the scale to maintain profitability, as advertising ceased to be cost-effective and negotiating power with suppliers dwindled. Etlin's team analyzed each of the com-pany's more than 900 stores and determined the appropriate footprint for Winn-Dixie's operations. Moving quickly so as to "right-size" the company within ninety days, the team settled on a group of 326 non-core stores to close or sell. These stores did not fit the new, refocused strategy of only operating stores where Winn-Dixie could hold a #1 or #2 market share.

Huffard's team enacted nine simultaneous M&A transactions selling approximately 130 such stores to other retailers, while Hilco Trading and Gordon Brothers liquidated the remaining 200 stores at much less lucrative prices. "When you sell it as a going concern you preserve the jobs of the employees at the store, as well as getting rid of the retail, the inventory, and the lease all in one package," Etlin said. "It's much messier to go through the other side of the process, but we did have to do it for more than 200 stores." Together, the efforts of Blackstone and the liquidators resulted in Winn-Dixie's complete exit from Ohio, North Carolina, South Carolina, Georgia, and northern Mississippi and Alabama. The company's refocused strategic footprint now focused entirely on Florida, the southern Gulf States, and Louisiana.

Those stores that remained had deteriorated to the point consumers shunned them for cleaner, better-lit competitors. Many stores hadn't seen any capital investment for over a decade, and it wasn't an appealing place to buy groceries. For example, the installation of lower-wattage light bulbs in an effort to decrease electricity costs had contributed to a cave-like atmosphere. In effect, Winn-Dixie had unconsciously ceded its competitive position to Publix on the high end, while Sam Walton had applied everything he learned from his tenure on the Winn-Dixie board to capture the value end of the market. With its renewed liquidity from the DIP financing, Winn-Dixie could finally make the necessary capital expenditures to bring its stores up to date.

Winn-Dixie also exited all of its manufacturing operations except for two dairies and the Chek Beverage operation. Given the plethora of lower-cost, higher-quality outsourced options, the company sold all twelve of the remaining manufacturing and processing plants to third parties. Most of the value of such assets came in the form of including the long-term contracts with Winn-Dixie, but until the Chapter 11 filing, those contracts bore a significant default risk, depressing their value. With a strong management team in place and under bankruptcy protection,

Winn-Dixie could at last realize some value from the sale of the manufacturing plants.

Lynch also began a herculean effort to change the company's ingrained culture, which had become complacent and lethargic. This dovetailed well with a 40 percent headcount reduction at headquarters, as they reduced the number of stores, which both slashed SG&A expenses and allowed management to select and retain those employees most capable of building a more urgent, customer-centric culture. The company also sought to retain its best store managers, offering court-approved retention and relocation packages to top performers at the defunct North Carolina stores. Meanwhile, Winn-Dixie's CIO began to address the company's technological approach, which lagged some twenty years behind the industry norm.

Throughout the company, Etlin's team found examples of low-hanging fruit that could reduce the company's cash burn, boost sales, and restore public confidence in the grocer's image. One example: Winn-Dixie stores lacked a kosher foods section in a state where certain counties' Jewish populations approach 15 percent.[16] By addressing local ethnicities and other seemingly obvious problems, Lynch and the streamlined Winn-Dixie management began to turn the company around.

By spring 2006, the strategic, operational, and financial changes made by management began to bear fruit. Winn-Dixie reported a 25 percent reduction in SG&A as a result of headcount reductions at headquarters to match stores closed and sold, with a 4.3 percent growth in same-store sales as a result of improved average sales per customer visit, due in part to improved customer service, the introduction of pricing and promotional programs, and new branding initiatives. Gross margin climbed by 30 basis points as a result of improved inventory shrink management. The company further managed to get its receivables and inventory turnover ratios under control by resuming the collection of receivables from vendors and liquidating approximately $300 million in inventory as part of the store and distribution center closures. With trade vendors reassured about the long-term viability of the grocer, Winn-Dixie ceased COD payment terms and stretched out its payables to a more normal level, thus allowing it to decrease its withdrawals on the DIP facility.

In the meantime, events had transpired in favor of the reorganizing company. Credit markets had loosened considerably during the first twelve months of the bankruptcy process; this allowed the company access to an additional $200 million in liquidity. The sales of stores, store leases, and the liquidation of inventory had also injected more than $300 million in cash into the company, thereby allowing it to pay down its DIP facility almost entirely, invest in store remodeling efforts, and satisfy many of its highest priority claims in cash.

Valuations Are Critical

With Winn-Dixie apparently on the right track at last, Huffard began the critical valuation analysis that would determine each of the creditors' recovery. In order to silence the bickering among creditors from its twenty-three separate Winn-Dixie-related entities in bankruptcy, the company reached a Substantive Consolidation compromise. This concept consolidated each Chapter 11 filing from all the various Winn-Dixie entities into one case, with all the property of Winn-Dixie effectively deemed the property of the consolidated estates, eliminating inter-company claims, distributions, and guarantees. This unusual tactic resulted from Winn-Dixie's unusually complex operating structure, and greatly simplified the process of identifying and sorting claimants into various classes based on order of recovery.[17]

Huffard briefly considered the liquidation analysis prepared by the team. Everyone but the noteholders did better under the consolidation of all the claims. (See Table 6.2.)

Although some creditor groups stood to gain from the consolidation as others lost, even an optimistic liquidation value left all of them far from a 100 percent recovery, thus decreasing the likelihood that they would approve a plan for liquidation. Such an asset-based valuation model ignored the company's value as a going concern. If the company left bankruptcy as an operating entity, the stock in the "new" company (referred to by the nickname Newco) would have real value that could exceed the liquidation values. This would yield more return for the creditors if they received stock in Newco.

Table 6.2. Winn-Dixie Liquidation Analysis

	Consolidated Case		Deconsolidated Case	
	Low	High	Low	High
Note holder recovery	$12,930	$39,458	$37,128	$112,854
Percentage recovery	4%	13%	12%	36%
Landlord recovery	$23,761	$72,510	$14,423	$44,150
Percentage recovery	4%	13%	3%	8%
Vendor / supplier recovery	$9,523	$29,060	$2,618	$7,989
Percentage recovery	4%	13%	1%	3%
Retirement plan recovery	$5,388	$16,443	$-	$-
Percentage recovery	0.04%	0.13%	0	0
Other unsecured recovery	$3,501	$10,683	$935	$3,162
Percentage recovery	4%	13%	1%	3%
Total	$55,103	$168,154	$55,104	$168,155
Percentage recovery	4%	13%	4%	13%

This then started another process, that of valuing the stock of Winn-Dixie as a new entity outside of Chapter 11. The company's depressed profitability made using comparable EBITDA multiples problematic, while a traditional capital asset pricing model (CAPM) significantly underestimated the true cost of equity for a company in a turnaround situation, even for one contemplating a balance sheet of 100 percent equity.[18]

Ultimately, Huffard relied primarily on a discounted cash flow (DCF) analysis, which relied on the financial projections, arriving at a valuation range of the reorganized Winn-Dixie entities of $625 to $890 million based upon an emergence from bankruptcy in the fall of 2006. Those projections included funded debt of only $10 million, resulting in an estimated midpoint equity value of approximately $750 million. The liquidity raised by the company's store divestitures and liquidations allowed it to pay down nearly all of its DIP facility and satisfy more than $400 million in claims through cash payment or assumption of the claims' contractual terms. Note holders, holders of landlord claims, and vendors received the lion's share of the $750 million in Newco common equity, with note holders receiving a 25 percent premium (95.6 percent recovery versus 70.6 percent for landlords and vendors) as compensation for the joint-and-several claims[19] they forfeited as part of the Substantive Consolidation Agreement. (See Table 6.3.[20])

Although Winn-Dixie had a very complex set of claims against it, and its subsidiaries, in the end the key to getting agreement was the value of the new stock and how to divide it up. With the emergence from Chapter 11, the officers and management and corporate structure changed. The plan established a new, nine-member board of directors, consisting of CEO Peter Lynch and an independent member deemed acceptable to the creditors, with the creditors' committee selecting the remaining seven members of the board. The reorganization plan also called for the new board to establish and implement a new equity incentive plan for management not to exceed 10 percent of the total outstanding shares of the new common stock.

With the U.S. Bankruptcy Court's approval of Winn-Dixie's final reorganization plan on August 4, 2006, and the $725 million in exit financing, the company emerged from Chapter 11 on November 21, 2006.[21] The total of 637 days spent in bankruptcy significantly exceeded the average restructuring process for a food retailer, reflecting management's determination to get it right the first time after several failed turnarounds outside of the bankruptcy process.[22] The reorganized company operated just 553 stores in only five states of the southeastern United States along with seven distribution centers and the three manufacturing facilities. Strategically, Winn-Dixie moved up-market to compete directly with Publix on service, convenience, and quality, abandoning the value end of the market to Wal-Mart and other bulk discount retailers. This drove the operational improvements, improving people, improving locations, improving the way they think about the business, the way they execute out in the stores.[23]

By January of 2008, Lynch and the Winn-Dixie management team had delivered four consecutive quarters at or above the Plan of Reorganization's projections. Same-store sales continued to grow, with margin expansion of more than 100 basis points due to reduced shrink. So successful was the turnaround that it received recognition from the Turnaround Management

Table 6.3. Summarized Treatment of Winn-Dixie Claims

Winn-Dixie Stores, Inc., Summary of Treatment of Claims

Class	Estimated Allowed Claims	Summary of Treatment	Estimated Percentage Recovery	Voting
Administrative Claims				
Post petition date costs, severance, fees, cure payments	$76,600,000	Cash payment or by contract	100.0%	No
DIP facility claims				
Revolving loans	$–			
Term loans	$40,000,000			
Letters of credit	$220,600,000			
Priority tax claims	$14,900,000	Cash payment, by contract, or deferred over six years	100.0%	No
Unimpaired Class of Claims and Interest				
Class 1—Other priority claims	$51,000,000	Cash payment or by contract	100.0%	No
Class 2—MSP death benefit claims		Per terms of benefit plan	100.0%	No
Class 3—Workman's comp claims		Per Workman's Corp laws of particular state	100.0%	No

Class	Amount	Treatment		
Class 4—Bond/letter of credit backed claims	$857,000	Claims backed by L/Cs. Amounts greater than amount available from the source of payment are unsecured. Cash payment or by contract.	100.0%	No
Class 5—Convenience claims	$35,200	Claims equal to or less than $100. Cash Payment or by contract.	100.0%	No
Class 6—Subsidiary interests	$—	Winn-Dixie to retain ownership interests in subsidiaries	N/A	No

Impaired/Voting Classes of Claims

Class	Amount	Treatment		
Class 7—AmSouth collateralized L/C claim	$17,000,000	Contractual rights to be reinstated	100.0%	Yes
Class 8—Thrivent/ Lutherans leasehold mortgage	$395,864	Contractual rights to be reinstated	100.0%	Yes
Class 9—Allowed NCR Purchase Money Security Interest Claims	$3,400,000	Per contract or 80% lump sum payment	100.0%	Yes
Class 10—Secured tax claims	$31,300,000	Holders to receive payment over a period of 6 years at 6% per annum	100.0%	Yes
Class 11—Other Secured Claims	$—	Rights reinstated by cash payment	100.0%	Yes

(Continued)

Table 6.3 (Continued)

Winn-Dixie Stores, Inc., Summary of Treatment of Claims

Class	Estimated Allowed Claims	Summary of Treatment	Estimated Percentage Recovery	Voting
Class 12—Note holder claims	$310,500,000	62.69 shares of New Common Stock for each $1,000 of secured claim, pro rata share of any excess common shares—may subject to Indenture Trustee liens	95.6%	Yes
Class 13—Landlord claims (greater than $3,000)	$284,100,000	46.26 shares of New Common Stock for each $1,000 of Allowed Claim, pro rata share of any excess common shares or cash payout through claim reduction fund	70.6%	Yes
Class 14—Vendor/supplier claims (greater than $3,000)	$218,900,000	46.26 shares of New Common Stock for each $1,000 of Allowed Claim, pro rata share of any excess common shares or cash payout through claim reduction fund	70.6%	Yes
Claim 15—Retirement plan claims (greater than $3,000)	$87,800,000	38.75 shares of New Common Stock for each $1,000 of Allowed Claim, pro rata share of any excess common shares or cash payout through claim reduction fund and 10% discount on Winn-Dixie purchases for a period of two years after distribution date	59.1%	Yes

Class	Estimated Amount	Treatment	Recovery	Voting
Class 16—Other unsecured claims (greater than $3,000)	$84,100,000	34.89 shares of New Common Stock for each $1,000 of Allowed Claim, pro rata share of any excess common shares or cash payout through claim reduction fund	53.2%	Yes
Class 17—Small claims (greater than $100, less than $3,000)	$3,200,000	Cash payment of 67% of allowed claim	67.0%	Yes
Impaired/nonvoting classes of claims				
Class 18—Intercompany claims		No payment unless for tax planning	0.0%	No
Class 19—Subordinated claims	$—	Discharged as of the Effective Date	0.0%	No
Class 20—*Noncompensatory damages claims*	$10,000,000	Discharged as of the Effective Date	0.0%	No
Class 21—Winn-Dixie interests		All Winn-Dixie interests will be cancelled	0.0%	No
Total estimated claims	$1,454,688,064			

Source: Winn-Dixie Stores, Inc., Disclosure Statement, June 29, 2006.

Association in the form of its 2007 Turnaround of the Year Award in the "Mega Company" category. As Huffard later recollected, "The thing that made it as successful as it was is the management team, especially in the form of Peter Lynch. He was an incredible force pushing that company in the right [strategic] direction."[24]

Winn-Dixie had good fortune in filing bankruptcy when it did. Less than a year later, Congress approved the BAPCPA's sweeping changes to the federal bankruptcy code, which made it significantly more challenging for a company in Chapter 11 to reorganize quickly and effectively. As a result of pressure from various lobbying groups, it became far more difficult to take the time to analyze the appropriate contracts and leases to reject, to retain and incentivize effective management teams, and to remain liquid at the outset of the bankruptcy process. Moreover, the credit markets softened greatly in 2007, which would have restricted Winn-Dixie's ability to raise the DIP financing necessary to execute its plan.

In addition to the company's timed bankruptcy filing, Winn-Dixie reacted well to a natural disaster as it prepared its plan of reorganization. In late August 2005, Hurricane Katrina devastated whole swaths of Mississippi and Louisiana, including New Orleans, one of Winn-Dixie's remaining core markets. Fortunately, the company had learned from the four hurricanes that had criss-crossed Florida the previous year and had developed rapid response protocols that enabled it to get its 110 Katrina-affected stores up and running faster than its competitors did. With employees and their families safely hunkered down in its Hammond, Louisiana, distribution center, Winn-Dixie was the first grocer to re-open in the heavily damaged areas of the state, going so far as to open mobile pharmacies to maintain the flow of prescription drugs to its customers. The crisis presented a powerful opportunity to revise customer perceptions of the company during a time of need, leading to sustained 20 percent comparable store growth in this core market.

Conclusion

The success of the Winn-Dixie reorganization demonstrates the overarching theme to bankruptcy: though it can wipe out shareholders and undermine customer and supplier confidence, it offers a company powers it would otherwise lack to enact sweeping changes in pursuit of a three-legged turnaround. The ability to reject executory leases represents an opportunity to discard a failed strategy (in Winn-Dixie's case, of northern expansion) in favor of a new one by escaping from leases on unprofitable or closed stores. The automatic stay grants the management team sufficient breathing room to undergo a genuine reengineering process and make the necessary operational improvements, such as Winn-Dixie's headcount reductions and improved information systems. The ability to raise DIP financing and sell assets free and clear out of bankruptcy represents an opportunity to make the financial changes needed to rationalize the company's balance sheet.

One last item about bankruptcy: Companies can declare bankruptcy more than once. That has given rise to nicknames, such as declaring Chapter 22 or 33. There are no such things; they simply refer to a company going into Chapter 11 for the second or third time, respectively.

A good example of multiple bankruptcies is Trump Entertainment Resorts, which filed for bankruptcy three times so far. "The Donald" claimed the recent filing in 2009 was again caused by creditors, owed almost $2 billion, and a general decline in Atlantic City's gambling revenue. One could claim there were even more Trump-related bankruptcies as some of the individual properties filed for bankruptcies along the way. Because of heavy debt always used by Trump it took substantial operating income just to cover debt payments. The Trump Taj Mahal in Atlantic City was financed mostly with $1 billion high-yield "junk bonds" and kept a lean staff to cover operations. This caused problems such as cleaning rooms only every other day as there were only 45 vacuum cleaners to service 904 rooms. They failed to capture high rollers because poor technology systems didn't track their preferences for food, nightlife, and so forth and didn't allow them to create a single loyalty card covering all three Atlantic City casinos owned by Trump. There was no clear strategy to differentiate the casinos, poor operations, and heavy debt load that caused the multiple filings. Each time, Trump himself managed to keep a substantial portion of the equity even when creditors received less than 100 percent of their bargains because he convinced everyone they needed him.

Pillowtex's board of directors similarly failed to observe clear warning signs, thus leading to its own multiple filings, with a less attractive outcome than Trump. The company became the leading U.S. pillow manufacturer, reaching $500 million in sales after twenty acquisitions. They then decided to buy Fieldcrest Cannon, a $1.1 billion towel and home furnishings manufacturer. The acquisition spree distracted management from the warning signs of the decline of the U.S. textile market. They also laid off the most critical Fieldcrest Cannon staff and mismanaged inventories while piling up debt. The abrasive, egotistical style of the CEO didn't help in negotiations with stakeholders when the company was bleeding cash. After the stock declined to less than $1, the CEO resigned and the company filed for Chapter 11 in November 2000. Pillowtex emerged from bankruptcy in May 2002, with only $200 million instead of $1.1 billion in debt. A new CEO was named to replace an interim one, who promptly decided to change the strategy laid out in the bankruptcy plan. That, coupled with increased competition, caused Pillowtex to default on its new, lower debt within four months of getting out of bankruptcy. At the same time, the company discovered that its pension plans were severely underfunded, just when losses instead of forecasted gains were reported. The company filed another bankruptcy petition. After unsuccessfully trying to sell the company and its retailers finding new suppliers, Pillowtex was liquidated in the new bankruptcy filing less than fourteen months after emerging from its first bankruptcy.

In summary, bankruptcy offers many advantages and disadvantages, which dictate whether a company on the brink should embrace it willingly or strive to avoid it at all costs. The Bankruptcy Code lays out how to deal with these advantages and disadvantages and many rules and regulations in one not too convenient package for U.S. companies. In the next chapter, we examine the regulations of other jurisdictions around the world, including the complex interaction of laws governing companies attempting to reorganize with operations in many different countries.

Chapter Seven

Managing International Turnarounds

In the days before globalization significantly flattened the business world, a turnaround took on an international character only for huge multinational organizations. This is no longer the case, as the increases in the global scope of even middle market businesses means that almost all turnarounds now have some international aspects that must be considered. This could be because the distressed company sources from foreign suppliers, has operations (perhaps a wholly owned subsidiary) overseas, serves international customers, has loans from different countries, or lists its securities on foreign exchanges.

A vast topic such as international turnarounds could fill many books, so this one chapter cannot cover it in its entirety. As a result, even more so than in other chapters of this book, my overruling advice is to consult a local attorney familiar with the rules of the relevant jurisdiction whenever you feel that you may be approaching a legal issue involving that country. The point of this chapter, then, is to alert you to examples of how and where such issues may arise, because turnarounds in multiple jurisdictions or with foreign creditors differ significantly from domestic turnarounds.

Many of these differences arise from the legacy legal and social environments that prompted the development of each country's regulations related to insolvency and financial distress. As explained in the previous chapter, America's more debtor-friendly Chapter 11 rules stemmed in part from the bankruptcy of a founding father and from the major role that railroads played in the nascent country's westward expansion. Most countries have economic histories, laws, political systems, and traditions much older than the United States' young two-and-a-third centuries.

As a result, regulations concerning insolvency and reorganization differ greatly from region to region. In a world where supply chains sprawl across the globe and companies have stakeholders from every continent, turnaround managers must be aware of the following differences:

1. *The causes of distress* are generally the same for all companies, no matter what the country, but may be more complex for companies with multiple international operations. This stems from lengths of supply chains, foreign exchange exposure, debt currency issues, and unanticipated regulatory changes. Even for companies without significant overseas footprints, international exposure can cause a liquidity crunch when heavy reliance on overseas vendors forces a company to carry higher levels of inventory to compensate for longer lead times, causing a significant drag on the company's cash flow collection cycle. Retailers such as Pier 1 Imports are particularly vulnerable to such liquidity concerns, as they typically build up inventory months in advance of converting it to cash in anticipation of seasonal sales trends.

Foreign exchange exposure represents another such cause of distress that can take on greater significance in international turnarounds, particularly those operating in countries where costs are denominated in the local currency but contracts are typically denominated in another. European aircraft manufacturer Airbus faces such exposure, as its massive aircraft contracts are typically denominated in U.S. dollars, leaving it especially vulnerable to the dollar's depreciation vis-à-vis the Euro; currency hedging contracts represent an imperfect and, particularly in volatile markets, potentially very costly mitigation strategy to this risk.

Debt payment terms in another currency can also lead a company into distress when the exchange rate turns against it. In the wake of a protracted legal battle, English entrepreneur Freddie Laker launched Laker Airlines in 1977, making two flights daily between London Gatwick and New York JFK. As one of the first no-frills discount air carriers, Laker proved extremely popular, prompting its expansion to include Miami, Tampa, and Los

Angeles as destinations. The weak U.S. dollar during this period made the airline particularly popular for U.K. residents, who could get to the United States for under £60. In order to fund this expansion with the purchase of new DC-10 aircraft, Laker issued debt with interest payments denominated in dollars, while continuing to accept the majority of its revenues in pounds. The 1981 rally of the dollar against all major European currencies squeezed Laker Airlines on both sides of the profitability equation; its revenues were worth less, and its debt payments were higher, ultimately leading to a bankruptcy filing the following year. This type of cross-border balance sheet problem continues today, when companies' efforts to hedge their currency risks have become ways to gamble on extra income.

   2. *The role of the government* can differ greatly across jurisdictions, and Airbus again represents one such unusual cause of distress. Airbus is a wholly owned subsidiary of European Aeronautic Defence & Space Company (EADS). Formed through the merger of French, German, Spanish, and U.K. entities, EADS has a complicated ownership structure, with Germany's Daimler Chrysler owning 22.46 percent, the French government and French conglomerate Lagardère Group each owning 11.23 percent, and the Spanish government owning 5.48 percent. (The remaining 49.15 percent trade freely on the Paris stock exchange, the Frankfurt stock exchange, and on stock exchanges in Madrid, Bilbao, Barcelona, and Valencia.)[1] In its constant struggle against duopolistic competitor Boeing, EADS has benefitted greatly from low- or no-interest loans, subsidized R&D, and debt forgiveness from the European governments that serve as both its equity holders and major creditors. (In fairness to Airbus, it has alleged that the U.S. government's high-margin defense contracts constitute *de facto* subsidies by another name.) In exchange for this broad-based support around the continent, these countries demand that Airbus use an unnecessarily convoluted supply chain, wherein each country's workers earn/receive a piece of the pie regardless of which one offers a true competitive advantage. Outsourcing the production of various parts is therefore not an option for Airbus; in 2006, Christian Streiff stated that he quit his position as CEO of Airbus after just three months because the governance structure of EADS preferred to maintain the balance

of power dictated by the company's Franco-German shareholder structure rather than make necessary operational changes.[2] This presents something of a double-edged sword for Airbus; on the one hand, its close ties with European governments and their role as both equity holders and creditors (as well as the potential arbiters of any insolvency proceedings) allows the company to absorb losses and renegotiate contracts that might sink other companies. On the other hand, this lax governance creates skewed incentives for management, who have little incentive to cut costs and improve operations in the face of such a substantial safety net. Unanticipated regulatory changes can affect international organizations in other ways. For example, companies such as Cemex and ExxonMobil have suffered from President Hugo Chavez's confiscation of their assets in Venezuela.

3. *The early warning signs of distress* may be more difficult to ascertain across jurisdictions, as some countries have significantly weaker reporting requirements, even for publically traded companies. The absence or differing forms of financial information will make it far more difficult for outsiders to determine if a company is facing a declining gross margin or negative cash flow. Similarly, different countries' accounting standards have varying methods of valuing inventory and writing off accounts receivable, which can obfuscate a company's failure to manage its working capital properly. Schwinn faced this when it discovered hundreds of bikes in the river behind its plant in Hungary—government rules didn't allow for the write-off of that inventory.

The turnaround of Parmalat USA—the American subsidiary of Italian dairy conglomerate Parmalat SpA—demonstrates how weak regulatory scrutiny can allow not simply aggressive accounting but out-and-out fraud to disguise a company's warning signs.[3] Parmalat management in Italy siphoned *billions* of dollars out of the company but managed to stave off detection for years by raising financing from indulgent capital markets and by producing false documentation suggesting that the company held significantly more capital reserves than it actually did. When Bank of America announced that the company's claim that it held a bank account at one of its affiliates for nearly $5 billion was false, Parmalat SpA and Parmalat USA filed for bankruptcy within one week. The document Parmalat had produced to demonstrate its liquidity was an obvious forgery that would not have evaded detection from more diligent regulatory or audit watchdogs.

External sources of corruption can also disguise a company's financial performance, complicating the detection of early warning signs. Although no nation is completely free of bribery and corruption scandals, these problems tend to be more pervasive in emerging markets. After seizing power from a corrupt management team and beginning a turnaround effort at Brasil Telecom, Angra Partners (a Brazilian firm tasked with the turnaround) suddenly found the company faced significant potential liabilities stemming from the departed management team's rampant bribery of legislators on matters related to the telecom industry.[4] It's interesting that the company also showed how turnaround managers sometimes have additional tools at their disposal in other jurisdictions; the company's corrupt former management had very strong personal ties with many of the managers who remained, and the taint of corruption threatened to undermine the new management team's turnaround strategy. In a move that probably would have been impossible in the United States for a variety of legal and professional reasons, Angra retained an Israeli security company to conduct extensive interviews (including lie detector tests) to determine each executive's risk profile, and terminated several senior executives based in part upon their findings.

Finally, Brasil Telecom also demonstrates how the volatility of emerging economies can mask the operational deterioration that eventually makes a turnaround necessary. Though it continued to post subscriber and revenue growth around the turn of the century, the Brazilian Internet market's 36 percent compound annual growth from 2000 to 2005 makes it clear that with such a powerful tailwind, incumbent management should have posted significantly more impressive performance than it did.[5] Similarly, emerging markets' stock exchanges can become wildly inflated, as investors chase returns in what they think will be the next overseas success story. Because the market value of equity is a significant input to Altman's Z-score calculation, inflated equity values can understate a company's likelihood of insolvency.

4. Director and officers take on very different *fiduciary duties* in various jurisdictions. In many European countries, directors

can be held personally liable for the company's debts in an insolvency situation. Whereas wily officers may be able to stave off bankruptcy for some time even when they are in the zone of insolvency in the United States, French directors who fail to file for bankruptcy within fifteen days of becoming unable to pay its due debts with available assets assume personal liability for creditors' claims.[6] Polish law is particularly strict, as directors are *required* to launch a bankruptcy proceeding if they feel that the company is unable to pay its debts as they come due, with punishment for failing to do so including personal liability for the company's debts and up to a year in prison.[7] Recent changes to the Spanish bankruptcy code similarly establish a concept of "preventative attachment," wherein directors guilty of various acts of mismanagement will see their personal assets used to satisfy creditors' claims.[8] Finally, some jurisdictions change the very party to whom directors owe a duty in the first place, such as Luxembourg, where directors are beholden to the company itself, rather than its shareholders.[9]

I saw this up close in the bankruptcy proceedings of a company called Breed Technologies, whose ill-advised and extremely rapid acquisition binge in the automotive safety-device space left it unable to make the *first* of its many expensive debt payments. Breed, also a manufacturer of airbags and seatbelts, threatened to shut down General Motors unless it advanced tens of millions in cash to keep Breed afloat; the next day, GM filed suit claiming Breed had attempted to extort it, and Breed filed for bankruptcy soon thereafter. Despite the approval of a reorganization plan that saw its more than $600 million in long-term secured debt wiped out entirely (along with $500 million for bondholders, shareholders, and all of its domestic accounts payable), the significant claims filed by vendors to and creditors of its foreign subsidiaries were made whole. The reason? Breed's officers and directors knew they could otherwise never again set foot in Germany or France, for fear of being held personally liable for the impaired claims, and therefore convinced the banks who wound up owning the company and the bankruptcy court to honor those claims in full. Bankrupting those subsidiaries would also have brought on further delays in their jurisdiction as well, slowing down Breed's emergence from the U.S. Bankruptcy Court.

5. _Creditor attitudes_ frequently differ across jurisdictions. Whereas American creditors are highly familiar with extended payment plans and offers of deferred interest that debtors may offer in an attempt to avoid insolvency—ever cognizant of the threat of a cram-down plan or preference claim in bankruptcy that could leave them even worse off—suppliers in other countries may be very comfortable negotiating far more aggressively, secure in their notion that "in Europe, vendors always get paid." The obstinacy of vendors in the turnaround of cable and Internet provider ish GmbH very nearly forced the company into a massive liquidation.[10]

6. _The bankruptcy trustee or its equivalent_ can play very different roles across jurisdictions. I encountered this type of situation in attempting to help a client purchase a competing German company that had filed an _Insolvenzplan_. A financial buyer had made what we considered to be an extremely lowball offer for the company's assets, and so my client requested a one-week extension of the thirty-day sale process that was about to end to allow sufficient time to travel there and conduct the necessary due diligence to make a competitive bid. The court-appointed administrator told him in no uncertain terms not to bother, because he was confident that the incumbent bidder could successfully complete the transaction at the offered price. Should the administrator approve an extension beyond the first thirty-day reorganization window only to see the transaction fall through, he would have been personally liable for the company's payroll, which was guaranteed by the German government only up to the first thirty days of the case. Naturally, this incentivized him to approve the most certain to succeed (read: lowest) bid possible to avoid finding himself on the hook to creditors.

7. International jurisdictions have very _different goals for the bankruptcy process_. While the U.S. bankruptcy code declares as its goal the maximum preservation of value for distribution to stakeholders (with a public policy justification of encouraging investment in private enterprises and a "fresh start" whenever possible), France's Law for Voluntary Arrangements stipulates that its aim is to maintain as high a level of employment as possible. Obviously, this is often at odds with the goal of preserving creditor value, as many companies enter distress precisely because they are

overstaffed. Similar laws exist for current (and even previous) Communist and Socialist countries.

8. _Procedural differences_ between jurisdictions are legion. French insolvency laws, for example, do not provide for the creation of creditor committees, and only gain access to certain debtor information if they successfully petition the court to appoint them as monitors.[11] In the Netherlands, however, the supervisory bankruptcy judge is barely involved, and the vast majority of negotiations take place directly between the purchaser of a bankrupt company and its creditors, with limited court oversight. Though foreign jurisdictions have increasingly adopted more debtor-friendly bankruptcy codes modeled on the United States' Chapter 11, in general most countries put a great deal more time pressure on debtors, and give them fewer options to restructure debt and reorganize their operations. As a result, most countries' courts have significantly lower rates of success in rehabilitating companies; one study estimated that more than 90 percent of bankruptcies in France end in liquidation, rather than in a sale or reorganization.[12] England suffered similar endings for many years.

Another frequent procedural challenge arises from some jurisdictions' (including the United States) usage of the principle of substantive consolidation. The Winn-Dixie case from the previous chapter involved substantive consolidation, which allows debtors from the same corporate family of parent and subsidiaries with largely intertwined ownership and financial operations to file jointly, with creditors filing their claims against the consolidated pool of assets, rather than against each subsidiary. This can cause problems when lenders in countries that do not use substantial consolidation have specifically extended credit only to one subsidiary and are sufficiently collateralized on their claim, but if forced to file the same claim against the consolidated pool would find their claim impaired. In order to protect such creditors, courts will often—but by no means always—allow creditors to carve out a portion of the assets to satisfy their claim before contributing any remaining value from their collateral to the consolidated pool.

9. _The priority of claims_ can vary across jurisdictions, although recently more countries follow a hierarchy generally similar to

that used in the United States. However, subtle differences often arise, such as from the treatment of tax liabilities, which in some jurisdictions rise above all others. In cases of fraud, these subtle differences can take on a great deal of importance, as a sizable claim held by the government can mean the difference between the secured lender being the first money out of a company or becoming the fulcrum security. More notable differences exist in France and Spain, where employee claims come first; in the case of France, employee claims for payment up to sixty days take absolute priority, followed by eleven months of social security unemployment pay, and only then are followed by administrative expenses. Sweden, by contrast, grants highest priority to maritime and aircraft liens, followed by landlord claims for up to three months of rent.[13]

10. *Plan confirmation* is determined very differently in certain jurisdictions, such as in China, where equity holders have the right to veto any plan that impairs the value of their shares.[14]

11. *Exchange commissions* in many countries operate very differently when a publicly traded company experiences distress. The shares of Chinese companies that have filed for bankruptcy continue to trade, whereas in Australia, a company that has not filed bankruptcy can nonetheless request that trading of its shares on the Australian Securities Exchange be suspended pending its efforts to raise additional financing. That suspension can last more than one year![15]

12. Some countries present *obstacles for resolution* that are commonplace in Chapter 11 proceedings. For example, though China in 2007 passed an Enterprise Bankruptcy Law that emulates the American Code, it potentially poses certain conflicts with the country's Commercial Banking Law, which prevents commercial banks from holding equity in nonfinancial institutions in all but a few situations. Because those same commercial banks are typically the largest creditors to bankrupt Chinese companies, Chinese courts may be reluctant to permit the type of debt-for-equity swap frequently seen in the United States.

13. *Labor regulations* differ vastly across various jurisdictions. Germany's equivalent of the WARN Act requires three months of notice rather than two, and layoffs of more than thirty individuals activate what is known as a Social Plan, which invokes a host of

very costly obligations on the part of the employer to make greater severance payments and provide for the retraining and placement of terminated employees. Many countries have similar provisions for Social Plans, but enforcement of those is sometimes less rigorous than the WARN Act, which establishes a six-month look-back window to ensure that a company does not attempt to avoid incurring WARN obligations by trickling out a smaller number of terminations every few weeks. The unique relationships between local office HR departments and local Works Councils can sometimes allow a company to pursue such a strategy, such as in one European turnaround where turnaround professionals made four monthly dismissals of fifteen workers, avoiding the trigger for a Social Plan.[16] This may appear to contradict our recommendation in Chapter Five, which suggests that such repeated rounds of layoffs can destroy morale. However, the vastly different employment regulations in European countries make workers far less fearful of headcount reductions. Severance packages are far more generous, and terminations much less frequent, so worker morale often proves more resilient, even in the wake of multiple rounds of layoffs. Of course, as in the United States, open communication is key here, so subsequent rounds of layoffs should not prove a surprise to survivors.

As a result, companies planning to downsize as part of a restructuring must take into account the differing costs of shutdowns and layoffs in the various jurisdictions in which they do business. In his turnaround of multinational pharmaceutical company Elan Corporation, Garo Armen had to balance the desire to exit certain businesses that operated primarily in Ireland with the higher costs that such layoffs would entail. In the end, Armen terminated a disproportionate number of jobs in Italy and the UK, whose labor laws are slightly less onerous to downsizing employers than are Irish ones.[17]

14. Different countries also offer *different terms of repayment* for creditors, even when made whole. For example, Mexican monetary law dictates that claims denominated in foreign currencies are fully enforceable, but if payment is made within Mexico's borders, debtors are permitted to pay in Mexican pesos at the Banco de México's official exchange rate, essentially shifting the cost of conversion onto the recipient. Savvy creditors may contract

around this by including terms in loan agreements that require payment made somewhere outside Mexico's borders.[18]

15. _Different market dynamics_ can lead to strategic dissonance for companies delivering the same product across borders. For example, McDonald's franchises in Iceland struggled for years because the country's geographic isolation was fundamentally incongruous with the company's strategy of providing a high value to customers, with value defined as quality divided by price. This metric required low costs to stand out from local competitors, so the company uses a regional sourcing strategy to achieve bulk discounts on input costs such as lettuce, beef, buns, and other ingredients. Though quality ratings at Icelandic stores met or exceeded benchmarks, the exorbitant cost of flying in the supplies to support just three locations prevented McDonald's franchises from delivering on the price side of the equation. Precisely the same strategy worked remarkably well in other European countries, but because McDonald's core competency of providing high value was negated by excessive shipping costs, the three Icelandic locations closed in late 2009.[19]

Clearly, these differences but scratch the surface in listing all the ways that cross-border insolvency cases present unique challenges. As always, managers should contact legal counsel with any questions regarding these or any other issues that could arise in the case of an international turnaround. The turnaround itself could also involve the following issues:

International turnarounds tend to involve a _higher degree of complexity_ for a company's operations, as diverse groups of creditors begin to assert different claims on different assets under different rules on different continents. Though the prevailing trend around the world is toward greater comity—that is, legal reciprocity among jurisdictions—while respecting the sovereignty of the nation in which the proceedings are taking place, the legacy barriers erected by the different goals and roles of the bankruptcy courts in various countries continue to paralyze companies with far-flung operations more than those with all of their facilities in one country.

Issues of nationalism can also arise in international turnarounds, both in terms of assigning blame for the distress and determining which facilities and jobs to retain. For example, constant conflict between the American board of Atari and the French board of its majority stockholder Infogrames took on overtones of "us versus them" that degenerated into finger-pointing over who was at fault for the company's declining performance. In another turnaround, executives at a European subsidiary of a bankrupt American parent company mistakenly felt no need to reduce their cost structure, believing that any problems had originated at the American parent and should therefore be solved there as well.[20]

Issues of nationalism presented significant challenges for Carlos Ghosn's turnaround of nearly bankrupt Japanese auto-maker Nissan, as it relied upon a tight alliance with France's Renault. It is hard to imagine two more vastly different cultures than the French and Japanese, and the pride of Japanese auto-workers threatened to derail collaboration with a country not known primarily for excellence in automotive engineering. A French citizen born in Brazil to Lebanese parents, Ghosn insisted that the combined entity adopt English as its working language to avoid inflaming language-based nationalistic sentiments and instead focus employees on appreciating the differences between their two cultures.

This nationalism can also impact market dynamics for com-panies attempting to grow out of distress in part by entering new markets, as Gerstner's IBM did in taking the fight for large gov-ernmental contracts to the home country of Japanese competitor Fujitsu Ltd. In the contract bidding for computerizing processes for both the city of Hiroshima's sewer department and Nagano's public library, Fujitsu bid one yen to demonstrate its willingness to defend its home turf at all costs.

When the new CEO took over at Breed as it emerged from bankruptcy, he discovered there were language, culture, work rule, and other differences among the plants in different coun-tries. He successfully changed every plant and subsidiary to the same measurement system. The overarching language became return on assets, with a target set for each unit; then ROA became the first thing discussed at every meeting.

Team diversity can prove helpful in the tense environment of a company in crisis. One successful turnaround intentionally drew high-potential middle managers from around Europe and re-assigned them to new markets, which created a cross-pollination of ideas and practices from around the company that contributed to the turnaround's success.

Turnarounds in developing markets can exhibit *geopolitical risks* with which domestic investors may be unfamiliar. For example, the recent outbreaks of drug-related violence in Mexico's Baja Peninsula have delayed a recent graduate's efforts to buy out his family's pharmacy chain and enact sweeping changes to restructure the business.

Fitting in can go a long way in providing a turnaround manager with credibility in a foreign context. One turnaround manager credited simple efforts, such as avoiding using American English spell-checker corrections on words like "centre" and "organisation" for lending it subtle credibility in a European turnaround. More demonstrative efforts included respecting local work ethics by not imposing American working hours on locals despite the company's impending crisis, and participating in local holidays or customs.[21]

Despite all of these challenges to foreign turnarounds, the international restructuring community has seen great advances over the past twenty years, with more than a dozen nations revising their bankruptcy laws and moving toward a flexible set of regulations that promote cooperation between courts in various jurisdictions. Many of these new regulatory regimes have openly declared their intention to emulate the United States' Chapter 11, which for all its shortcomings remains the gold standard in the world for presenting a set of rules that fairly balance the goals of the debtor and its creditors in the hopes of maximizing the value to be distributed. Several now promote the goal of a "fresh start."

More important, the distinct trend has been toward a scheme of cooperation between various jurisdictions, with courts establishing cross-border insolvency protocols in an effort to increase the efficiency of the process and discourage forum-shopping. In one notable example regarding Everfresh Beverages' 1996 bankruptcy filings in both the United States and Canada, courts held the first joint cross-border hearing in order to ensure the proper coordination of timing in both cases. After the case's conclusion—which involved a sale of the entire business—the stakeholders' legal counsel estimated that the value recovered had increased by approximately 40 percent as a result of the cooperation between the two courts. In other cases involving both Canadian and American courts, judges on both sides of the border have held live hearings by videoconference so as to coordinate their efforts more cohesively.[22] Fanny May Candy's sale of its profitable Canadian Subsidiary, Laura Secort candy and ice cream company, required it to avail itself of Canadian law and lawyers. They cooperated with their U.S. counterparts to get the deal closed.

This trend toward greater cooperation has benefited from the United Nations Commission on International Trade Law (UNCITRAL) Model Law. In addition to UNCITRAL's rotating list of member nations, representatives from the World Bank, the European Commission, the American Bar Association, the American Bar Foundation, the Center for International Legal Studies, the Groupe de Reflexion Sur L'Insolvabilite et Sa Prevention, INSOL International, the International Bar Association, the International Insolvency Institute, the International Women's Insolvency and Restructuring Confederation, and the International Working Group on European Insolvency Law came together in 1997 to promote the Model Law, a set of best practices intended to encourage cooperation between courts in different jurisdictions during insolvency cases.

The Model Law does not attempt to usurp the practical insolvency laws of each country, but rather streamline the procedures of the jurisdiction overseeing the bankruptcy to facilitate cooperation between foreign courts. Thus far the following countries (in the denoted years) have passed legislation based on the Model Law: Australia (2008), British Virgin Islands (2003), Canada (2009), Colombia (2006), Eritrea (1998), Great Britain (2006), Greece (2010), Japan (2000), Mauritius (2009), Mexico (2000), Montenegro (2002), New Zealand (2006), Poland (2003), Republic of Korea (2006), Romania (2003), Serbia (2004), Slovenia (2007), South Africa (2000), and the United States (2005).[23] The Model Law runs a full eighty pages in length, so naturally a full discussion of its suggested best practices is beyond the purview of this book. However, creditors from around the world should not hesitate to contact legal counsel if one of their borrowers is involved in insolvency in a country that has adopted the Model Law. The U.S. version is the aforementioned Chapter 15 of the Bankruptcy Code.

A Word on Fraud

As mentioned previously, the risk of fraud is significantly higher in international turnarounds, where regulatory oversight may be spotty. Fraud can create uniquely challenging engagements for turnaround professionals. Although the cause of the company's distress is an exogenous factor that upon detection is typically removed, the surviving company can suffer such a loss of reputation with suppliers and creditors and a devastation of employee morale that an otherwise healthy company brought low by fraud can become troubled very quickly.

Parmalat represents a perfect example of such a situation. The Italian parent company was accused of a massive, multiyear fraud. Upon its detection, the senior managers in Parmalat's U.S. subsidiary cleaned out their offices and disappeared on planes back to Italy almost overnight. As Jim Mesterharm of Alix Partners sifted through the company's data to determine its true financial condition, it became clear that management embezzlement had been pervasive for the past twenty years, with funds siphoned off from the parent company's frequent debt offerings to pay officers huge sums of money. Tellingly, Parmalat USA had never really received any revenue targets or hurdles from its Italian parent; its main mission was to promote the Parmalat brand in the United States. Mesterharm later learned that some U.S. managers believed the only reason that Parmalat SpA expanded into the United States by buying fresh-milk operations was to give senior management an opportunity to go shopping in New York.

In any turnaround, the process of forming an accurate picture of the company's liquidity and the timeline upon which various creditors needed to be paid in the near term is a critical first step. The outright embezzlement by departed management made this already difficult process even more challenging, for executives guilty of fraud rarely leave behind accurate company records that might include illegal disbursements, and they rarely respond to requests for clarification of the victim company's muddled income statements. Mesterharm's team knew they would face an unusually difficult job of assessing the company's true financial situation when their request for the company's books was met with a question from the company's controller: "Which set of numbers would you like to see, the one we report, or the real numbers?"

Operating in the dairy industry exacerbated this already exceptional time crunch, for failure to pay key vendors would result in an immediate shutdown and likely liquidation. Renegotiation of payments to farmers was out of the question, because milk prices and payment terms were determined by the state regulatory board. Truck drivers would leave on Thursday to pick up milk, and they usually carried checks from Parmalat with them to pay the supplier dairy farmers. Despite this unusually profound time pressure, Mesterharm's team fought through the distortions and fabrications on the company's income statements, some $300 million of which involved prior management reversing expenses and moving them into accounts receivable as "credits," effectively booking them as revenue. They also discovered the prevalent use of special-purpose entities (SPEs) to hide dubious perquisite expenses and create fictitious overseas sales, such as the questionable claim that Parmalat sold to Cuba 55 gallons of milk, per year per inhabitant. After a grueling process of fact-checking and forensic accounting that required numerous interviews with employees at all levels of the organization, Mesterharm's team produced a reliable 13-Week Cash Flow Model that painted a clear picture of the company's dire liquidity situation.

Mesterharm immediately called the Italian Court-appointed turnaround consultant hired to oversee the Italian parent company's bankruptcy and requested financing to keep the company afloat. Naturally, the parent was receiving identical calls from subsidiaries all over the globe that had been left similarly high-and-dry by the embezzlement. After procuring an $8 million unsecured junior loan from Parmalat SpA, Mesterharm had to turn to the company's second-largest creditor—GE Capital—for additional financing. Even making such a request took a great deal of both diplomacy and nerve, for just two weeks before the bankruptcy filing, GE had engaged in a sale-leaseback transaction with Parmalat USA for almost all of its manufacturing and distribution assets . . . and just weeks later, not a penny remained because it had been stolen in its entirety.

Naturally, GE twice refused Mesterharm's request that they consider offering Parmalat USA the DIP financing necessary to remain operational, expressing the sense of indignation and betrayal typically felt by a creditor who has fallen victim to fraud. Fortunately, Mesterharm entered the situation as a fresh face, one unsullied by the fraud of the departed executives, and as such he possessed the credibility of an innocent outsider. Delicately balancing the need for immediate financing with the desire to wait for GE to come to grips with the fact that it had been defrauded, Mesterharm engaged Lazard's restructuring team to value the business while giving GE's lending team time to cool off. Over a three-day weekend that included Valentine's Day and the President's Day holiday, after which the company would have to liquidate on Tuesday, Lazard drummed up three fire sale bidders, whose willingness to pay a price greater than $50 million demonstrated to GE that a going concern sale would reap enough to increase its recovery from the estimated $0.05 on the dollar it expected in a liquidation. Reluctantly, GE realized that in spite of the still stinging wound left from the embezzlement, it would benefit from injecting more capital into Parmalat USA in the form of temporary DIP financing, so the company could live and retain value as a going concern.

Ironically, Mesterharm's team continued to uncover inappropriate behavior above and beyond the theft by former managers, and yet found a way to use it as leverage in addressing the company's operational challenges. The day before Alix's engagement, Parmalat USA's general manager (GM) left the company to join a major competitor as a sales representative, and immediately began to steal major customers. In the absence of any red flags explaining why customers would leave so quickly, Mesterharm spoke with Parmalat's head of sales, who explained "[the former GM] has those guys in his back pocket . . . he's tight with all the buyers at the major Northeast grocery chains." A thorough review of the GM's expense reports revealed that he had made nearly five times his expected annual salary of $200,000, with payments deposited to his account at infrequent periods that just so happened to occur immediately before the awarding of large contracts. Using the power of the bankruptcy courts, Mesterharm subpoenaed the former GM, his bank records, and any other relevant information, threatening to go public with his belief that the GM owned an inflated payroll of $4 million because he had pocketed significant portions of it but also used it to pay his buyers kickbacks for signing new contract agreements. Extravagant expense reports included such items as $50,000 worth of Louis Vuitton luggage provided to a buyer as a gift, the rental of an island in the Caribbean for a month for another buyer and his family, and trips to Las Vegas with thousands of dollars of payments provided to customers for suspiciously labeled "gambling and entertainment expenses." As many of these buyers were married men and their names appeared in the subpoenaed records, the threat to go public with such information made many in the industry nervous.

Dean Foods nonetheless had the temerity to file a large claim in Parmalat USA's bankruptcy case, on the grounds that Parmalat USA's closure of its Brooklyn plant led to the rejection of a contract to supply Dean Foods with milk at a below-market rate. With a competitor as its largest unsecured creditor, Parmalat would face significant headwinds in attempting to reorganize, as a powerful stakeholder would have a perverse incentive to force the company's liquidation. By researching why Parmalat had entered into an unprofitable contract in the first place, Mesterharm learned that the contract had probably been anti competitive from day one, with a lowball price offered to Dean Foods in exchange for Dean Foods closing a plant and cooperating on pricing. With Dean Foods under pressure from the U.S. Department of Justice for anticompetitive behavior, Mesterharm negotiated aggressively with the company, with the threat of voiding this below-market contract as a fraudulent conveyance and revealing possible unethical behavior of its newest sales representative looming ominously in the background. Forced to choose between advancing their claim and avoiding messy litigation and a public relations nightmare, Dean Foods capitulated and backed out of its claim, and soon thereafter the former GM left Dean Foods.

Aspects of the original fraud ultimately resulted in additional leverage, this time against the Italian parent from which it unquestionably had to make a clean break. However, Parmalat USA required two things from Parmalat SpA: technical support and, more important, the right to use the Parmalat name, logo, and related IP. Now sitting on the same side of the table with GE representatives eager to maximize their recovery by suing the Italian parent, Mesterharm found himself negotiating against the very same parties that had originally turned to him to restructure Parmalat USA. Both sides of the ocean had filed claims against each other, but the claims of the parent were deemed to have no basis in fact, so Mesterharm used the company's far-flung operational structure against it. Finding that the $100 million from the GE transaction had passed through Parmalat's Canadian operations—which represented a key asset of the Parmalat SpA Group—Mesterharm threatened to sue the Canadian business, which might have forced its own bankruptcy filling and possibly derailed Parmalat's Italian bankruptcy proceedings, preventing it from reorganizing. Knowing how the insolvency of the Canadian operations would throw an even larger monkey wrench into its own reorganization, Parmalat SpA settled, withdrawing its claim against Parmalat USA and agreeing to let it use the Parmalat name.

Fraud rarely occurs in as blatant a manner as it did at Parmalat, with the guilty executives fleeing under cover of darkness and most absconding with their ill-gotten gains. As brazen as it was, it probably made recovery for survivors at the company easier, as there were no shades of grey in determining who was at fault; the villains were easily identifiable. Typically, fraud is far more painful, for it is difficult to be defrauded by someone you do not already trust. A far more common situation occurs when a debtor's management team finds itself overextended, without any unencumbered assets that could support additional leverage, and begins a slippery slope into fraudulent behavior. They might stop delivering proceeds to the lender in order to make payroll, for example, or they may sell items without reporting it to their lender, thereby masking a degradation of their borrowing base. Another common example arises when payroll comes due and there is no availability under the revolver, so the company begins invoicing on Thursday for goods shipping on Friday or even next week or next month; this increases the receivables balance that serves as the basis for many asset based loans, providing them borrowing availability to meet payroll. It might work once, or twice, or even a dozen times, but if the company does not actually improve its performance, it tends to slide further down the distress curve, until management begins invoicing for goods well before they even arrive from suppliers. Eventually, a frustrated supplier can derail the entire scheme by putting the company on cash on delivery, and suddenly the manager is trapped in his own web of deception.[24]

In turning around a company that has fallen victim to fraud, communications to employees, customers, and suppliers takes on an even greater role than in most turnarounds. Employee morale is less likely to plummet, and customers and vendors are less likely to panic and switch to a competitor if they find out the truth directly from the source, with an appropriate degree of contrition and apology even from new management. Competitors will already be advertising the company's misadventures, so it is better to get the company's message out in front of the news. As with most communications of a sensitive nature, it is best to make these communications in person to put a human face on the tragic news and restore faith that it will be addressed.

It is particularly important to find the guilty parties and remove them from the company as soon as possible. In many—but not all—situations, it will make sense to involve the relevant law enforcement bodies immediately, but above all, the turnaround manager must restore credibility to an organization that has almost certainly lost it from its creditors and other stakeholders.

As with many aspects of the turnaround field, an ounce of prevention is worth a pound of cure in dealing with fraud. Extensive background checks, diligent expense reimbursement monitoring, following up on signs that employees are living beyond their means and therefore possibly accepting kickbacks, and handing out payroll checks in person to avoid no-show jobs on the payroll are just some of the steps companies can take to protect themselves. It is a good idea to check directly with financial institutions to ensure the amount of cash shown on the company's books matches the banks' records.

Elan Corporation

There are many other examples how international jurisdictions play a role in key turnaround decisions even when bankruptcy is not directly involved. Founded in Dublin in 1969, Elan Corporation became a diversified specialty pharmaceutical player, with various products and services in pain management, neurology, dermatology, infectious diseases, oncology, and diagnostics. Led by CEO Donal Geaney, Elan became one of the most significant Irish companies by 2001, with a market capitalization of approximately $20 billion, which accounted for almost 20 percent of the total value of the Irish Stock Exchange.[25] It had also become a major international company, with offices, laboratories, and manufacturing facilities in four countries.

Two developments in early 2002 changed Elan's situation dramatically. First, the *Wall Street Journal* indicated that Elan's fifty-five licensing arrangements could be artificially inflating revenue.[26] They were recorded as investment assets and thus not expensed on the income statement, but the upfront technology licensing fees paid by the ventures were recognized as revenue by Elan.[27] The *Wall Street Journal* estimated that Elan's 2001 revenue would have been 40 percent lower had these business ventures been consolidated. Government agencies quickly launched investigations of Elan's accounting practices.

Shortly after the accusations of accounting improprieties emerged, a midstage clinical trial of a high-potential Alzheimer's disease drug was discontinued. Fifteen patients in the study had developed a dangerous inflammation of the brain and spinal cord, and Elan was forced to terminate the study, casting doubts on the future of one of its most promising products.

These two setbacks led to a precipitous drop in Elan's stock price, thereby triggering a vicious cycle. Elan's near-term debt obligations were significant, and the company had traditionally satisfied its debts through conversions into equity. This would not be feasible because of the reduced share price, leading to internal and external concerns about the firm's viability and even further declines in the share price. By July 2002, Elan was trading down approximately 96 percent from its price at the start of the year.

Meanwhile, Elan's leadership was paralyzed. Internal and external communications were unclear and concealed the extent of the company's problems, and managerial inertia led the board of directors to seek a replacement for longtime CEO Geaney. Garo Armen, then an Elan board member, blamed the lack of a strong leadership response on decision-making paralysis. He was appointed chairman and interim CEO of Elan in July 2002, and was concurrently chairman and CEO of Antigenics Inc., based in New York, and chairman and interim CEO of Elan, based in Dublin. He faced an extensive list of challenges on both sides of the Atlantic that needed immediate and decisive action.

Armen knew that success in turning Elan around would require him to avoid the decision-making paralysis that had plagued his predecessors. To that end, he quickly took steps to restore trust and calm among his various constituents. Externally, he quickly addressed an SEC investigation with investors, as well the international ramifications. He charged the board of directors to meet their fiduciary duties and to conduct an internal accounting investigation. It would later show there was no fraud, just "aggressive, but legal accounting." He also promised that Elan would more transparently communicate its finances with the public while acting more prudently in its financing practices by avoiding its extensive borrowing. Internally, Armen took a similar approach. He implemented a series of town hall meetings, flying to Elan's various facilities to answer employees' questions. He promised full transparency, telling employees, "You now know what I know."

Strategy Considerations

Armen faced important decisions regarding the company's scale and scope within the context of almost immediate cash needs to satisfy upcoming debt maturity. He saw three potential company strategies for the future:

- Pure commercial organization
- Pure biotech company
- Blended commercial and R&D organization

Armen and Elan's board ultimately decided on the third option, choosing to retain certain commercial and research assets that reflected their core competencies while attempting to divest others. What resulted was the establishment of Core Elan which consisted of a commercial business with previously approved products in neurology, pain management, and infectious diseases, a biopharmaceutical research unit with three key development programs, and one contract manufacturing unit. He also created Elan Enterprises, which consisted of the business and products to be divested, including the drug delivery business, multiple approved products, and various research programs.

Operations

Regardless of the strategy Elan adopted, the new company would clearly have to be a leaner organization with scaled-back operations, if only to conserve capital. Thus, Armen implemented a restructuring plan to bring down operating expenses by $300 million per year. Two significant cost centers comprised the bulk of the austerity program—properties and employees.

At the start of the crisis, Elan operated nine facilities in four countries, Ireland, Italy, the United Kingdom, and the United States. Armen knew that the four properties owned outright by the company were clear targets for divestiture to generate cash. However, one of the four was Élan's most significant Irish property, and Armen preferred to maintain the company's historical presence in Ireland. Following the sale of the owned properties in Italy and the United States, Élan had to decide which of its leased facilities to retain. Based on the decision to pursue a strategy that involved a more limited focus on commercial and research programs, Armen decided to retain the two most significant U.S. properties—in San Francisco and San Diego, both hubs of pharmaceutical research—and exit the others. In addition, a small facility in the United Kingdom was retained.

The labor market characteristics of the countries in which an international company such as Élan operates complicate the shutdowns of its locations. For example, trade union density, a measure of the wage and salary earners that were unionized versus non-unionized, was 12.6 percent in the United States and 36.3 percent in Ireland in 2002.[28] The more centralized bargaining arrangements with labor due to unionization in Ireland and a more labor-focused legal framework due to the Irish Industrial Relations Acts would have made it more costly to close facilities in Ireland than the United States.

The Irish model was similar to the U.S. WARN Act but with extra requirements. For companies with 300 or more employees (such as Elan), a layoff of thirty or more employees required notification to the employees and the government employment ministry. The notice period of thirty days was more lenient than the WARN Act, but during the interim period the company was required to work with the affected employees and the government to seek alternatives to dismissal and approaches to reduce its negative effects. Normally required severance pay per person was typically increased in the case of collective dismissals.

Italian law was similar to Ireland's. Regulations specific to collective dismissals of five or more employees required the company to notify both the employees (and/or their representatives) and the public authorities (local, regional, or national, depending on the number of people affected). After notification, a forty-five-day examination period followed, in which a committee composed of representatives from each group met to discuss alternatives to dismissal, alternative employment possibilities, and severance. The layoffs and business unit closure could be implemented after the examination committee discussions were held.

U.K. law was less onerous than those of its European counterparts. Notice had to be given to the employees as well as government authorities, but the company was less obligated to participate in discussions on reemployment of the affected employees. For changes affecting 20–99 and 100 or more workers, after giving notice the company was required to wait 30 and 90 days, respectively, before implementation.

Financial Issues

Elan's financial position was deteriorating fast. It had an extremely low Z-score, indicating a very high probability of bankruptcy, and a low quick ratio, indicating an inability to meet short-term debt obligations. In Ireland there were three insolvency options when a business was unable to meet its debt obligations: liquidation, receivership, and examination. Liquidation was the termination process whereby the assets of the company were dissolved to pay creditors in order of a priority similar to the United States, but with more protection for employees. Receivership was the process by which secured lenders took control of a company's assets to liquidate and receive payment. Examination was introduced in 1990 to provide an opportunity for insolvent companies to remain in business. Modeled on Chapter 11 in the United States, in examination the court provided the company protection from debt obligations through the appointment of an examiner for a seventy- to hundred-day period. However, in Ireland only 2 percent of insolvent companies entered examination, compared with more than 20 percent of insolvent U.S. companies entering Chapter 11.

For Elan, the time that examination would have afforded to reorganize the business would have been a huge asset because of its aforementioned "decision-making paralysis." Despite this, after weighing the pros and cons of bankruptcy, Armen chose instead to begin its own divestment process to generate cash for the business. He felt the business was much more likely to survive without bankruptcy and Elan needed to generate a high value from its divestments, which was more likely if the company was not going through bankruptcy proceedings. Armen also believed he would be better able to convince talented employees to remain at Elan outside of bankruptcy.

When he took control of Elan, Armen faced a daunting list of debt repayments due, with more than $800 million due in the rest of 2002 alone. He was confident Elan could meet these short-term debt obligations; however, he knew he would need to increase his cash position to meet obligations beyond the next five months.

By the end of 2002, Elan was well along in its recovery plan. Through the sale of various assets, the company had raised cash totaling approximately $1.3 billion. A number of liabilities had been eliminated, which further mitigated concerns over liquidity and insolvency. The restructuring plan of reducing headcount by a thousand employees by concentrating on their revised strategy and reducing operating expenses by $300 million was under way.

Armen had to return to his own business in the United States and launched a search for his replacement. He ultimately chose to hire Kelly Martin, a forty-four-year-old senior executive at Merrill Lynch who had focused for most of his career on fixing units within Merrill that faced operational and financial troubles. Martin was American. The market's reaction was mixed. Many questioned his qualifications to run a pharmaceutical company and his decision to be based in San Diego rather than Dublin. Others saw Martin's appointment as a sign that, as a turnaround banker, he would work to rejuvenate the company and make it attractive for sale to a bigger pharmaceutical.

As a good example of how one executive can make or break a turnaround, after taking the reins in 2003 Martin made a number of missteps related to the operational side of the business. In one instance, he mishandled the withdrawal of a drug from the market due to unexpected side effects. In another, he over-stated the success of an ongoing clinical trial that turned out to have negative results, resulting in shareholder lawsuits. He was criticized for mishandling other deals, wasting money on private jets and multiple offices, and other botched programs.[29] The Street.com's biotech analyst Adam Feuerstein named Martin the Worst Biotech CEO of 2008. Still hanging on in 2010, Martin finally announced he would retire in 2012, while shareholders and analysts still called for his resignation. Elan will need a real turnaround person like Armen again.

LEGO Group

Identifying one's core competency is important no matter what jurisdiction is involved. The Danish company LEGO Group had to do this to flourish again. It reached €1 billion in sales, and *Fortune* magazine declared their product "the toy of the century."[30] In the late 1990s, however, the company stopped its focus on designs customers wanted. Company executives thought extending the brand was the way to go. For example, they launched a line called Galidor in 2002, which included action figures with little more than their arms being able to be changed.[31] There were no build-ing skills required and not much imagination needed compared to its other toys. They also used the characters to co-produce a TV show for kids on Saturday morning. The show was not a success and sales of the toys plummeted. Management also let the design-ers go off unrestricted; they created models that needed 5,400 additional components, causing supply chain problems, and the new models didn't do well with the children. They also went into clothing, theme parks, retail, and video game businesses.

LEGO lost money in four out of the seven years through 2004; sales dropped 30 percent and then 10 percent more in 2003 and 2004, respectively. Profit margins went to a negative 30 percent and executives estimated the company every day was destroying €250,000 in value.

In 2004, the company had been led by the founder's grandson who was CEO since 1980. It was another example of the worldwide phrase "rags to riches to rags in three generations." The family finally decided an outsider was needed. They turned to their director of strategic development, Jorgen Knudstorp, as the new CEO. First, he recognized that they needed a strategy that returned them to their core competency of LEGO toys that inspired imagination for three generations, in most countries around the world. He made sure the marketing department worked with the designers to make models their research showed their customers really wanted. They eliminated models and businesses that didn't fit the revised strategy.

From an operations standpoint they particularly focused on the supply chain which managed 11,000 suppliers, twice as many as Boeing needed to make airplanes. LEGO had little buying power when they spread their purchases around. Their own manufacturing facilities, mostly in high-cost places such as Switzerland, the United States, and Denmark, were inefficient. Its Danish factory alone, with 800 machines, was one of the largest injection molding operations in the world, but had to handle short runs of many products due to the growth in stock-keeping units (SKUs). Similar problems existed in IT, how large big box chains were handled, the use of hard-to-find colorants, and many more places in the company.

Meanwhile, the culture of the family-owned Danish company required that they needed to keep the workforce loyal through the downsizing required to meet the revised strategy. Knudstorp set a course of complete transparency with everyone, so they understood the problems and the proposed solutions. Input was sought from all levels. Meanwhile, the chief financial officer was put in charge of finding cost savings and divesting certain assets.

All these efforts paid off. LEGO returned to €61 million profitability in 2005, and in 2006 profits were up by 240 percent over the prior year.

In summary, no matter what the country involved, a turn-around still revolves around *strategy,* including finding the core competency to build around; *operations,* including reengineering and fitting the downsizing of people and facilities to the strategy; and *finance,* including the selling of assets that don't fit the strategy. The differences from jurisdiction to jurisdiction do affect these decisions, particularly labor issues, the local priority of claims, and liabilities of officers and directors.

Chapter Eight

Turnarounds at (Intentionally) Nonprofit Organizations

Many turnaround managers joke about having worked with dozens of nonprofit organizations, a few of which were even intentionally so. Each semester, I always dedicate one full class session to the topic of turnarounds at nonprofit organizations, for two reasons. First, more and more managers are pursuing roles in such groups as concepts of sustainability and social entrepreneurship become more popular. Second, even the would-be investment bankers and corporate litigators that I teach will one day serve on nonprofit boards, whether their motivation is altruism or a desire to get better seats at the opera or symphony. Many are surprised to find that though nonprofit organizations have unique idiosyncrasies that can make their turnarounds differ only slightly from for-profit organizations, they actually have far more similarities to corporate turnarounds than they have differences.

Nonprofit Organizations: A Brief Definition and Primer

So-called nonprofits differ from for-profit entities because they enjoy protection under section 501(c) of the United States Internal Revenue Code, which establishes twenty-six types of organizations exempt from federal (and often state) income taxes. The most prevalent of these organizations tend to fall under section 501(c)3, which identifies organizations devoted to religious, charitable, scientific, public safety testing, literary, educational, athletics, artistic, or social (e.g., for the prevention of cruelty to children or animals) causes. In order to qualify for tax exemption, such organizations must not distribute its surplus funds (i.e., profits) to shareholders or members, but must instead use them to advance its stated mission. The largest American 501(c)3 organization is the Bill & Melinda Gates Foundation, which has a very broad mandate of solving hunger, health care challenges, and poverty abroad while increasing access to information technology and education in the United States. Other 501(c)3 organizations have narrower, slightly less ambitious missions, such as the Society for the Preservation and Advancement of the Harmonica (SPAH) which aims to "cultivate, develop, improve, foster, promote, preserve and advance the harmonica and harmonica playing."[1]

Similarities to For-Profit Turnarounds

A similar environment exists for nonprofits in trouble. Recognizing their distress, suppliers to nonprofits will grow increasingly wary of advancing them any trade credit, demanding cash in advance. Lenders and donors may grow hesitant to cut checks to an organization in fear that it may soon shut its doors. Donors to nonprofits want to feel that their funds went to accomplish that organization's mission, not pay the last Comcast or PG&E bill before it closed up shop.

Nonprofits face many of the same external causes of distress that for-profit companies experience. For example, the recent economic downturn has crippled many nonprofits, who rely heavily upon donations that come from disposable personal income or draw operating capital from shrinking endowments. Such economic turmoil can be especially painful for organizations focused on addressing poverty or homelessness, which face a spike in demand for services just as funding sources dry up.

Just as with for-profit companies, economic downturns do not need to be global in their scale to affect nonprofits. In the Introduction, we discussed how the closing of the Fore River Shipyard in Quincy, Massachusetts, destroyed local restaurants and bars that relied on the lunch and after-work traffic of shipyard workers. Similarly, the creeping decay of the Detroit metropolitan area in general and the U.S. automotive industry in particular throughout the 1980s and 1990s saw Detroit's Temple Baptist Church lose some 75 percent of its weekly attendance base, driven in large part by the dramatic demographic shift that saw residents flee Detroit in droves.

Changes in technology can throw nonprofits into disarray, requiring strategic refocusing. The March of Dimes was originally founded with a goal of eradicating polio, and supported that mission for seventeen years. Upon Dr. Jonas Salk's development of a vaccine that effectively accomplished this goal, the organization found itself without a mission, and eventually revised its charter to refocus upon preventing birth defects and premature births.

Shifts in consumer demand can affect nonprofits, as some donors may be less loyal to any one particular mission and may instead donate to whatever cause has received recent significant media coverage. For example, in the wake of September 11, many local charitable organizations noted significant decreases in donations, as donors gave to funds such as the Survivor's Fund in lieu of their traditional charities. Similarly, the rise in popularity of long-distance air travel forced Amtrak to operate at a loss ever since its creation in the early 1970s, because the massive fixed costs of operating a national passenger railway require demand levels that have been siphoned away by air carriers.

Industrywide issues can plague nonprofits, particularly those focused on regulatory-intensive sectors such as health care. Visiting Nurse Service System suffered along with hundreds of other home health agencies in the wake of Congress's 1997 Balanced Budget Act, which resulted in major reductions in Medicare reimbursement. Many similar nonprofits counted Medicare reimbursements as the primary driver of their revenues, so the bill put a great deal of pressure on their operating budgets.[2] State delays in Medicaid payments caused small pharmacies and medical practices to declare bankruptcy.

Other seemingly unrelated changes in regulation can also challenge nonprofits by spurring demographic changes. Many urban school districts struggled mightily in the wake of the desegregation mandated by 1954's *Brown vs. Board of Education*. The resultant "white flight" from urban areas to the suburbs and to private and Catholic schools left urban school districts significantly underfunded and struggling to attract top educational talent. Some have only recently turned to outside turnaround experts to strengthen the delivery of their education mission, as discussed later.

Internal causes of distress are also similar in the nonprofit environment.

The same blind pursuit of growth that plagued Sara Lee has crippled more than a few nonprofit organizations. From 1985 to 1991, Greenpeace's total income grew fourfold to $179 million, but its headcount grew proportionately such that when income dipped to $130 million in 1995, the organization had to resort to significant layoffs to break even.[3]

Drifts from core competency akin to the strategic drift that plagued Krispy Kreme can plague the nonprofit world, in which such lack of focus is referred to as "mission drift." Big Brothers Big Sisters of Metropolitan Chicago (BBBSMC), a nonprofit organization affiliated with the larger Big Brothers Big Sisters of America, is a mentoring organization that has been active in the Chicago community for over forty years. The mission of the Chicago Chapter is to empower youth by mentoring children through one-to-one mentoring relationships in community-based and school-based programs. Fueled by rapid growth into fourteen new programs during the 2000 to 2005 period, fundamental organizational problems became more apparent and ultimately came to a peak in 2006. The symptoms were classic, with no clear strategy, revenues barely covering the organization's overhead cost, funding payroll difficult most weeks, and a $350,000 line of credit from a local bank that was fully used. The local group depended on two sources for the vast majority of its revenues—grant money from United Way and from the United States government. Its antiquated IT infrastructure did not allow it to fully coordinate fundraising and marketing activities. After thoroughly investigating their options, the board of directors asked Art Mollenhauer, a member of the BBBS Lake County Board of Directors, to spearhead the turnaround efforts as CEO. The turnaround he attempted is discussed later in this chapter.

Not surprisingly, insufficient capital hamstrings many nonprofits. Failed charities abound more than people realize. About

30,000 to 60,000 charities disappear from IRS files each year, presumed to go out of business, with about as many new ones formed each year.[4] Charities can fail because their key donors go bankrupt or because the charities put their funds into failed organizations, such as massive funds lost by charities who had invested in Enron or in failed Icelandic banks. These issues exist worldwide. In the United Kingdom, for example, a charity that gave legal assistance to migrants and refugees left 13,000 adults and children facing uncertainty when it entered liquidation administration.[5] The managers blamed external factors, particularly late payment of governmental legal aid, but the government noted that "every other organization" was more efficient and coped with timing of legal aid payments.[6]

Despite the even worse societal effect implied by such actions, fraud and dishonesty can also submarine nonprofits. In late 2008, the JEHT Foundation—devoted to reforming the U.S. criminal justice system—had to close its doors, having lost almost its entire endowment to Bernie Madoff's Ponzi scheme.[7] Fraud is also an all too frequent problem within nonprofits themselves.

Nonprofits travel down the very same organizational distress curve, through the blinded, inaction, faulty action, and crisis phases. The primary difference is that until recently, nonprofit organizations have proceeded much more rapidly and consistently from the crisis phase to dissolution than their for-profit counterparts. This has probably resulted from the fact that an extremely troubled nonprofit typically lacks a sophisticated creditor base that is motivated to maximize its recovery, so inertia (and the desire to save face by frustrated donors) drives nonprofits into a quiet shutdown with few objections if they can't raise sufficient new money.

Nonprofits exhibit many of the same warning signs as do corporations. For example:

- Management analysis can reveal executive teams ill-equipped to deal with sudden downturns, input cost spikes, or other adversity.
- High staff turnover is even more indicative of trouble in a nonprofit, where the expected duration of an employee is much higher given the nonpecuniary rewards offered to employees

of such organizations. When turnover occurs frequently at the leadership level of nonprofits, this can be both a sign and cause of organizational distress, for stakeholders intent on preserving the status quo can easily resist change, knowing that any reform-minded leaders will soon leave or be replaced.

- Trend analysis will similarly provide clues about the organization's health, although the metrics differ slightly in the not-for-profit world. Declines in fundraising are analogous to sales declines, and the organizational efficiency—a measure of the portion of what a nonprofit raises that actually goes toward accomplishing its stated mission—is roughly comparable to a company's gross margin; declines in either should raise the same red flags. Declining cash balances, liquidity crises, and fundraising shortfalls need no translation, as they are clear indicators that the nonprofit has begun sliding down the organizational distress curve. A/R collections can even be analogous to the percentage of pledged dollars that a nonprofit actually collects; naturally, a decline in this ratio should be met with alarm.

Just as for other organizations, protecting intellectual property is very important for nonprofits. After "for the cure" became a successful slogan for the Susan G. Komen for the Cure breast-cancer charity, others began to copy it. With many charities trade-marking slogans with the three-word phrase, the Komen group felt they had to stop the proliferation of group names such as Kites for the Cure, Bark for the Cure, Juggling for the Cure, Blondes for the Cure, and Kayaking for the Cure. The Komen group had launched legal battles against these and even against those who use their signature pink ribbons, stating "We see it as responsible stewardship of our donor's funds."[8]

Nonprofits can pay as well as their for-profit counterparts when new leadership is needed. When a fairly new Tampa area hospital defaulted on its $80 million in loans due to mismanagement, the lenders foreclosed into bankruptcy after a multiyear court battle. The county board which was supposed to oversee the county's hospital insisted that the auction for the sale and operation of the facility be limited to nonprofit hospital entities. The board balked when they learned the nonprofit chain that was the high bidder had a CEO who earned $17 million the prior year, which was a comparable salary for his for-profit counterparts. The delay was temporary until the Tampa bankruptcy judge approved the sale.

Turnarounds Are Similar

When a nonprofit begins to struggle, it should immediately build a 13-Week Cash Flow Model, just as a for-profit company would, for they must immediately determine which creditors must be paid without delay, which can be placated for the time being, and when cash will come in and out of the organization's bank accounts, with the ultimate goal of determining exactly how much cash is need (and how quickly) in order to assure survival.

For nonprofits, the challenge of estimating sales is replaced by the difficulty of forecasting donations. Organizations reliant on governmental funding face an even greater seasonal challenge, as governmental budgets are typically planned only once annually. Publicly funded railroad system Amtrak faced precisely this difficulty in attempting to enact its own turnaround, for it based its capital budgeting process on the amount of funding Congress would appropriate for it each new fiscal year. The organization's resultant need to wait until the passage of a new budget sometimes prevented it from utilizing its full budget appropriation before the end of the fiscal year, when the budgeting process began anew. In response, Amtrak began preparing longer-term budgets with scenario analysis built in to provide for a more flexible response to each year's federal grant amount. In many for-profits' departments as well as most government agencies, there is a rush to spend money left at the end of the year for fear lower spending would lead to a lower budget next year.

Turnarounds at nonprofits still require the use of the turnaround tripod, with the strategic aspect requiring the identification of the organization's true intended mission. The operational change will involve reengineering the organization to identify every process that contributes to that mission, and stripping out any assets, operations, or employees that do not. Finally, the financial restructuring may require renegotiation with any creditors, a burst of fundraising, or increasing the price (if any) charged for the organization's services. Art Mollenhauer did all of these when he turned around Big Brothers Big Sisters.[9]

Mollenhauer had a twenty-four-year career with Baxter Healthcare in general management and had been a volunteer as a big brother for over ten years. Because the organization had a history of receiving bailouts from either United Way or the U.S. government when necessary, the management team had never considered implementing a more sustainable revenue model. Lack of diversity by the board of directors made it unable to anticipate and understand the challenges faced by the communities that the agency was trying to reach. Mollenhauer recognized that the agency's lack of interest in marketing seemed illogical for a nonprofit that relied on donations from outside the organization. Antiquated technology limited the ability of multiple chapters of Big Brothers Big Sisters in the Chicago area to coordinate and target their fundraising efforts effectively. Further, the agency offered fourteen different types of programs across the entire metropolitan area. This fragmented approach increased the cost of delivering services. Their reliance on unpaid volunteers helped the organization ensure passion and a sincere desire to help, but it also limited the quality control process and made succession planning very difficult. It is difficult to fire someone who truly wants to help, but may not be performing to expectations. The high turnover rate among the paid staff was another indicator that there were problems. To accomplish the turnaround and as part of strategic due diligence, Mollenhauer and many of the directors went out and met every single donor and volunteer in the program.

First, Mollenhauer refocused the strategy and mission to get the organization down to its core competency. Overall, ten programs were eliminated, which meant a cut of over 70 percent of the offerings. The new agency was going to strategically focus on just four programs across twelve zones throughout the Chicago metropolitan area. This included a reduction of underperforming and money-draining programs. The main program of community mentors and students would remain the most prevalent program, plus the continuation of three partnership programs that provided site-based mentoring. The three variations of site-based are a group of adults from a corporation or university providing tutoring at a specific school, a group of students going to a workplace setting for mentoring, and a hybrid program that focused on targeting a specialized group of students. An example of the latter is the African American executives from McDonald's who mentor African American students at a specific school. Changes were also made to the IT systems to create a centralized donation database. Mollenhauer made a significant donation, which encouraged many others to do the same. Once he focused on creating a comprehensive plan to trim costs, he then went on to another phase which focused on growing the organization in a controlled manner. The agency increased the number of students served under the various retained programs, and revenues grew from $600,000 to $2,000,000. Corporate partners grew from six to twenty-six. University partners grew from one to six. The agency went from about 70 percent of their funding being from the government or United Way to now only about 7 percent. A line of credit is now used only to address seasonality issues, just like a for-profit company.

The turnaround of BBBSMC clearly demonstrates that in order to successfully turn around an organization, strategy, operations, and the finances must all be addressed. Mollenhauer completely reshaped the strategy of the organization. He recognized the need to stop pursuing activities that were not contributing and refocused on its core competencies to grow from there. He changed consolidated operations for the decentralized activities of the county-run branches to help everyone streamline fundraising, as well as mentoring efforts, thus reducing turnover, and was able to pay more realistic wages and employee benefits to the paid staff. It has been a successful turnaround.

Just as at Fortune 500 companies, turnarounds at nonprofits require entrepreneurial, out-of-the box thinking to break through the status quo and return the organization to health. One must find or rediscover the core competency of the organization.

Leadership is every bit as important in turning around a faltering nonprofit organization, as executives must use different levers to unite a unique set of constituencies. Any creditors will invariably be nervous about advancing any goods to a nonprofit that has fallen behind on its bills, and employee morale can crash when it seems that an organization will fail to meet its ambitious mission, so leaders must gain credibility quickly and demonstrate the courage necessary to make difficult decisions.

Former Brigadier General Michael Mulqueen won national recognition for the leadership he displayed in turning around the Greater Chicago Food Depository, which has become the food bank industry standard for efficiency. Though many expected that the "command and control" style of leadership prevalent in the military would clash with nonprofit culture, Mulqueen has proven successful by setting very high standards for discipline and account-ability for his staff. He recruited staff from for-profit organizations, and compensates them based on performance to ensure that the organization's mission of feeding the hungry is not the only thing incentivizing them. This increased the group's organizational efficiency to 94 percent, attracting many more small donors who want to know that their funds are going to support the organization's mission.[10]

Board members of nonprofit organizations hold similar fiduciary duties as do directors at for-profit corporations: the duty of care and the duty of loyalty, with the slight difference that the duty is owed to the beneficiaries, rather than to its shareholders. Board members must keep informed about the organization's operational and financial performance, attend board meetings, and generally serve the best interests of the nonprofit. Allegations to the contrary generally pertain to overpaying management, failing to maintain adequate cost controls, frittering away corporate assets, mismanaging endowments, or keeping inadequate records required by law. The business judgment rule offers the same protections to such claims, and will generally prove sufficient except in cases of dishonesty or not acting in good faith. The duty of loyalty similarly prohibits self-dealing, as it does in for-profit corporations. A nonprofit can drift into the zone of insolvency, at which point its board's duties expand to a broader requirement to balance the interests of all the organization's stakeholders, including the community it serves, its creditors, donors, any customers, and employees. Furthermore, boards must take every action possible to attempt to exit the zone of insolvency, either by a turnaround, a merger with a healthier organization, or dissolution.[11]

Nonprofits often demonstrate the same reluctance to change management or hire outside consultants as do managers at for-profit companies. Both types of executives will look to shift blame to vague "market forces," reluctant to be held accountable for the organization's distress. Nonprofit managers will express the same belief that an outsider couldn't possibly understand or demonstrate the same passion for their mission, and may make even more pointed remarks that outside consultants are "only in it for the money." Nonetheless, they are highly likely to need such outside assistance.

Bankruptcy is an option for troubled nonprofits, although until recently, few had availed themselves of the protections offered by Chapter 11. Historically, troubled nonprofits would occasionally find a healthier organization with which to partner, but in the vast majority of cases, they would simply liquidate rather than reorganize. According to *Nonprofit Quarterly*, nonprofit organizations represent 30 percent of all corporations but only 1 percent of corporate bankruptcy cases, perhaps because non-profit management teams would prefer to liquidate rather than admit to financial distress.[12]

Nonprofits that do file for Chapter 11 enjoy all of the same pros and cons of bankruptcy explained in Chapter Six of this book. While there can be no debt-for-equity swap, as nonprofits lack equity holders to begin with, organizations can use the automatic stay to work out payment plans with their creditors and make strategic and operational changes. The downside of the cost of paying professional fees is particularly difficult for nonprofits, as such fees must be paid upon emergence as administrative claims, and the filing will make it difficult to raise funding in such situations when DIP financing is out of the question.

Multiple bankruptcies exist for nonprofits. One of the biggest was St. Vincent's Hospital in New York. The causes and warning signs were well chronicled, including mismanagement and over-aggressive expansion. St Vincent's went into bankruptcy in 2005, with $250 million in debt, caused partly by earlier decisions to form a network with other hospitals, many of which were failing themselves. It emerged from bankruptcy in 2007, with an incredible $700 million in obligations, which included liabilities for medical malpractice, pension obligations, and the debt of the networked hospitals. It still had bloated administrative costs, was paying too many consultants, had 120 different IT systems, and needed to cut back from its forty shelters, 500 housing units for the mentally-ill, fifty-four outreach clinics, and 50 percent over capacity at the main hospital.[13] All these things took money, and donors were scarce. Turning to the government didn't help because there were problems in the governor's office and the city of New York had budget problems of its own. The hospital closed in 2010 under the weight of massive operating losses and its crushing debt. The lawsuits, however, live on.

Unique Challenges with Nonprofit Turnarounds

The *payer is often not the customer* in nonprofits. Doctors and hospitals are often paid by insurance companies. Public school systems get their revenues from taxes, not from the pupils. Donations keep most charities functioning, not money from the people they are trying to help.

There are clearly *different sources of capital* for nonprofits. They cannot raise equity or avail themselves of the stock market to raise funds if needed. They can sell bonds or take out loans, often to build new facilities. There are numerous municipal bonds that default every year, when projects such as the Las Vegas monorail cannot make payments.

They cannot change their mission easily. Whereas a board of directors of a for-profit company can go into new lines of business or reinvent themselves if needed, it is problematic for a nonprofit. If a large university were to lose its nonprofit status because it used significant donations for unrelated for-profit businesses, all those prime acres of land would become subject to property taxes. Any donations to a charity that loses its nonprofit status would no longer be tax deductible to the donors.

In general, there is a *mission versus margin* tension that does not officially exist in a for-profit company. Although many public company CEOs believe their shareholders are better off if all stakeholders are well treated, they are in a minority. Nonprofit CEOs have a more delicate balancing act to all their stakeholders.

As discussed earlier, nonprofit boards take on many of the same fiduciary duties in nonprofits as in for-profits, but they play a *very different role*. In for-profit corporations, the board has little involvement in the company's operations, but rather serves as an overseer of management's actions on behalf of the shareholders. In nonprofit situations, the board often takes a far more active role as the organization's major revenue generator.[14] In addition, all but the largest, most professionally run nonprofits tend to have less savvy boards with limited financial or management experience. While this is obviously a generalization, the very nature of nonprofit culture can make governance challenging, as board members can rise to their positions less through an efficient, merit-based search process and more because they happen to share a passion for that organization's particular mission.

The nonprofit world typically *moves much slower*, due to many stakeholders weighing in which can make it very difficult to impart a sense of urgency to its employees. Overcoming the inertia of the status quo is already challenging at for-profit companies, but nonprofit employees tend to be even more resistant to change.

As a result, in nonprofit turnarounds, *morale is even more important, but motivation to change is more difficult* because many of the usual motivational levers are unavailable. Nonprofit managers rarely have the ability to offer performance-based compensation because it often rankles employees preferring a more egalitarian atmosphere, and granting stock options is impossible in the absence of equity in the organization. Even in the rare situations where nonprofit turnaround managers can offer the possibility of pay raises, such offers are less effective in nonprofit environments, where employees generally derive far less of their job satisfaction from pecuniary rewards. Because they often accept lower pay than they might earn in the private sector in exchange for a feeling that they are doing good rather than doing well, nonprofit employees sometimes demand greater autonomy, with an implicit bargain of "I'll take less money to work for a cause I believe in, but if I wanted to get bossed around, I would work for a corporation." This attitude can make it very difficult to inspire the kind of radical thinking necessary to reengineer a company from a blank sheet of paper. If their passion can be reignited by the right leadership, however, the employees can be a powerful force to make changes.

Nonprofits are *overseen by the attorney general of each state* where first licensed rather than the typical secretary of state's office. Attorneys general often seek involuntary dissolution of charities who fail to live up to their missions. Such charities are accused of conspiracy to defraud donors, distributing funds to directors, failure to use contributions for the purpose stated, illegal distribution, and other breach of fiduciary duty charges. For example, the California attorney general targeted a long list of charities, including one that used aggressive telemarketing techniques to raise funds supposedly to help police, firefighters, and veterans. Almost all the millions went to bloated overhead and expenses such as sailboats for directors of the charity.[15] The fundraisers and directors were sued by the state as well as the donors.

It is often *difficult to fire customers* of a nonprofit. A nonprofit hospital is not supposed to turn away emergency cases even if they cannot pay. Public school systems must take on all children that live in their district even if it overburdens their facilities.

Nonprofits also lack the singular metric of success offered by bottom-line profitability, so *measuring performance* can be very challenging. Sales and gross and net margins make it easy to monitor corporations' performance, but the success of a nonprofit is more nebulous, particularly for nonprofits with broad, ambitious social missions. Consider a church, whose success might be measured by the average weekly attendance at services, the number of new official members (to the extent such a designation exists), or value of total donations received; all of these measure success, but they are imperfect proxies for determining the extent to which the church has accomplished its mission of spreading the gospel. This lack of measurability also extends to trend and benchmarking analyses, such as the Z-score, which currently has no widely accepted nonprofit analogue. One accounting firm has promoted a twelve-factor model that purports to measure the financial stability of nonprofit organizations, but this so-called "A-Score" lacks the statistical rigor that produced Altman's Z-score because it did not regress a large data set of nonprofits' financial information against a binary variable of whether they filed for bankruptcy or liquidated. Instead, it represents more of a commonsense approach to nonprofit financial management; organizations with high levels of cash and low debt have high A-scores, and so on.[16]

Board composition is often a weakness in nonprofit organizations, as many directors may join for the same reason, such as having lost a loved one to a particular disease for organizations devoted to finding a cure, or a love of hunting for organizations devoted to defending the Second Amendment. While this can create passionate, committed boards, it can also lead to homogeneity, with executive teams lacking the complementary skill sets necessary for effective management. The Joffrey Ballet found itself suffering from an unusual governance problem, as its two locations (Los Angeles and New York City) each had its own board with separate fundraising responsibilities. This decentralized approach bred dissension, as each board felt that the other city's ballet received a disproportionate share of attention and resources.[17] Such infighting can prove all too typical of nonprofit companies, where the absence of a uniting goal like share price increases can lead to highly politicized decision making, with board members pursuing their own conflicting agendas.

In the case of the Joffrey Ballet, fewer people seemed to be interested in seeing ballet in person, as cable television became a cheaper alternative for ballet connoisseurs in other cities to experience it. The organization decided to move all operations to Chicago in 1995, a faulty action that only exacerbated the organization's problems. They left behind their New York and Los Angeles donors and had to build a whole new audience. In its struggles to establish itself as a Chicago company, problems were magnified by the fact that the company did not have a home performance location, and without one it was hard to sell season tickets. They bounced from the Opera House to various theaters, fitting around each one's schedules. Finally, the mayor stepped in and convinced Commonwealth Edison to donate a building to the Joffrey in 1999. After raising almost $1.4 million to renovate the building, they discovered their CFO had left their books in disarray.

By the time the accountants could make sense of the books, they had to inform the board that the Joffrey wouldn't make payroll that month. The campaign changed from a capital campaign to a "save the Joffrey" campaign. When the board tried to convert the building renovation pledges into operating funds, this infuriated some supporters who believed that the company was mismanaging their operations and misrepresenting their pledge drives. Joffrey mortgaged everything they could and had amassed $3 million in debt by mid 2001 and still did not have a turnaround plan or renovated the building, which aggravated donors even more. Management and the board finally took action. They first targeted strategic solutions to identify their target audience. Previously, the Joffrey had focused their dance and advertising campaign on their more athletic performance than most ballet companies; their belief was to attract men who would then bring their families. It didn't work, and only through an insightful marketing research study did management finally realize that their main customer base was the thirty-five- to fifty-five-year-old woman who had lost touch with her inner ballerina. To attract that profile, they realigned the marketing and production efforts toward a more graceful and beautiful traditional aspect of their ballet performance. To create local buzz and support from the Chicago community, management invited local heavyweights, such as CEOs from several local companies, to join the board.

As part of the company's restructured operations, Executive Director Jon Teeuwissea realized they couldn't play taped music on some of their performances and persuaded several foundations to underwrite a switch to live music by a professional orchestra. Analysis of weekday and weekend ticket sales showed that just 21 percent of customers came to shows on weekdays, versus 79 percent on weekends. He cut to a sole weekday performance on Wednesday, which then became a high subscription request, cutting out historically unprofitable shows on other weekdays. The financial reorganization was carried out on multiple fronts— reduction in costs and an increase in grants and subscriptions for a steady income. The company was small by any standards but had bloated operating costs, largely due to a unionized workforce of fifty artists, six artistic staff, eight production staff, and thirty administrative staff. Based on the new strategy, Jon successfully renegotiated labor contracts with unions representing the artists and the production specialists. Jon altered touring activities to reduce costs. In 2005, at the peak of the real estate boom, they sold the building they had acquired free from Commonwealth Edison, for $6.5 million, which paid off debt as well as gave them remaining money as operating cash going forward. Although the building was originally donated to use as a home for the Joffrey, it was deemed cost prohibitive to convert the building into the necessary open space, free of structural support pillars for studios or performances. They increased fundraising efforts by reaching across three influential pillars of the Chicago community—large foundations, large corporations, and political contributions. To create buzz toward subscriptions and ticket sales in the target audience, a women's board was started, led by socialite philanthropists. These women would have fundraising parties and invite all their friends and became the largest single donor group to the Joffrey Ballet. The company's new home, the Joffrey Tower, was soon built as a mixed-use building right in the heart of the theater district in downtown Chicago.

Politics and Nonprofits

Politics often gets in the way of trying to turn around not-for-profits, particularly quasigovernment agencies.

United States Postal Service

The United States Postal Service (USPS) has faced turnaround problems sporadically over its lifetime. More recently, beginning with the collapse of the U.S. housing market in late 2007 and the subsequent collapse of the global credit markets in late 2008, more problems were added to USPS's usual ones when it then faced a decline in volume of 9.5 billion pieces, which resulted in a budget deficit of $2.8 billion.[18] In fiscal year 2009, mail volume dropped another 30 billion pieces, presenting them with a budget deficit of over $8 billion. The USPS is "rooted in a single, great principle: that every person in the United States—no matter who, no matter where—has the right to equal access to secure, efficient, and affordable mail service."[19] Since Benjamin Franklin served as the first Postmaster General in 1775, the quasigovernment institution established by the U.S. Constitution has had bumps along the way, such as periodic logjams of millions of pieces of mail, bringing them to a grinding halt, and volume declines at the turn of the millennium. Legislative actions have been both a blessing and a curse. For example, congressional changes in 2006 resulted in increased health care obligations and translated into more frequent stamp price increases. However, the same legislation reduced pension liabilities and allowed the growing Express Mail business to compete at market rates. The USPS provides mail delivery to 149 million delivery points, employs almost 700,000 workers, and processes about 200 billion pieces of mail annually. If it were a U.S. corporation, it would rank number 26 on the Fortune 500 list with $75 billion in annual revenue. The organization is 85 percent unionized and governed by an eleven-member board appointed by the president of the United States. With people going to electronic mail, electronic bill payment, and a societal shift toward environmental responsibility by avoiding paper waste from mail, this has reduced demand for USPS services for traditional mail volume. The increasing use of the Internet to purchase goods, however, has actually increased traffic of package delivery due to e-tail sites such as eBay and Amazon.com. Unfortunately, this volume is much more directly competitive with other delivery services. While the USPS cannot issue equity, it does have a large line of credit from the Federal Bank's financing arm and has access to overnight borrowing markets, similar to banks, which traditionally have extremely low interest rates. USPS, however, has a maximum debt ceiling of $15 billion.

Beyond the normal strategic, operational, and financial issues faced by companies, the USPS faces a high level of political and social scrutiny. Making simple changes such as raising stamp prices or closing a branch location can result in protests or congressional action. Competitors such as UPS and FedEx are integrated more tightly with many customer companies to improve supply chain logistics and customer service. For example, Dell co-locates with FedEx hubs so that as soon as a computer is built, it is immediately shipped to the consumer, resulting in incredibly fast delivery that becomes competitive with in-store purchase models.[20] Because of direct government involvement, the early warning signs that have been repeated many times through the press are largely ignored. Cash flow and return on assets have been negative since 2007, so debt is heading toward its maximum ceiling. Approximately one million additional route stops are added each year due to the increasing population of the United

States, thus deliveries are being made to more places with less volume per stop. The union contracts are a particular problem because of fringe benefits greater than other federal workers, no layoff clauses, starting salaries nearly 30 percent higher than for comparable-skilled private workers, and a no-transfer clause that doesn't allow assignment between post offices, even if one gets much busier than another due to growth or decline of neighborhoods. The postmaster general and the deputy postmaster general usually come up from the ranks, most often starting as a postal clerk. They find it difficult to make serious changes within the organization. They have focused recently on cost reductions, particularly efficiency improvements, but the strategy appears to lack any emphasis in driving volume or utilizing its infrastructure to unlock new revenue streams. Some turnaround changes have been well-conceived, such as expanding options to provide customers access to its services without visiting a physical location by selling stamps by phone, mail, and from the Web site. Customers can use the Web site to print postage labels, including for Priority Mail, Express Mail and even International Mail, and scheduling package pickup. The USPS is reviewing products and services that customers might value when visiting a post office, so they can leverage their network of retail locations (including the sale of office supplies, print and copy services), exploring a partnership with OfficeMax, and looking at how other countries use their post offices. For example, in Australia you can renew a driver's license; in Japan, get life insurance; in Italy, do banking; in France, you can buy prepaid cell phones. USPS is working to close thousands of obsolete post offices, many of which serve towns with fewer than 250 people, and even cut back on Saturday delivery.

Whereas a board of directors of a company might take a while to wake up to what's happening within its organization, once they do, they are reasonably free to take action, but in the USPS politics often interferes. It's interesting that much of its ability to make changes will depend on public perception, as well as support. Many people see the USPS as a bureaucratic federal service provided by the government, not a business. However, USPS is rated as one of the most trusted organizations, public or private, and has a 97 percent service level on delivery. The question is whether or not they understand that that is part of their core competency and the need to leverage their brand, such as through e-mail services of your name, such as jamessmith@USPS.com, or any of the services performed by their international counterparts. The key is to have Congress require the postal service to shrink and adapt to today's realities rather than focus on being personally reelected.

Indian Railways

Politics interfering with nonprofit turnarounds is a worldwide issue. Indian Railways has been a government of India owned enterprise since its inception in 1948, which combined forty-two railroads that started over a hundred years earlier.[21] It operates a network of 63,000 kilometers of rails transporting seven million passengers and two million tons of freight every day. Because Indian Railways is classified as a strategic entity by the government, it imparts a social obligation in operating unprofitable routes and transporting certain commodities and passenger segments at or below cost. Only two other sectors are designated as strategic by the Indian government: its military and its nuclear energy program. By the mid-1990s, Indian Railways lost its high margin first-class passengers to air travel. Meanwhile, Indian Railways employs more than 1.5 million people and is run by the minister of railways, who is actually directly appointed by the prime minister of India. Indian Railways employees form unions at all levels and enjoy high job security and exceptional benefits. In over one hundred years of operations the company has had no layoffs. As a result of its government affiliations and strong employee unions, the company's leadership team has had little leeway to make changes in personnel strategy and was also influenced by corrupt politicians. As the Indian government invested heavily in good roads to move goods, more freight traffic was being lost to truckers who were privately owned. With the minister of railways a public appointment, it is a highly politicized position. Thus, those appointed to the post usually have personal and political goals that usually do not align with the long-term sustainability of the railroad or even that discourage ministers to take on unpopular tasks that would correctly manage risks facing the company.

With crowded passenger trains and huge financial losses, the turnaround finally started with Nitish Kumar, railway minister from 2001, and his efforts were continued by his successor, Lalu Prasad Yadav, who took over in 2004. The actions they took included longer trains. In the 1990s, the average length of an Indian Railways train was fourteen coach cars for passenger trains and forty wagon cars for freight trains, relatively short compared to other international railway transportation companies. The strategy options were limited but they knew they had to focus on moving the passengers, attracting more freight, and cutting the losses. To move longer trains and heavier loads meant they had to invest in higher-horsepower locomotives. It also meant that they would have to remodel train station platforms to be able to handle longer trains. By creating a passenger profile management system and working to make operations more efficient, they were able to focus on increasing wagon turnaround from seven days to five days, a turnaround that would enable the Indian Railways to operate an additional 800 trains each day with its then existing equipment. Freight terminals were modernized into around-the-clock mechanized handling facilities with full train length platforms within only six months. This allowed a significant reduction in wagon turnaround time. Freight is the largest and most profitable source of revenue, but customers tended to only be charged on a per wagon basis. Companies therefore overloaded the cars but Indian Railways did not receive the additional revenue. Changing the official weight limit and now actually weighing the cars allowed Indian Railways to receive compensation for the load the company carried. Because there was little latitude to fire employees, they developed a plan to provide bonuses to employees after they had taken training to become solution-oriented on the job. Simply providing necessary winter gear to employees who worked outdoors in winter months also helped. Finally, they did not fill positions of employees who left the company or retired, the only way they could cut down the total number of employees. Indian Railways soon found itself in a much better position by 2008 with $4.7 billion in profits. Both passenger travel and freight shipping increased and Indian Railways was regaining its share with both customer segments. Because of the close connection with the government and politics, however, it will be curious to observe whether the efforts and sweeping changes will be altered by another minister who seeks to fulfill his own political agenda.

Nonprofit Turnarounds in Action: A Perfect Storm in the Big Easy

The New Orleans Parish School Board (OPSB) deteriorated rapidly in the late twentieth century, decimated by budget short-falls, constant staff turnover (the parish had nine different super-intendents between 1996 and 2005 alone), and woefully lax financial controls. By 2005, the district's budget hadn't been bal-anced in five years, and 65 percent of its schools failed to meet the state's performance standards; in fact, one high school vale-dictorian in 2003 needed seven tries to pass the state's tenth-grade math test.[22] Clearly, the organization was failing to accomplish its mission or preserve its margin, and so despite exhibiting the very common reluctance to hire outside advisors, the parish's board voted 4–3 in May 2005 to hire turnaround consultancy Alvarez & Marsal to fix the financial and administrative elements of the school system. Alvarez managing director Bill Roberti took on the role of chief restructuring officer, while managing director Sajan George served as interim COO.

Roberti's team began conducting the same forensic account-ing it would have conducted at a for-profit company, and quickly identified dozens of examples of outrageously poor cash manage-ment. Several employees had been receiving fifty hours of over-time pay, fifty weeks a year, while another had been on paid leave for three decades. An FBI investigation of the district's accounting department had resulted in twenty-six indictments and twenty guilty pleas, one of which involved a payroll employee who began writing herself checks that totaled nearly one-quarter of a million dollars.[23] The Alvarez team had won the engagement on the strength of their performance in turning around the St. Louis Public Schools, but George found New Orleans so much further down the organizational distress curve that he claimed it made "St. Louis look like a Fortune 100 company."[24]

The team quickly developed a 13-Week Cash Flow Model, which determined that the OPSB's purported cash balance of $29 million was significantly overstated because its accounting staff was incapable of identifying which payables checks had been issued and remained outstanding. Instead, this apparent cash cushion would turn negative by September, requiring immediate financing to continue the board's operations in face of a newly predicted $48 million deficit. The team seized control of OPSB's cash disbursement processes to limit cash outflows, and used its 13WCFM to convince JP Morgan Chase to fund a short-term $50 million revenue anticipation note (RAN) just days before the start of the 2005–2006 school year.

Having made the necessary financial changes to ease the OPSB's liquidity crisis, the consulting team then accepted as a given its strategic mission of educating the children of the Orleans Parish and set about making operational changes to support that strategy. Just as in a for-profit turnaround, the team reengineered various processes at the organization by rejecting the status quo and starting from scratch on its procurement, HR, payroll, and information technology departments, thereby leading to the following operational changes:

- The previously lax controls on purchasing began to be enforced to the letter, thus preventing the unauthorized spending that had led to several departments spending over their approved budgets and now allowing the district to enjoy volume discounts from combined purchases.
- As in for-profit companies, bureaucracy and fiefdom-building had led to improper promotion standards, siloed divisions, and underutilization of business systems and technology, so the team revised and communicated staffing control policies, oversaw staffing conferences with principals, developed a process for "no shows" to ensure that those who abandoned their jobs did not receive a paycheck, and developed a revised substitute teacher placement system to fill the remaining vacancies for the first day of school.
- HR, finance, benefits, accounting, and tax departments were forced to communicate more efficiently with each other through the creation of cross-functional teams with regularly scheduled meetings.
- Employees were cross-trained for various IT positions, thus creating redundancies that mitigated the risks of employee turnover or illness.[25]

Just six weeks into their engagement at the OPSB, Roberti's team had stopped the bleeding, raised emergency financing, and begun to make the operational changes necessary to return the school district to health.

And then, the levees broke.

On August 29, three days after the closing of the RAN transaction, Hurricane Katrina smashed through the state of Louisiana, precipitating "the worst engineering disaster in U.S. history." Within forty-eight hours, 80 percent of New Orleans had flooded, with some areas under fifteen feet of water. As with the rest of the city, the school system was shattered; buildings ruined, financial records destroyed, and students and teachers scattered across the southeastern United States. An organization that had previously found itself slowly but surely enacting a turnaround from the crisis phase suddenly found itself on the precipice of dissolution.

Although it is hard to consider New Orleans and its school system in any way fortunate after suffering the most concentrated destruction of an American city in history, its prior engagement with A&M meant that trained crisis managers were already on the ground and involved in the school system. Recognizing that the engagement had just become vastly more complicated, the state revised its contract with the consultants, and the school system began the long process of rebuilding.

However, the catastrophe did give the turnaround team two additional tools. First, its almost total devastation meant that the status quo no longer existed, and as such, the school districts could be started over from scratch, without legacy infrastructure serving as an obstacle to progress. Second, the frenzy of emergency activity following Katrina prompted the state legislature to hand control of the districts' schools over to the Louisiana Recovery School District (RSD), an organization created in 2003 to allow the state to take over failing schools and operate them according to accountability metrics established by the Louisiana Board on Elementary and Secondary Education (BESE) as mandated by the No Child Left Behind federal law.

RSD stated its mission as creating a world-class public education system in New Orleans in which every decision focuses on the best interest of the children, but the destruction of records and scattering of institutional knowledge meant it had to do so in a situation with much uncertainty and missing information.[26] Officials reported that forty-seven of the 128 New Orleans public schools had suffered severe damage and thirty-eight more had moderate damage, prompting many to predict that schools would not reopen for at least a year. Furthermore, officials had no idea how to estimate the number of students that would return to the system, as Katrina had created a sudden, violent diaspora the likes of which had never been seen in the United States.

In conjunction with RSD's takeover, the executive team had to help lay off the vast majority of existing school district staff, requiring sophisticated HR policies to mitigate the threat of lawsuits and preserve morale. They set up telephone hotlines, posted information on the RSD Web site, and provided information through the media regarding the changes that would take place. That served as a precursor to a new three-stage turnaround plan, which focused first on stabilizing the crisis with a twenty-person crisis call center and teams that examined facilities to determine the extent of the destruction. Second, the team developed an emergency restructuring plan to gain governmental approval to open up to eight new schools and execute all the necessary hiring and procurement of related janitorial, food, and transportation services. Finally, they executed this plan, and also received permission to expand their focus to include a real estate footprint rationalization analysis and an insurance claims and recovery management strategy to ensure that the necessary federal and state funding was procured to finance the restructuring plan along with insurance proceeds.

Because the OPSB could no longer rely on the previous $50 million RAN because its local revenue was materially and adversely affected, making its collection uncertain, they needed to secure alternative financing sources. They began by petitioning the much-maligned Federal Emergency Management Agency's (FEMA) Community Disaster Loan (CDL) program, and followed up by securing a Community Development Block Grant (CDBG) from the state of Louisiana. Lastly, the school board sought to use the Gulf Opportunity Zone Tax Credit Bonds as a source of relief. By filing timely and compelling appeals to these financing sources, the turnaround consultants managed to assist the OPSB in securing more than $320 million to fund the restructuring.

A&M's strong work prior to the hurricane eased the district through the post-Katrina turnaround, as it allowed them to update their previous forecasts and get an understanding of the financial situation quickly. From there, it was a matter of obtaining the capital necessary to fund the revamped 13WCFM and identifying the needed operational changes to improve the organization's performance. In September of 2007, the Louisiana Department of Education issued a press release thanking the turnaround consultants (as well as numerous other service providers) for their help in returning New Orleans schools to fully operational, with eighty schools serving 34,000 children.[27]

In the process, the New Orleans schools' turnaround demonstrates many of the similarities and differences between for-profit and nonprofit turnarounds, while its unique circumstances create an interesting parallel to the for-profit bankruptcy process. Although the school district could have filed for Chapter 9 bankruptcy proceedings (see Box 9 regarding Chapter 9 bankruptcies and how they compare to Chapter 11), it managed to avoid such a filing despite its almost impossibly dire situation. However, Katrina threw the entire system so out of whack that the A&M team had options not usually available to nonprofits outside of bankruptcy. For example, union rules providing for tenure make terminating underperforming teachers incredibly challenging, so blatantly poor teachers often end up getting shuffled to low-performing schools rather than fired, while skilled teachers tend towards schools in richer areas with already high-performing students. Therefore, the post-hurricane chaos in a sense simulated a bankruptcy proceeding in that it allowed the school district to reject executory contracts with teachers that it otherwise could not have. Similarly, an organization in bankruptcy would have had the opportunity to raise DIP financing to fund its operations; the New Orleans schools instead enjoyed the unusual opportunity to raise emergency funding from a variety of other governmental sources. The post-Katrina frenzy imparted the same sense of urgency in the company that a bankruptcy filing typically does, and the disarray into which the entire region had been thrust acted as a de facto automatic stay, since so many of the district's creditors were slow to demand payment because they were scattered around the southern United States. Finally, the disaster

Box 9: Chapter 9 Bankruptcy

Chapter 9 of the Federal Bankruptcy Code gets little attention, as it pertains to municipalities—which can include public agencies, cities, towns, counties, and other political subdivisions seeking relief from their creditors.[28] The highest-profile bankruptcy took place in 1994, when Orange County in California filed for the largest municipal bankruptcy in American history. Chapter 9 has taken on a higher profile in recent years, as the real estate crash depressed property values and therefore property taxes for many municipalities.

Chapter 9 debtors enjoy the same automatic stay as do Chapter 11 debtors, and have additional protections relating to sovereignty; while creditors in Chapter 11 can demand that a court fire a management team or attempt to sell a certain asset, Chapter 9 creditors cannot demand nearly the same level of control over the debtor's operations. They cannot request the dismissal of elected officials, or interfere with any of the debtor's political powers, unless some level of criminality is discovered.

Creditors still form committees in Chapter 9 proceedings, which carry out substantially the same functions, with the exception that creditors cannot file plans of reorganization, a power reserved only to the debtor municipality. Notably, municipalities may also reject collective bargaining agreements and retiree benefit plans, a critical provision given the fact that many Chapter 9 debtors find themselves in financial distress owing to onerous pension plans and union contracts. Vallejo, a city in California's East Bay, filed for Chapter 9 in 2008, largely because approximately three-quarters of its general fund budget was consumed by expensive police and fire department union agreements. Municipalities may also borrow funds during bankruptcy proceedings, which would become an administrative claim unless court approval authorized it to become a super-priority claim.

The unique debt structures of reorganizing municipalities changes typical recoveries. Certain bondholders tend to enjoy higher recoveries in Chapter 9 proceedings, with special revenue bonds (paid by revenue streams such as the tolls on the bridges built by the original debt financing) receiving higher priority than general obligation bonds, which join the great unwashed as general unsecured creditors. All such bondholders are safe from

(Continued)

Box 9: (Continued)

allegations of preference payments. It's important to note that the automatic stay does not prevent the holder of a special revenue bond from applying those special revenues to pay down its debt outstanding, and, in fact, the holder can continue to receive debt service payments post-petition.

Plan confirmation follows the same general structure as under Chapter 11, with the exception that the test to demonstrate that creditors are receiving at least as much as they would in a liquidation becomes irrelevant because municipalities cannot liquidate. In its place, Chapter 9 uses a unique test measuring whether the proposed plan is "in the best interests of creditors," which typically means that it must offer higher recoveries to creditors than any other available option.

As in Chapter 11, debtors can use Chapter 9 to reject onerous contracts, renegotiate lower debt payments, and identify the aspects of its operations that no longer make sense. Though strategic options are often limited compared to those in Chapter 11, as the expectation is that the municipality will continue to serve the same constituents in the same region with largely the same services, the flexibility it offers for both operational and financial changes are powerful. Creditors can end up owning assets of municipalities if that was their collateral, subject to court approval and certain voting mechanisms. Creditors cannot, however, end up owning municipalities.

allowed the creation of a system of charter schools, something that politics and union contracts prevented previously. Only time will tell if all those turnaround efforts will pay off in full, but so far, so good.

Chapter Nine

Turning Duds into Dreams

Long before I became a consultant, then an attorney advising companies in distress, I made my reputation in the turnaround industry by buying underperforming companies, guiding their return to profitability, and exiting via a sale as a healthy, restructured entity. My experiences cover but one of the many facets of the world of distressed investing, however. Investment vehicles of all stripes have proliferated, including investment funds advertising themselves as focusing on "distressed" assets. One could be a real estate fund focusing entirely on purchasing small REO ("real estate owned," or a situation where a bank has unsuccessfully attempted to sell a property at a foreclosure auction) opportunities in one part of the United States. Another fund might focus entirely on buying and selling the publicly traded debt of companies that are in crisis or have already filed for Chapter 11. Both of the aforementioned approaches can be very lucrative but are fundamentally different, simply because they tend to be *trading* strategies rather than *turnaround* strategies.

Many of my colleagues in the Turnaround Management Association (a global organization of turnaround professionals) have made millions—if not billions—pursuing such trading strategies for themselves or their institutions, so I want in no way to demean them. Instead, one must understand the difference between the two; if, for example, you have picked up this book and skipped to this chapter, you may find in dismay that it will not teach you how to identify an undervalued bond trading at 10 cents on the dollar and then sell it for 22, which is good work if you can get it. My approach was always to find companies whose distress *seemed* so catastrophic that they had greatly diminished value, and instead fix their problems to preserve and increase the value that remained despite appearances.

Passive investors usually focus on trading in liquid securities higher up on the capital structure, to find mispricing or undervaluations in bond pricing for example. Active investors seek to control a target company after restructuring, whether through direct purchase of a company's assets or via a debt for equity swap. Note that *having a control position is critical* for the active investor.

Why Buy a Distressed Company?

Returns on an investment can be high. While each transaction has its own probability for success or failure, pros in this field try to average a 25 to 45 percent return on their money per year. There are home runs such as Sun Capital Partners receiving sixty-eight times its investment in a mattress retail chain, a transaction discussed in more detail later in this chapter. There are also many stories of small, local businesses purchased through the bankruptcy courts that succeed under new management. Some small companies do poorly, ending up in bankruptcy again. Be warned that even the pros can fail at buyouts, such as Cerberus Capital, a $27 billion private equity firm that specializes in investing in undervalued companies. Cerberus, named for the mythical three-headed dog that guards the gates of Hades, lost its entire multibillion dollar equity stake in Chrysler as part of the U.S. Treasury Department's bailout deal for Chrysler. Similarly, Texas Pacific Group and friends sank $7 billion into Washington Mutual in spring 2009. Only months later, the FDIC forced WaMu into a merger with JP Morgan Chase, losing the investment group over $5 billion on the deal.

Wanxiang American Corp., a subsidiary of a Chinese $4 billion auto parts company has purchased a number of underperforming companies. One of them was Rockford Powertrain, a maker of powertrain components for road graders, bulldozers, tractors, and other off-road heavy equipment. No surprise that they moved parts of the manufacturing to China, but about one-third of the U.S. jobs were saved. Design, quality, and supply chain problems were solved and the company was sold only a few years later for a 200 percent internal rate of return (IRR) for Wanxiang.

Another reason is to *find a strategic fit with your existing business,* which could be for a product extension or additional distribution. The French gaming company, Infogrames, made a successful tender offer for debt-swamped Atari in 2009. They were able to increase their game portfolio somewhat, but more important, they acquired (inherited?) Atari's game distribution contracts with thousands of retail outlets. New York Wire acquired Hanover Wire, both makers of co-axial cable and other wire products, to expand their product line and take over a company that was lowering prices in the market.

Defensive moves can drive acquisitions of troubled companies such as when Aleris tried to buy a smaller competing aluminum producer from a bankruptcy sale process. They wanted that plant dismantled and used for parts, taking the capacity out of the market place. Alcoa outbid them by a substantial margin and did the same thing, effectively taking overcapacity out of the market just as Aleris wanted.

If you have *a customer in trouble*, your own company may be at risk due to lost business. One could purchase a controlling position by trading money owed for a secured loan (being careful to avoid preferences or fraudulent conveyance) or give them additional capital in return for a controlling position.

A *supplier in trouble* could cause serious problems to a company's supply chain. A power company in Texas bought the short line railroad that delivered its coal when the railroad was headed for the bankruptcy court. There are many examples of a manufacturer buying a troubled component maker to protect their sources of supply.

Investors pursuing an active investment strategy generally follow a six-step process:

1. Searching for opportunities
2. Assessing each company's viability
3. Valuation
4. Structuring a transaction
5. Managing the turnaround
6. Exiting via a sale, recapitalization, or public offering

Searching

In general, the process will entail a search for a company (or part of one) that has a core competency to grow; assets to support the core; adequate financing available, including working capital; a plan to turn the company around; and an exit strategy if appropriate. Finding a distressed company to acquire is in many ways similar to the search for a healthy company, with various sources of opportunities.

Intermediaries often advertise companies for sale, and it is a simple matter of reaching to join their distribution lists whenever they engage a new sell-side client. These intermediaries come in many forms, from solo proprietor business brokers representing hair salons and restaurants to global investment banks representing Fortune 100 conglomerates with all or part up for sale. Working with brokers and their twenty-first-century equivalents—Web sites such as www.bizbuysell.com, which lists thousands of small businesses for sale all over the country, and www.bizben.com, which lists mostly California businesses—offers the primary advantage of deal flow. They will typically represent many different businesses and can send information on a variety of opportunities to ensure that a prospective acquirer sees a broad array of deals.

The downside, of course, is that this deal flow is by definition being shopped to a vast universe of potential buyers in the hopes of creating a competitive auction that maximizes sale values. Although distressed situations slightly mitigate this risk, as there are fewer investors interested in struggling companies than there are in healthy ones, the fact that there are many potential buyers viewing the deal makes a true bargain basement price less likely.

Private equity funds therefore pride themselves on developing so-called "proprietary" deal flow, where transactions are not marketed so widely and there are fewer prospective buyers bidding on the sale. The various interrelated parties in distressed situations can provide such deal flow, and a shrewd buyer will attempt to engage with all of them.

Lenders can be a great source of potential acquisition opportunities, as they may be seeking to modify or exit their loans to struggling borrowers, who are likely to have tripped one or more of the covenants explained in Box 1 in the Introduction. If a borrower has taken write-downs of unsalable inventory or uncollectible accounts receivable—which often serve as the foundation upon which its borrowing base is calculated—a lender can find itself in a situation of overadvance, where it has extended more credit than its loan officers originally intended by the formulas in the loan documents. At that point, the lender often approaches the equity holders, frequently the management team in lower middle market or family-held businesses, and requests that they make an equity infusion to address the overadvance. Various factors may make such an infusion impossible. At that point, the lender may begin to put pressure on the management team to begin seeking a buyer.

From a buyer's perspective, a key transition occurs when the responsibility for a loan is transferred from the loan's originator to the bank's workout group, also commonly known as a SAG, or special assets group. At this point, the bank has recognized that the borrower is in trouble, and repayment is in doubt, so it transfers the loan from the originator's balance sheet to that of the workout group, which specializes in maximizing recovery from troubled loans. This creates two key benefits for potential buyers: first, the workout group is accustomed to distressed situations, and is therefore less likely to suffer from paralysis as the loan originator, who may feel the same temptation felt by management to pretend that the problems are temporary and act as if the loan will be repaid. Second, the transfer of the loan to the workout group is often—but not always—done in conjunction with some write-down of the loan's expected value. For example, an originator might have carried the loan on her balance sheet at $10 million (the amount extended to the borrower), but the workout group may receive it on its balance sheet already written down 20 percent to just $8 million. The combination of these two effects—a comfort with distressed situations and a lower hurdle rate for success—tends to make workout groups more likely to force a sale (or other transaction) in order to speed the bank's recovery, unburdened by the fear that the originator might feel of recognizing that the loan was a mistake. The workout departments of lenders are often the best business minds in the institutions, but are also the toughest negotiators with recalcitrant borrowers.

With time, a buyer can develop relationships with such work-out groups, and become one of the first people they call when they believe that they need to force a sale. The advantage to such sources of opportunities is that they may offer truly proprietary deal flow and an opportunity to work with a company long before a bankruptcy filing is necessary; the disadvantage is the difficulty of establishing such relationships without a past track record of working with the workout group. They must believe that you have the resources to close on a transaction fairly quickly. Once in a while, banks will foreclose on a borrower and "toss the keys" to someone like you. This will only happen if you can convince them you bring industry or other turnaround expertise—and you will keep a significant part of their debt on the books, even if con-verted to non-recourse debt if possible.

PACER, or Public Access to Court Electronic Records, is a good source for any *bankruptcy filings*, which are a matter of public record. Located at www.pacer.gov, the PACER system will contain the initial filing and then various highly detailed schedules of every bankruptcy filing in the United States, searchable at $0.08 per page. PACER is inexpensive, exceptionally thorough, and contains companies who have already reached a stage where they are likely to be receptive to purchase offers, but it has the disad-vantage that as a public document, any opportunities it contains will probably have been seen by many other potential purchasers. This is also where you could learn of parts of a company you could buy.

Attorneys can occasionally represent good sources of deal flow, particularly those who focus on bankruptcies, restructuring, and insolvency. As mentioned above, any bankruptcy will be a matter of public record. Attorneys who work with troubled companies are sometimes hired well before a filing becomes necessary, and so they may be able to make introductions to potential buyers while the troubled company still has enough breathing room to review its strategic alternatives. Note, however, that such introduc-tions are outside the typical restructuring attorney's job descrip-tion, and unlike investment bankers and brokers (who get paid a success fee upon the closing of any transaction), attorneys will not have the same financial incentive to consummate a deal, and may even fear losing the client in the event of a change of control.

With almost 10,000 businesses filing for bankruptcy each year, there are plenty of opportunities as well as traps. Attorneys in the field know each other and can help as sources of deals.

Turnaround consultants can become a source of investment opportunities for interested buyers, although a raft of tricky incentive problems may make them less practical as a reliable referral source. On the one hand, if a company hires a turnaround consultant, it has either been forced to by a fed-up lender or it has recognized its own distress; either way, it generally indicates a greater receptiveness to sale proposals. On the other hand, turnaround consultants may have limited incentive to refer the company to potential acquirers, instead preferring to attempt the turnaround on their own. This can create an adverse selection problem; if a turnaround consultant who has been hired as a chief restructuring officer recommends that management sell the company, she probably does not believe in the success of the turnaround, suggesting that the company is not a perfect acquisition opportunity. These consultants often work as receivers for companies going through an assignment for the benefit of creditors, the state law version of bankruptcy. These deals may be "shopped" less than bankruptcy.

10-K and 10-Q forms from public companies can suggest targets to buyers, as one of the most attractive opportunities can come in the form of neglected subsidiaries of larger public conglomerates, such as Middleby's 2001 acquisition of Blodgett from Maytag as discussed in Chapter Three. Often, trouble at the parent level can cause management distraction, driving a decision to exit struggling business lines at bargain prices. Alternatively, a subsidiary's struggles may stem directly from its inclusion under a larger corporate umbrella, either because the subsidiary is prevented from targeting certain customers due to a conflict of interest from the parent, or because it is forced to use the parent's product as an input when that input may not be competitive or cost effective.

News sources can unofficially signal a company's impending trouble, which could presage its becoming available for a distressed sale. Any time a newspaper reports a plant closing, a hiring freeze, mass layoffs, or the discontinuation of a product line, a shrewd observer can conclude that the company may be considering selling some or all of its assets. In the electronic age, one need not read dozens of newspapers, but can instead set up a focused set of daily searches on Google or other search engines, which deliver daily e-mail alerts anytime phrases such as "plant closing" or "as a going concern" appear in a major news bulletin.

In the past decade, news services have even emerged with a specialized focus on the distressed world, such as Beard Publications and its Troubled Company Reporter. Recently, another company called Indicium Solutions has begun offering a subscription service that delivers daily batches of leads on potentially distressed companies. Indicium's proprietary software tool scrapes the pages of every state and federal courthouse in the United States, identifying situations where a company has become delinquent in paying its taxes, has been sued for nonpayment of an outstanding debt, or has had a judgment issued against it by a court, all of which are early-stage indicators of distress.

Wealth management firms are a good source for family-owned firms that may have problems. Sale of the company may be the only way to satisfy unhappy heirs. Family offices are a similar source if you can get an introduction.

Finally, *professional networks* can produce serendipitous introductions to companies whose distress has yet to become public knowledge. Frequently in my career, I have been approached by an acquaintance, colleague, or former student, asking a question about the bankruptcy process, or what they should do regarding a customer who has begun stretching out payments. It's impossible to tell from where the next opportunity might come, but it always helps to keep one's ear to the ground. For more targeted networking, I have found my membership in (and occasional leadership of) the Turnaround Management Association invaluable, as it surrounds a turnaround practitioner with all of the various turnaround stakeholders in a professional setting. Other relevant professional organizations include the Association of Insolvency and Restructuring Advisors and the American Bankruptcy Institute, each with its own niche focus within the larger turnaround world. Your own network of friends may yield a conversation of employers having problems with an underperforming subsidiary or division.

Assessing

In assessing a distressed acquisition target, an acquirer must go through precisely the same steps outlined at the beginning chapters of this book. The first step is to identify both the external and internal causes of the company's distress; each cause presents a different level of risk going forward, some of which can be mitigated, and others which cannot.

Generally speaking, external forces will be more difficult to change, and therefore a company struggling with external causes of distress will—all else being equal—present a less attractive turnaround candidate for an active investor. For example, most if not all distressed companies will blame some sort of economic downturn for their struggles, particularly in any recessionary environment. However, shrewd investors are highly reluctant to bet on a company's recovery based entirely on taking advantage of a cyclical recovery, for downturns can and have lasted far longer than the investor's ability to fund working capital during a period of sustained losses. If a recovery is included as a key assumption in the acquirer's turnaround plan, however, it should be highly conservative, such as when HIG Capital invested in troubled homebuilder Coachmen Industries in late 2009, when the collapse of the housing industry had forced dozens of other homebuilders into bankruptcy filings.[1] An HIG representative later explained their willingness to invest in such a downtrodden industry because their analysis suggested that Coachmen would not require a return to the housing boom of 2005–2007, but rather just a return to a historically low level of homebuilding activity.

Similarly, industrywide issues can be so profound that they make an investment in the space out of the question for most distressed investors. The question is one of permanence: Will the issue resolve itself naturally, or does it represent a permanent drag on the profitability of companies in the industry? For example, Walmart's stranglehold on the American retail supply chain may wax and wane over time, but for the purposes of anyone considering acquiring a vendor selling to the gargantuan retailer, it has to be taken as a given for the indefinite future. But sugar growers in Brazil had no less viable a business in 1999 simply because a statistically foreseeable drought had plunged many of them into bankruptcy; even a merely *bad* season of weather in 2000 would return them at least to break-even. Government regulation that has directly or indirectly caused distress also falls into this category, although the slow pace of legislative change means that it will probably fall to the more permanent end of the spectrum. In both cases, however, a buyer must determine which issues can be expected to change, and which will remain a cause of distress for the foreseeable future.

Other external causes present a different question; rather than asking whether the external environment will remain the same, the buyer must determine whether the company can adapt (quickly and effectively) to this new environment. A company may find the ability to respond to changes in technology, such as in 1993, when IBM finally shed its mainframe mentality and embraced the client/server architecture. IBM could do this because its core competency lay not simply in that particular product, the mainframe computer, but in engineering effective solutions and marketing them on the strength of its historically pristine brand. Other companies may find that their core competence lies too far afield from this new change in technology, such as the carriage makers whose expertise in woodworking failed to translate to the construction of the newfangled automobile. (By contrast, the Studebaker Brothers Manufacturing Company was one company that had begun its life as a blacksmithing shop, giving it a core competency that allowed for a transition to automobile manufacturing so successful that it became the second-largest automaker in the world by 1913.)[2]

Changes in business model and shifts in consumer demand present the same challenge to potential buyers of companies facing these external causes of distress. It remains to be seen whether newspapers can successfully translate their core competency as a trusted source of information into an online world with depressed advertising rates and customer reluctance to pay for content; it's hard to get the moth back into the cocoon. Investors in Krispy Kreme also had to evaluate whether low-carbohydrate diets were simply a fad that had depressed the donut maker's sales, or a wave that would leave the company as a niche provider with a mass-market cost structure. Schwinn actually presents a small success story in such a situation, but it took several owners to recognize how the brand could change to meet these changing consumer needs. After Sam Zell's group purchased the brand at bankruptcy auction and failed to turn it around, private equity fund Wind Point Partners acquired Schwinn as an add-on acquisition to an existing portfolio company called Pacific Cycle. Recognizing the brand's name recognition and its distribution agreements with large retailers such as Walmart, Wind Point acquired the company in a 363 bankruptcy sale. By leveraging Schwinn's distribution agreements, Pacific Cycle was able to address its significantly concentrated customer base, reducing Toys R Us from 90 percent of revenues to just 15 percent. This required a fundamental shift in the Schwinn business model, as it transitioned from being a bike manufacturer and marketer to essentially a licenser of its brand, with all of its production offshore. Wind Point ultimately sold the Pacific Cycle platform—which had also rolled up other distressed brands like Mongoose and GT Bicycles—for some fifteen times its investment.

Finally, a change in interest rates is one external change that can be fixed, although it may require tough negotiations with creditors with the extreme threat of a bankruptcy filing looming in the background. If the company is simply paying too high an interest rate on its floating rate debt, a renegotiation with creditors could address the problem, or a debt-for-equity swap in Chapter 11 reorganization could reduce that interest rate exposure.

In terms of internal causes, insufficient capital is perhaps the easiest one to address, as the rationale exists that a better capitalized company could fund the necessary capital expenditures and working capital needs to return to profitability. This can be tricky, however; many a reckless management team has bemoaned their simple need for additional working capital and short-term financing, when in fact their own leadership shortcomings have led the company to require capital infusions. A buyer who can identify a company that has genuinely struggled due to undercapitalization, however, has a relatively simple fix, with one caveat. While my colleague Professor Steve Rogers suggests that a buyer of a healthy company should reserve between 15–20 percent of the company's purchase price to fund working capital and any operational changes, savvy turnaround investors know that a distressed purchase will require a great deal more capital in reserve. The thirteen-week cash flow forecast, pushed out monthly for the rest of a year's period, should help determine how much is needed. The reason is that the depressed prices paid in distressed situations are just part of the capital need, because turnarounds always take longer and drain cash more than one can anticipate. In this way, they have many similarities to entrepreneurial startups (as discussed in the Introduction), which almost always require more time and capital than originally expected.

The blind pursuit of growth can also generally be addressed with a solid turnaround plan, as the buyer can restructure the organization by stripping out the business lines or assets that no longer support the company's revamped strategic focus. In the case of Flying J, the previous CEO's unchecked acquisition spree had led to the company owning two oil refineries and a 700-mile oil pipeline that any purchaser would be likely to divest in reorganizing the company. From the buyer's perspective, Flying J's decision to file for bankruptcy offered both advantages and disadvantages; the power of the bankruptcy court made it easier to strip out underperforming assets and created a streamlined process for the sale of assets free and clear of any liens, but the filing also meant that the company's availability had been publicized and there was a competitive bidding process. The company's advisors and its new CEO, Crystal Maggelet, did an outstanding job in negotiating deals that led to higher than expected selling prices for the cash-draining California refinery and the pipeline. In fact, one of the creditors offered to buy one oil and gas subsidiary for $30 million and was turned down. Thanks to an auction, it went for over $100 million.

Another example is Cannondale Bicycle, the leading producer of high-end bicycles, which in the late 1990s went into the motorsport business. These efforts at growth diverted management attention and created severe financial problems for the then public company. Pegasus Capital got involved prebankruptcy with loans in mid-2002. Cannondale went into Chapter 11 in January 2003 and Pegasus converted its loan and additional cash into ownership of the company. Pegasus recruited new senior management, who focused on the company's core bicycle business, selling off the motorsports group. They also worked on improving dealer relationships and supply chain efficiencies. With higher sales and profit margins, Pegasus sold Cannondale five years later for a large profit and won *Buyouts Magazine*'s "Turnaround of the Year" award for the transaction.

Bankruptcy also makes it easier to address the overextension of credit, as the purchaser can renegotiate with lenders or pursue debt-for-equity swaps as mentioned above. Product issues can present slightly trickier problems, as consumer perceptions of poor product quality or an antiquated brand tend to be sticky, making it more difficult to change them. However, as the successful turnarounds at Gucci and Harley-Davidson demonstrate, such efforts are not impossible. Any prospective buyer must first evaluate whether the product issues can be fixed as well as whether the customer can be convinced as such, and then finally, whether this transformation can occur within an affordable timeframe.

Lastly, fraud and dishonesty can create attractive buying opportunities for investors when they bring about a company's distress, but the buyer must make absolutely certain that she has made a clean sweep of any bad actors within the organization. Because suppliers, customers, and lenders are likely to feel hurt and act with suspicion toward the besmirched organization, any new buyer will need to enter the situation cognizant of that fact. The buyer's newness to the situation may offer a clean slate, but that slate has to stay spotless, as even the appearance of any impropriety will look like backsliding to fatigued stakeholders. As the experiences of both Brasil Telecom and Symbol Technology show, any ties to past malfeasance must be eliminated rapidly in order to preserve credibility and inspire new faith among surviving employees.

After analyzing the causes of the company's distress, the prospective buyer can then identify where the company lies on the organizational distress curve. As explained in Chapter One, the further a company has slid down the curve, the greater the effort required to enact a successful turnaround and the lower the likelihood of success. In the context of buying a company, this means that a company at the crisis phase should sell for a lower price— all else being equal—than a company in the faulty action phase, and buyers should target a higher expected internal rate of return (IRR) on the investment to account for this increased risk.

Generally speaking, traditional private equity firms focusing on healthy companies target a minimum IRR of 20 to 25 percent. While no empirical data exist on the subject, those target IRRs should increase at each subsequent phase on the curve. Example target returns might be healthy/blinded ≈20–25 percent; inaction ≈25–30 percent; faulty action ≈30–35 percent; and crisis/ bankruptcy ≈35 percent or more. Remember that these are averages. Because there will be full losses sometimes one must actually target a rate over double those stated when determining a reasonable upside to the transaction.

After identifying the company's stage on the organizational distress curve, a buyer should research the company's warning signs. This should not, however, be an entirely retrospective activity, as it will do little good to determine what incumbent management *should have* seen before experiencing the current level of distress. Rather, the warning sign analysis should be conducted as of the present date, in order to determine what potential threats loom for the company going forward. Trend analysis of profitability and asset management indicators, an industry and product analysis, and review of diagnostic prediction models such as the Z-score, DuPont, and SWOT analyses can help a prospective buyer decide whether a target company has bottomed out at the faulty action phase, or whether further degradation in its financial performance seems likely, bringing it to the crisis phase.

The last stage in assessing the opportunity is to use as much information as is available to construct a preliminary 13-Week Cash Flow Model in order to get a clear picture of the company's near-term liquidity needs. This can prove very difficult in distressed situations, especially when a disgruntled lender is forcing a transaction on management, who may rebel by attempting to withhold information or provide inaccurate records to potential buyers. One company had been cutting checks to pay vendors, reducing the accounts payable accordingly, and then the CEO would put the checks in his desk drawer because he knew they needed the cash for payroll. Even if numbers are given in good faith, it's difficult to get comfort in the accuracy of a troubled company's financial records. Typical adjustments that are used to recast a seller's income statement include

- Reduction in cost of goods sold, supposedly because vendors were charging more to a company with credit problems, projects were "rushed" because of "poor planning," and U.S. vendors were used rather than overseas only because of poor credit
- Adjustments downward to professional fees, due to the company's need for more legal and other professional advisors, including taking out costs to defend against lawsuits
- Decrease in SG&A by assuming they wasted marketing expenses on poor products
- Adjustments for paying too much in salaries, especially to family members
- Assumed reductions in lease rates by a new, better-capitalized buyer

Many other changes may have been made as well. Of course, any of these should be adjusted back up by the buyer, who must demand full disclosure of all such recasting. These adjustments on the part of the seller are often more than offset by the costs that will be incurred by the new turnaround team, the hiring of competent managers, suppliers who want to make up for prior losses, the need for better advisors, and so on. In general, skepticism should reign, as inventory will often be burned through, working capital balances will have been overstated in order to increase the borrowing base, and cash balances will be inaccurate. As always, caveat emptor.

Pro formas purportedly showing *future* financial performance as improving on its own soon always makes me think the translation from the Latin *pro forma* means "if we are incredibly lucky" or "no-way, no-how." However, even with imperfect information, the 13WCFM is a crucial step, as it serves as the foundation for understanding how much excess capital will be needed to fund the turnaround process. As explained above, the purchase price of a distressed company can be as little as half of the total capital need.

All of these assessments of the company, its situation, its customers, its suppliers, its management, and its liquidity needs fall under the broad category of what M&A investment bankers and attorneys call "due diligence." The irony arises from the fact that due diligence takes on twice as much importance in a distressed situation, and yet must be conducted in less than half the time. This results in the paradoxical allure of buying distressed companies; it is a harrowing experience, fraught with unfathomable stress and anxiety and the constant risk of losing every penny of investment capital, and yet the stress junkies who are drawn to it consider it more addictive than any drug, and it can fill your wallet instead of emptying it.

Valuation

The purchase price of an underperforming company is much more difficult to negotiate than for a normal company. The main reasons are that there are more stakeholders than usual involved in the negotiations, valuation is even less precise, and there are arguments over who should pay for the turnaround. The negotiations for the price per share of a normal company usually take place between the buyer and the owner or board of directors representing the owners. In the case of a troubled company, particularly one near the crisis stage, there could also be the banks and bondholders at the table. If the company is in bankruptcy, one can add the unpaid vendors, lessors, unions, the PBGC, the U.S. trustee, and the judge.

Valuations of troubled companies are always imprecise. Generally speaking, there are three ways to value a company: income-based approaches, market-based approaches, and asset-based approaches. Income-based valuation methods rely on the assumption that any asset is worth the future cash flows it will generate, which must be discounted back at an appropriate interest rate to reflect the time value of money. The discounted cash flow (DCF) model therefore requires assumptions regarding the timing and magnitude of a company's cash flows. A related, less complicated income-based approach would disregard the company as a going concern and instead forecast how long it would take and what value could be received in an orderly sale of all of the company's assets, whether business unit by business unit or in its entirety.

Market-based approaches compare the company for sale to related companies (typically those in the same industry, geography, and general size range) to determine the appropriate multiple to apply to some measure of the company's profitability, such as net income, cash flow, or EBITDA. For example, if ten generally similar public companies ("comparables" or "comps") are trading at an average of 7.5 times their last twelve months of EBITDA, one could argue that the company with $1 million in EBITDA over the same period is worth $7.5 million. A related approach uses recently announced M&A transactions to identify a similar multiple to apply to whatever metric of profitability has been selected. Naturally, these approaches can be garbage-in, garbage-out, as the selection of an overly friendly set of comparables, a timeframe that intentionally includes or excludes outlying transactions, and the measure of profitability selected can greatly influence one's conclusion on valuation. It goes almost without saying that a buyer should rely only on his own assumptions in using either such valuations, as sellers will invariably be overly optimistic regarding future projections, and will try to paint historical performance in as positive a light as possible; even in the absence of outright distortions and deception, sellers will often attempt to add back "one-time" expenses to produce a much healthier-looking "normalized EBITDA" or "normalized cash flow" when such expenses are in fact likely to recur. Buyers should therefore always value a company based on their own multiple of their own projections, rather than simply accepting the seller's proposed multiple of the seller's projections or claimed historical financials.

Both the income-based and market-based approaches encounter significant difficulties in their application to distressed companies. In the case of income methods, the selection of an appropriate discount rate is very challenging, because it must be *significantly* higher than its competitors to reflect the extreme riskiness of a company in distress. (Flip Huffard commented that in his opinion, the discount rates used in DCF models for distressed companies are chronically underestimated, and should approach 20 percent.)[3] In the case of market-based approaches, it is fundamentally difficult to apply a multiple to a distressed company, because any measure of its profitability is so likely to be depressed that the multiple would be meaningless, or even negative.

The final type of valuation methodology is an asset-based approach, typically the liquidation value, or the amount that each individual asset of the company could fetch at a forced auction. Buyers would prefer to pay no more than liquidation value, because it limits their downside. That's literally the last thing anyone, other than maybe the senior bank, would want. That senior lender may already be playing hardball, restricting working capital borrowings, and forcing the payable to be stretched. These three types of valuation are summarized in Table 9.1.

Books and articles abound on these subjects, and should be consulted, along with an attorney who has negotiated distressed M&A deals and an investment banker if the size of the deal justifies it. (See Box 10 for more information on items that may affect the valuation of distressed companies.)

The biggest argument often centers around who will pay for the turnaround. The sellers will say, "This company can be returned to profitability again, so you have to pay extra for the potential." Your answer would have to be, "Then go ahead and do it yourself. If I am to take the risk of the turnaround, I cannot pay you for it." In the end, the price usually is negotiated somewhere closer to the current value.

The key is for you to determine what the company is worth to you, including what portion of what debt you'll assume, what working capital you want, and what liabilities, if any, will be assumed. Then, let the stakeholders sort out how they'll divide up the proceeds and the carcass. Remember that ultimately the price will also depend upon the structure of the deal.

Structuring

It is possible to purchase a distressed company through several different structures and processes, each with its own advantages and disadvantages. The categories listed below are just typical examples, for each distressed acquisition has so many nuances that no two deals are exactly alike. In general, the bankruptcy process offers the most buyer protection from pre-sale claims, as a federal judge officially declares the termination of such claims in most bankruptcy-related transactions. However, this protection comes at the added expense of the bankruptcy process. All the

Table 9.1. Overview of Valuation Methodologies

APPROACH:	MARKET		INCOME	ASSET	
Methodology:	Comparable Public Company	Comparable M&A Transaction	Discounted Cash Flow	Forced Sale	Orderly Liquidation Value
Key Factors	• Choice of company set • Multiple • Timeframe (historical vs. forward) • Size, mix of products/services, customers, other comparison items	• Choice of transaction set • Multiple • Length of timeframe • Size, mix of products/services, customers, other comparison items	• Projected cash flows • Cost of capital • Risk premiums • Terminal value	• Proceeds expected from an auction or other time-limited disposition of assets, typically piecemeal (e.g., Article 9 or foreclosure sale)	• Prices expected for individual or aggregated assets from reasonable marketing and sale efforts over an appropriate period of time

Source: "Triple Trouble: Valuating Companies in Chapter 11," *Journal of Corporate Renewal*, September 2008.

Box 10: Additional Issues in Valuing Distressed Companies

Purchasers of distressed companies will necessarily have to consider additional issues in valuing their acquisition targets. While there are countless issues that can arise, the following represent some of the more common questions to address:

Working Capital Adjustments

The valuation of a healthy company often uses an industry-specific multiple of some measure of profitability; for example, manufacturing companies in 2007 were generally being acquired between six and nine times their last twelve months of EBITDA. Several years later, that range has both compressed and shrunk to somewhere between five and seven times. However, these types of valuation metrics assume a normalized level of working capital, a rarity in distressed companies, whose poor quality makes receivables less likely to be collected and inventories less likely to sell. As a result, a working capital (WC) adjustment is often necessary in calculating a "true" purchase price. For example, a buyer might acquire the assets of the following company for $1 million, knowing that it had the following working capital deficiencies:

	Inventory	A/R	A/P	Total WC
Company A's reported WC while in distress	$400,000	$200,000	$800,000	–$200,000
Company A's actual WC while in distress	$250,000	$50,000	$800,000	–$500,000
Healthy Company A with normalized WC	$500,000	$100,000	$300,000	$300,000

In order to acquire this company and fund a turnaround, a buyer would not merely need to pay the $1 million purchase price, but also add the $800,000 difference between the company's actual working capital position (a deficit of $500,000) and the normalized level of working capital for a healthy version of that company ($300,000). As such, the true purchase price of this company would actually be $1.8 million, and might therefore make the deal unpalatable to a buyer wishing to pay only $1 million.

Capital Expenditure Adjustments

Similar to working capital adjustments, buyers must take into account any short-to-medium-term capital expenditures that will be necessary upon closing the purchase. Many distressed companies will have delayed important upgrades to plants and equipment in an attempt to stem liquidity crises, so these additional expenses must also be added to the price paid to the seller.

Underfunded Defined Benefit Pension Plan Obligations

The legacy costs of defined benefit plans—which promise a certain monthly benefit to retirees based on years of service and salary during employment—can influence the valuation of a company purchased out of distress. Companies rarely offer such plans anymore because of their exorbitant cost, but in the past, they would make various actuarial assumptions based on the number of retirees in the plan, how long they would live (and therefore how many payments they would receive), and what the future return on investments would be in order to determine the company's required contribution to the plan in any given year. Because companies in crisis have limited cash on hand, many companies attempt to justify decreased contributions to the pension plan with overly aggressive actuarial assumptions; for example, even a 50 basis point increase in the assumed annual rate of return on assets can imply that contributions could be cut in half in a given year. However, the status of a pension plan when a company files for bankruptcy has been the subject of ceaseless litigation over the past few decades, which makes the task of challenging a company with such a shortfall very challenging and brings the PBGC to the negotiating table, potentially sinking a transaction if the PBGC is demanding too large a slice of a reorganized company.

Tax Attributes

Companies in distress typically have lost money over recent timeframes, so investors may find value in the opportunity to use historical net operating losses (NOLs) to reduce income tax payments going forward. Naturally, this will only increase the value of the

(Continued)

Box 10: (Continued)

company to buyers able to use these NOLs. Section 382 of the Internal Revenue Code offers strict regulations as to whether NOLs are preserved following a change of control. Generally speaking, you should consult a tax professional to determine whether a distressed business's NOLs would be available to you in the event of an acquisition.

---

other transactions fall further to the other side of the spectrum, where protection is limited but time to closing and transaction costs drop accordingly.

Stock and Asset Purchases

For our purposes, these are just standard M&A transactions that happen to target a distressed company that is not so distressed that the equity holders are completely out of the money. A stock purchase refers to a transaction where the buyer acquires the actual shares of the target, whereas in an asset purchase, the buyer actually purchases the assets of the business, and the seller retains the shares of the corporation (which typically liquidates following the transaction). In a stock purchase, therefore, the same entity continues to exist, with the buyer essentially replacing the seller without interrupting the company's operations. Buyers generally prefer asset purchases, because they can identify exactly which liabilities will be transferred in the sale, and which will remain with the seller. This can help avoid successor liability issues for the buyer, such as product liability issues for products manufactured by the previous owners. Sellers therefore tend to prefer stock sales, because they cut all ties with the business entirely, and because stock deals generally result in lower capital gains taxes. Note that asset sales do also occur in troubled situations, but usually through one of the structures outlined below.

Loan-to-Own

In a credit bid or "loan-to-own" scenario, an investor can purchase the target company's debt without any intention of simply collecting the interest payments due to the debtholder, but instead with the plan of converting that debt to a controlling equity share of the business. This debt-for-equity swap can take place inside of a Chapter 11 proceeding, particularly if the investor provides DIP financing to the debtor. (This is much easier to do if the investor is also a pre-petition secured creditor.) As the DIP lender, the investor can exert a great deal of control over the plan of reorganization, and can use that control to compel the debtor to sell certain assets, upon which it can then bid. The DIP lender can also take control of the company if its experts can convince the bankruptcy court that the company's value is approximately equal to the amount of the DIP loan, leaving no additional equity in a reorganized entity to be distributed to lower classes of claimants.

An investor can also seize control by determining and taking a major position in the class of claims in the company's capital structure which represents the "fulcrum security," or the one that will receive equity in the reorganized entity upon emergence from Chapter 11. This is typically the first impaired class; in a company with $500 million in secured debt, $300 million in unsecured debt, $200 million in preferred stock, and a court-determined enterprise value of $600 million, the unsecured debt is the fulcrum security because its holders will probably receive equity in the reorganized company. (The preferred stockholders and common equity holders will receive nothing.) When the market recognizes that the unsecured debt will be impaired (in this case, they would only recover one-third of the $300 million in outstanding claims), these claims will trade down to approximately 33 cents on the dollar (or even less, due to the uncertainty of the case) to reflect that discount, and an investor could purchase them at a discount and receive equity based on the full, face amount upon reorganization. With a sufficient share of the unsecured debt, an investor could join the official creditors' committee, gaining both access to material nonpublic information on the company's operations and greater voice over the reorganization plan. However, as mentioned in Chapter Six, an investor on the official creditors' committee would probably be barred from continuing to trade in the company's securities. The challenge of this fulcrum security approach comes in identifying exactly where the waterfall will stop; that is, what the court will determine to be the company's enterprise value, how much debt it will be deemed capable of supporting, whether the court will consolidate the claims on various subsidiaries, and so on. This problem becomes especially thorny in large companies with complex capital structures and convertible securities; an investor can guess incorrectly as to what will be the fulcrum security, and find themselves on the outside looking in, holding either debt in the reorganized company when they wanted equity, or holding a worthless claim in a class that gets crammed down. If the enterprise value is sufficient, even claims lower than the fulcrum security can receive something.

These loan-to-own approaches can also work outside of a bankruptcy process, if the existing loan agreement has sufficient covenants and provisions that allow the lender to exert pressure on management. In small and middle market businesses, this most often comes about in the form of a personal guarantee on the loan; an investor might purchase the loan at a discount and threaten to foreclose on the owner's personal assets if he does not agree to exchange their debt for equity.

Article 9 Sales

Upon default, a secured creditor can use Section 9–610(a) of the Uniform Commercial Code to sell the assets of a distressed debtor, while avoiding the lengthy and expensive bankruptcy process. In order to do so, it must be absolutely certain that it has perfected its liens. Such sales can take place as so-called "friendly foreclosures," where the debtor cooperates, or as highly contentious affairs. In either case, the secured creditor controls the sale process, either publically or privately, and must demonstrate that the sale is "commercially reasonable" in every way, such as its bidding mechanisms, timing, and location. Secured creditors can in fact credit-bid their claim in this sale process in a modification of the aforementioned "loan-to-own" strategy; essentially, they bid the value of their claim for the assets, acquiring them if no one bids a larger amount.

Assignment for the Benefit of Creditors

An assignment for the benefit of creditors (ABC) is a liquidation process under state laws that allows a buyer to purchase a troubled business or its assets free of unsecured claims—and possibly secured claims as well if the secured creditors consent—without invoking state bulk sales laws. In an ABC, the debtor engages a third party (the "assignee") to solicit bids for the business or its assets; as a result of this arrangement, the assignee takes on a fiduciary duty to the creditors, and the distressed company transfers all of its interests in its property to the assignee. Unsecured creditors cannot pursue the assets assigned to the assignee, and instead have to submit evidence proving the validity of their claims in order to receive a share of the distributed funds.

State regulations vary regarding the level of court involvement in ABCs. In California, the process has no court involvement, and as such is often used in the rapid wind-down of troubled technology and life sciences startup ventures. Other states require significant court involvement in overseeing the process. Overall, however, an ABC is much more expedient and less expensive than a bankruptcy court liquidation, and allows buyers to purchase a business that has been cleansed of its unsecured claims. In addition, the seller in an ABC chooses its own assignee, allowing for the selection of someone with particular industry or geographic expertise.

Receiverships

Similar to an ABC, a receivership is a situation where a third party (here, the "receiver") is appointed to sell a distressed company or its assets for the benefit of its creditors. In this case, however, the receiver is appointed by a state or federal court, and the sale requires court approval, making it slightly slower and more expensive than an ABC. Such proceedings are therefore more commonly initiated by a creditor demanding repayment, whereas an ABC is typically initiated by the company in cooperation with its creditors. Courts will often also issue an injunction analogous to bankruptcy's automatic stay, preventing other creditors from foreclosing on assets and eroding the company's value.

363 Sales

A 363 sale process takes place inside of Chapter 11 bankruptcy proceedings, and provides the debtor with certain protections that can incentivize prospective buyers to bid. The bankruptcy court oversees the auction process, making it more time-intensive and costly than most other sales processes, but its primary advantage stems from the fact that buyers can purchases assets free and clear of any liens, with a court order enforcing that termination of any potential successor liability. It can be an efficient process with no likelihood that the seller will decide to back out at the last minute without penalty; it allows buyers to take advantage of other Chapter 11 protections such as the ability to reject executory contracts; and it offers several potential bidding strategies.

Once a debtor files for Chapter 11 and elects to execute a 363 sale (whether or not part of a plan of reorganization), the court holds a hearing to determine the bidding procedures, which entail when the auction will take place, how buyers will be deemed financially qualified, what the bidding increment shall be, and so on. In this hearing, a so-called "stalking horse" bidder is often identified, and a stalking horse agreement is approved by the court. The stalking horse is a bidder who has elected to place the initial binding bid on the company's assets, which then serves as a floor for the auction price. This same concept is often used in normal M&A deals. Occasionally, a creditor will act as the stalking horse and credit-bid the value of its claim. In exchange for revealing its intentions early, the stalking horse receives certain incentives, such as a break-up fee (generally between 2 and 4 percent of the purchase price) if another party overbids the stalking horse, which should cover full expense reimbursement and then some. The stalking horse also negotiates the purchase agreement and has the most time for due diligence. However, the stalking horse bidder has the upfront legal bills and is bidding in a vacuum without knowing how low the bidding could have started.

With or without the establishment of a stalking horse bid, the court then operates an auction, sometimes allowing the stalking horse or other bids to continue escalating until a winner is determined, at which point there is a sale approval hearing to finalize the transaction. This can be a lengthy and costly process, but the significant advantages of the bankruptcy process can make it an attractive transaction structure.

The differences among these various sale processes are summarized in Table 9.2.

Table 9.2. Various Distressed Purchase Options

Structure	Description	Advantages	Disadvantages	Appropriate when …
Stock purchase	Purchase of an equity stake of a company, just as in a healthy situation	No court involvement Generally less time pressure, given the absence of a court process	Likely to be more expensive, as the buyer pays some multiple on earnings All liabilities are purchased	The company is not so distressed that the equity holders are completely underwater
Asset purchase	Purchasing the assets of a company, rather than its equity	No court involvement Buyer can specify exactly which liabilities are transferred in the sale, and which remain with the seller	May invoke state laws on bulk sales, which can require notification of all creditors Sellers may demand a higher price in exchange for the higher tax rate on sellers	The business has the significant potential liabilities that cannot be valued with precision or buyer unwilling to accept

(Continued)

Table 9.2. (Continued)

Structure	Description	Advantages	Disadvantages	Appropriate when …
Loan-to-own	This entails acquiring a company's debt (often at a discount) and then using that leverage to control the company.	No court involvement Often a quiet process, leading to depressed sale prices Motivated creditor can sometimes force a transaction quickly Lower cost than bankruptcy	Risk of assuming lender liability Purchased security may not ultimately become the fulcrum security, leaving the credit bidder with less leverage A bankruptcy filing's automatic stay can involve many other stakeholders, delaying the sale Can lead to a highly contentious battle for control of the company	The company has contentious relations with its fulcrum lender, who simply wants out and is willing to take a haircut in order to do so, and the fulcrum security is clearly identified The "lender" is willing to take charge and own the company

Article 9 sales	A process under a state's Uniform Commercial Code where a financially challenged borrower cooperates with its lender to enact a foreclosure sale on assets	Speed & simplicity, so DIP financing not necessary Lower cost than bankruptcy	The burden is on the secured creditor to demonstrate that its perfected claim exceeds the value of the assets; any dispute by junior creditors could delay the transaction, as they are owed any surplus Cannot include real estate	The secured creditor is underwater and wants to foreclose rather than give management the opportunity to reorganize
Assignments for the benefit of creditors (ABC)	A procedure where a distressed company assigns all of its assets to an assignee, who then liquidates the assets and distributes the proceeds to creditors	Offers some of the protections of a bankruptcy sale without the related cost and delay The debtor can choose the third-party assignee Less publicity for a privately owned company	Selling "free & clear of liens" requires approval of either court or secured lender Lack of transparency and court oversight may compel creditors to file an involuntary bankruptcy	A smaller company's management has decided to capitulate and allow the company to be someone else's headache

(Continued)

Table 9.2. (Continued)

Structure	Description	Advantages	Disadvantages	Appropriate when ...
Receiverships	A state court appoints a third-party to operate or liquidate the assets of a struggling company	Like bankruptcy, a state law receivership forces all creditors to the same negotiating table and may stay collection efforts Lower cost than bankruptcy	Limited ability to void preference actions	Creditors are attempting to protect their collateral value pending a foreclosure process
363 sale of all or part of a company	A process inside of Chapter 7 or Chapter 11 wherein the assets of a company are transferred free-and-clear of existing liens	Court involvement streamlines process Possibility of buying assets free-and-clear Various strategies (e.g. as stalking horse or overbidder)	Public auction may increase bidding war Financial buyers may struggle to move quickly enough to be considered credible Nonstalking horse bidders face economic disadvantage Bankruptcy costs	A company has filed for bankruptcy but creditors believe that selling will maximize recovery Buyer wants to be certain that liabilities and liens are gone

There has been a trend over the last few years for buyers of companies in or near the crisis phase to demand the purchase be made through bankruptcy. The buyer would be the stalking horse bidder in a prepackaged fast track bankruptcy filing. While this adds to the transaction costs for everyone, it eliminates for the buyer uncertainty regarding title to the assets and the elimination of liabilities.

Managing the Turnaround: "Uh Oh!"

Sometimes buyers of distressed businesses are so focused on winning the deal that they are startled when they find they own it and now must laser in on managing the purchased company and enact a turnaround. The buyers should have already determined the core competency and the new strategy of the company, and are starting from behind if they haven't. The first critical step of managing a recently purchased distressed company is to ask the most difficult question a board or an owner ever faces: whether to retain the existing management, particularly the CEO. There will necessarily be many factors driving this decision; some may argue against "changing horses in the middle of a stream," suggesting that despite a few mistakes, the incumbent CEO knows the company and the industry better than any available replacement, for whom the learning curve would prove too steep in a time-sensitive environment. Others will recognize that the company's slide down the organizational distress curve happened under *someone's* watch, and that someone should likely be held accountable.

For me, this decision hit home when I learned (through an investment banker) of the opportunity to acquire a subsidiary of a public company, a plant in Alabama that made appliance and automotive parts. The parts that accounted for the most revenue were the "dashboards" or front control panels of washers and dryers, sold to almost every manufacturer. They were made by first stamping the forms out of coils of cold rolled steel, putting those through an anodizing bath, then silk screening the appropriate color and customer logo on each. The painted parts went by conveyor belt through ovens, to bake the paint into the shiny, enameled colors that will match the body of the washers and dryers. We were given access to the company's books and records and flew down for a plant tour. This company was making some money and running at full capacity. The parent company did not have the capital for expansion or to make changes that would lower their high internal scrap rates on the dashboards and on some of the auto parts. As part of my due diligence I informed the sellers that conversations with their largest customers were required. They agreed.

In a phone conversation, the head of purchasing for General Electric's Appliance Group stated, "If all my suppliers were like them, I'd be out of a job!" I immediately expressed my alarm about problems I'd missed. He laughed and said, "They are one of our only suppliers, out of 20,000, that my records show have never had a part rejected for failing a quality test. That's why they get most of our business for the dashboards as well as for our refrigerator and oven door handles. They say they don't have more capacity for other parts." Relieved, due diligence continued with an additional plant tour with an outside consultant who was an expert in manufacturing, meetings with management, deeper digging into their books, and reviewing contracts with customers, suppliers, and labor. After raising debt from banks to cover 50 percent of the purchase price and giving a minority position in the company to the seller to cover the rest, we closed the deal.

A plan was created with the current CEO of that unit for the needed strategic, operational, and financial changes. This was the executive described in the Introduction who split our agreed plan into two lists, those he couldn't do and those he didn't know how to do. Our team and a replacement CEO moved soon to implement the plans. As to strategy, the decision was made to eliminate the products made for the auto industry and focus on the company's core competency of appliance parts manufacturing. On the operating front, the first priority centered around the reason for the high scrap rate. Conversations with employees and plant visits showed that the inspectors, all women, were told "to examine the painted surfaces carefully and reject any that don't look perfect!" They used large mounted magnifying glasses to look for almost microscopic flaws and scrapped a significant number of parts. After conferring with the customers and testing inspectors' eyesight for normal reading power, the magnifying glasses were eliminated. If a defect couldn't be seen with the naked eye, even on close inspection, there was no rejection. Scrap rates dropped in half. New dies for the stamping machines dropped the scrap rates to almost zero.

As far as the rest of the manufacturing process was concerned, finding ways to give employees more authority to make changes in efficiency paid off as well, when they suggested how fewer people could be used to run various groups of machinery. The excess personnel were used to increase capacity for new appliance parts. The company's improved performance led to its sale a few years later to a strategic buyer for a 74 percent internal rate of return on the investment.

In my experience, the phase of distress at which the company finds itself on the curve is not a strong indicator as to whether replacing the CEO is the right move. Rather, it is a highly idiosyncratic process, wherein a rigorous management analysis of the type discussed in Chapter One is necessary to determine whether the incumbent has the tools necessary to lead a turnaround. Other factors include the structure that the transaction took; under a 363 sale, for example, it is possible to enact "key man" retention plans that could incentivize a skilled CEO to remain despite the washout of his or her previous equity holdings. (Winn-Dixie did precisely that in order to convince Peter Lynch to oversee the turnaround after the company filed for Chapter 11 protection.) The CEO may not even be willing to remain on the job, particularly in smaller family businesses where the transaction marks the end of the ability to treat the company like a piggy bank for rich perquisites.

Overall, the best indicator of whether a regime change is in order is a look back at the identified causes of distress. If a company truly has fallen victim to a perfect storm of economic downturn, rising input costs, and temporary overcapacity—as so many CEOs of troubled companies will invariably claim—then the existing team may well have the ability to turn the company around if they agree with the proposed strategy. Note that all of those causes can be classified as external ones. If, however, the major causes of distress are internal, such as the blind pursuit of growth or major product issues, that represents a strong indication that new management would be better suited to leading a turnaround. Obviously, any credible evidence of fraud or dishonesty in the executive suite—or even the tacit permission of it at lower levels, such as a laissez-faire attitude toward kickbacks or expense padding—should be considered a clear and unambiguous indication that anyone implicated needs to go. Turnarounds require a tight ship, with integrity and credibility above all else, and anyone involved in such misconduct cannot be allowed to taint the new turnaround effort.

Regardless of whether the CEO leading the turnaround is old or new, the management of an acquired distressed company follows precisely the same process as explained in Chapter Two, with a three-pronged approach to strategy, finance, and operations. The new owner will enjoy one advantage in this process in that his or her newness to the situation will make a true reengineering more easily attainable. He can analyze the business as a true outsider, lacking in preconceptions built up by years on the job, and start with a clean sheet of paper in determining exactly what is important to customers and what is not. Upon initiating the turnaround plan, the CEO must then keep a relentless focus upon the 13-Week Cash Flow Model, in order to monitor its effectiveness and prevent any backsliding into complacency after the quick initial gains from low-hanging fruit. In winning *Buyouts Magazine*'s award for the 2008 turnaround of the year, $8 billion private equity firm Sun Capital, which has invested in 230 distressed companies, was cited for increasing retailer Mattress Firm's EBITDA twenty-two fold. The company was purchased from a grateful parent company, happy to get rid of its underperforming subsidiary. Sun paid $4.5 million in equity and added $30 million in debt. The unit owned 200 stores and had no idea how many potential customers came through its doors each day. Sun decided to keep the CEO, strategically decided to make the stores more homelike by installing wood floors and artwork on the walls, and became supercenters for mattresses. They were praised for operating changes such as closing unprofitable stores, opening others in growing markets, and upgrading their sales force. After changes in how working capital and inventories were handled, profits began to soar. Sun sold the company after four years of ownership for $450 million.

Strong leadership will prove critical throughout the process in order to unite an anxious stakeholder base. This leadership becomes particularly important when layoffs threaten to depress morale, for employees take their cues directly from senior executives during periods of adversity. Now, if you are scratching your head and muttering that these two paragraphs sound like a reiteration of all of the chapters of this book, you have not only been paying attention, but you are beginning to take an appropriately holistic view of the process of buying a distressed company. Once acquired, it is almost no different from any other turnaround, with the major difference stemming from the buyer's novelty to existing stakeholders, which both puts pressure on the buyer to develop credibility and provides a clean slate with respect to past mistakes or underperformance.

Executing a turnaround based on the "tripod" approach with a fundamental reengineering as its centerpiece sounds terribly complicated, but successful distressed investors know that the process is not, as they say, rocket science. The goal of increasing cash flow has several major levers; top-line revenue, gross margin, SG&A, and interest expense. The three-pronged turnaround approach can use various strategies to push those levers. Raising prices, niches for old products, and new product development can increase revenues; more intelligent input sourcing can expand gross margins; outsourcing nonessential functions can decrease SG&A; and better working capital management can reduce interest expense. The particular strategies themselves are tricky, particularly in a company swimming in reams and reams of complicated, sometimes conflicting data, but keeping those major levers in mind can help guide one through the forest. It has been chronicled how private equity players and other value builders move quickly to do extensive due diligence, then move again at surprising speed to put their plan into action.[4] It helps that private equity players are just that—private. They don't have the pressure of a public company's quarterly earnings report, giving them (or you) the edge in building value, where the biggest failure will be the failure to act.[5]

Acquiring Gerber

Gerber Plumbing was founded in 1932 and built a reputation for quality manufacturing of bathroom sanitary ware and faucets.[6] It remained family owned until 2002, and enjoyed a reputation of customer and employee loyalty. Signs of problems, however, showed up in the mid-1990s. Due to federal mandates and state subsidies, the sale of low-flow toilets temporarily sky-rocketed and Gerber's three plants, all in the United States, ran at capacity. Meanwhile, nearly every plumbing manufacturer had already moved its production overseas, most to China. Then-CEO Harriett Gerber was fiercely loyal to her employees and their communities and refused to move production. She raised additional debt to buy out family members who disagreed with her strategy and to increase capacity at the Alabama plant. That plant never did gain the increased efficiencies.

The increase in housing starts and demand spikes from temporary government legislation led to a false sense of security for Gerber. Meanwhile, competitors were developing innovative new designs and finding ways to improve quality while reducing costs. The company was actually losing market share, and its costs were 25 percent above its competition. By the time of Harriet's death in 2001, the company had been losing money for three years. A new, third generation management team took over and things went south even faster. By late 2002, the company was projected to lose almost $12 million per year.[7] An investment bank tried to sell the company, but buyers shied away from environmental, union, product liability, and pension issues faced by a low-margin business with a shrinking market share. The two strengths of Gerber were its brand heritage and distribution network, but these weren't enough to appeal to financial or strategic buyers such as competitors.

With Gerber on the verge of filing bankruptcy, the investment bankers went back to a small company they had dismissed earlier, Globe Union, based in Taiwan but led by U.S.-based CEO Michael Warner. To buy time to do due diligence, Globe Union provided Gerber a bridge loan secured by intellectual property and some unencumbered real estate. Globe Union was already in the same business and wanted the brand and distribution presence in North America, but all the liabilities couldn't justify a positive value for Gerber. They thought if they could get it essentially for free it could be worth it.

Michael considered whether to wait for Gerber to enter bankruptcy and acquire it coming out, minus its liabilities. He concluded that the probability of liquidation was too high and decided to acquire it "as is," offering to take the stock, with all the liabilities. Gerber's shareholders received nothing, other than knowing the family company would stay alive and employees would have a job for as long as possible. The family would get future compensation if the liabilities turned out to be less than anticipated.

Globe Union had its turnaround plan laid out before they even closed the deal. It included changes in strategy, operations, and finance. Strategic changes would include development of new products, cost competitiveness, and "customer delight." New products were essential and that project started right away. Cost competitiveness meant off-shoring some production, since prices had dropped enough compared to costs that for some basic toilets, it was like taping a $20 bill to each one.

With Mexican labor at 10 percent of Gerber's union costs and Chinese at 3 percent, the U.S. plants had to eventually close. Brand loyalty stopped after a contractor had to spend more than a few extra dollars. Michael decided that the Kokomo, Indiana, facility would stay open as long as possible. He personally delivered the bad news to the other plants, beginning the town hall meetings by asking who purchased clothes and other products from Wal-Mart or similar stores. They soon realized how many of their purchases were made overseas. It took four years to transition everything to a Chinese manufacturer they bought, with the help of then current Gerber employees. To keep "Made in America" on some of their products, particularly those going to unionized plumbers, Gerber opened a facility just on the U.S. side of the Mexican border, where there was some wage competition for the U.S.-based employees.

As far as finances were concerned, the new owners used thirteen-week and twenty-six-week rolling cash flow forecasts to manage the company. They also changed lenders. Running a lean organization meant management pitching in whenever needed to save costs and keep expenses down.

Customer delight took longer than expected. It turns out that due diligence efforts missed an important issue: Gerber's quality had plummeted. By putting in strict production controls at the old and new plants and benchmarking against best-in-class, quality problems abated. In fact, the August 2009 issue of *Consumer Reports* listed four Gerber products among the Top 10 Performing Toilets for quality.

Despite the recent housing downturn and recession in 2009, Gerber achieved the best performance in the company's seventy-seven-year history. Their motto of "strength first, then growth" is paying off. Gerber was a smart acquisition because of the implementation of a good turnaround plan.

Small Deals Work Too

Investing in smaller transactions equates in most peoples' minds with entrepreneurship, yet investing in any-sized troubled company is a true form of entrepreneurship, as discussed in the Introduction. Several friends recently invested in a struggling small company with less than $100,000 in sales. The stockholder and inventor of the electrical product needed capital to grow. He received 35 percent of the company in return for all the new cash going into working capital. Not too long into the venture, we realized that a very large company had probably violated our patent. When letters to cease and desist were ignored, our attorneys informed us that a patent fight would cost over $1 million, about ten times our working capital. We stayed entrepreneurial in every way, taking advantage of a huge annual trade show coming up in a month. Like many shows in a variety of industries, the first night of the show is not open to the public; it is the night when the company executives are there and the press is invited.

For only one thousand dollars, we had a patent attorney draw up a lawsuit against the big company for the patent infringement. We hired a deputy sheriff, paying the $100 statutory fee, to serve the lawsuit during the opening night festivities. The deputy was the size of a pro linebacker, wearing aviator style sunglasses. He walked briskly into the conference center, one hand holding the document, the other resting on the grip of his holstered forty-five. The startled security people got out of his way, following him on his mission. Soon the press followed as well. The deputy went right to the CEO of the infringing company and served him the lawsuit in full view of the growing audience. A press release was handed out by a volunteer at the program, detailing how the big company had infringed on the patent of the little company that invented the product. By the next morning, the embarrassed CEO called and agreed to stop the infringement.

Although this bought us time (as well as grudging respect in the industry), it still left us to accomplish the turnaround. We're still working on it, and have made some progress. Our lesson here was that we became too enamored with the energy-saving feature of the invention, which can be a hard sell during a slow economy. It's too soon to report any success, as we still have to compete with inventions from better capitalized competitors who know how to invent without stepping on your patent. Sales have been modest and we will probably be happy if we score a double, rather than a home run.

The Other Side of the Table

It is important to understand the pressures that may occur for sellers. In the Atari deal mentioned earlier, the directors of Atari were between a rock and a hard place. Infogrames, the French parent of the venerable but troubled video game publisher, was proposing to buy out minority shareholders for $1.68 per share.[8] It was a tough proposition for Atari's directors, who had joined the company only five months earlier when the company went through a refinancing. The offer from Infogrames did not reflect a premium over the trading price, and disgruntled minority share-holders were threatening lawsuits.

Atari had few realistic options. The company had been losing money and depended on financing from a London hedge fund to stay afloat. Atari's outside accountant had questioned the company's ability to continue as a going concern. Could Atari find a new backer? Without additional financing, it would be required to liquidate or seek Chapter 11 protection, which would most likely offer no recovery for shareholders of a company with a storied history.

Moments of Glory, Years of Trouble

Atari was founded in California by computer enthusiast Nolan Bushnell, a fan of midway arcade games and a product of the San

Francisco counterculture. He developed the sensation Pong, a two-dimensional game of table tennis. The game was a huge hit, paving the way for Atari's 1976 acquisition by Warner Communications for $28 million. Bushnell, who was said to be a terrific innovator and salesman but a weak manager, was frequently at odds with Warner managers and was fired in December 1978. He went on to start the Chuck E. Cheese pizza chain.

Atari reached a commanding market share of 80 percent of the video game industry. Its cash flow represented a third of Warner's income that year with sales of $2 billion. The growth was chaotic, however. Bushnell's successor, Ray Kassar, was quoted as saying he had "no idea how many buildings I have or people working for me."

In the faddish and volatile game industry, Atari's 1981 sales had fallen by half as a result of increased competition and high inventories. Market share dropped to 66 percent in 1982 and to 40 percent in 1984. The company was crashing, and Warner managers decided to cut their losses, selling the high-profile consumer division to Jack Tramiel, the founder of the early computer company Commodore. It was a rocky decade under Tramiel, who emphasized computers rather than game consoles. Manufacturers of computers with their own operating systems were falling victim to Microsoft's success. Competition from Nintendo, Sega, and Sony led to multiple sales of the company to different owners, including sale of the Atari name and assets to Hasbro Interactive for $5 million in 1998. By that time, the company's market share had dwindled to less than 2 percent.

A Fresh Start?

Atari seemingly got a fresh start in 2000, when Infogrames acquired the rights to the Atari name. They aimed to reinvent the Atari brand with new games. Infogrames grouped its U.S. operations under the Atari name and also used the moniker for its European operations. The parent's ownership share was eventually reduced to 51.6 percent by September 2005 through a public offering, creating a complicated two-tier ownership structure that would bedevil both companies. But neither side proved capable of generating hits, and this, combined with delays and operating difficulties, led to declines in sales and operating income.

By 2005 the Atari board was forced to cut back on game development and sell assets to its parent, including the rights to the Atari trademark license. Atari was soon reduced to a mere game distributor.

Running out of cash in 2006, Atari secured a credit facility through Guggenheim Corporate Funding. It started with a revolving credit line of up to $15 million, but it soon found itself in violation of the loan covenants. Guggenheim issued waivers but reduced the loan availability to $3 million.

Infogrames had its own problems and in 2006 obtained financing from London hedge fund BlueBay Asset Management, which the following year became Infograme's largest shareholder with a 31.5 percent stake (convertible with the exercise of warrants and bonds to 54.9 percent). BlueBay soon was appalled at how poorly the French company and Atari were run.

That September, Atari's auditor Deloitte & Touche had expressed doubt that Atari could continue as a going concern. Losses were running at $25 million per year while sales plummeted to $79.2 million. Infogrames was losing even more money. Soon the NASDAQ threatened to delist Atari because its $15 million capitalization was too small.

BlueBay sprung into action. It brought in Curtis Solsvig of Alix Partners to take the reins as chief restructuring officer. It removed five Atari directors and appointed four independent replacements. It accepted the CEO's resignation. It desperately needed funds— the company had not yet started production of its holiday titles. BlueBay acquired the $3 million Guggenheim loan at par and boosted the credit facility first to $10 million, then to $14 million.

In return, Atari renegotiated the licensing agreements under which Infogrames had Atari market its games in the United States, and the royalties were small. It was reduced to a distribution subsidiary with no capital to invest in its own business. Atari also launched another round of layoffs, reducing the headcount at the New York headquarters by about 40 percent, to about seventy-two staff members.

The Takeover

BlueBay decided they needed to take complete control and to eliminate the two-layer managements. It made its move five months later with a March 5 letter to the Atari board offering $1.68 per share for all the minority shares. Evaluating the proposal fell to a special committee made up of the new independent directors. The committee swung into action. It hired Duff & Phelps as its investment advisor to deliver a fairness opinion, as well as the New York law firm of Milbank, Tweed, Hadley & McCloy LLP. Uppermost in the members' minds was adhering to good corporate governance principles. (See Box 11.) The independent directors wanted to make sure they fairly represented the interests of the minority shareholders and explored all avenues. They also did not want to leave the company vulnerable to lawsuits.

The alternative, of course, was to find new outside financing or a white knight. That was unlikely, Duff analysts told the special

---

Box 11: Fiduciary Duties of Directors in M&A Transactions

Duty of Care

Act in good faith, in an informed manner, and with the same degree of care that a reasonably prudent person would use.

Duty of Loyalty

Act in good faith and in the best interests of the company and its stockholders. Directors affiliated with a particular group of stockholders owe their fiduciary duties to all stockholders. They must be disinterested, independent, and consider potential conflicts of interest.

Good Faith and Candor

Disclose fully and fairly all information material to the decision.

Standards of Judicial Review: Business Judgment Rule

If challenged, a court presumes the directors of a corporation acted on an informed basis, in good faith, and in the honest belief that the action taken was in the best interests. A court will not substitute its own business judgment for that of informed, disinterested directors.

Standards of Judicial Review: Sale of Control

Directors are required to act reasonably to maximize stockholder value, i.e., to obtain the transaction most favorable to the stockholders that is reasonably available in the short term.

Standard of Review in Going Private Transactions: Merger

A merger with a controlling stockholder is always subject to the entire fairness standard of review. Here, there is potential for exploitation by a powerful controlling stockholder that has more information at its disposal. But the burden is on the plaintiff to show the transaction was unfair if the transaction was negotiated and approved by a special committee and subject to the majority of the minority of disinterested shares.

Standard of Review in Going Private Transactions: Tender Offer

A tender offer is subject to the business judgment rule instead of the entire fairness standard because only stockholder action is required; no target board approval is necessary.

Special Committee Duties in Going Private Transactions

In a merger, actions will be evaluated using the entire fairness standard. The special committee should be insulated from undue influence by the controlling shareholder, be able to select its own legal and financial advisors, have the authority to reject offers and negotiate higher prices, and have access to all relevant information concerning the company and the risks to the controlling stockholder. In a tender offer, a special committee must hire its own advisors, provide a recommendation to minority stockholders, disclose adequate information for minority stockholders to make an informed judgment, and pursue the best interests of the minority stockholders.

Presentation from Milbank, Tweed, Hadley & McCloy LLP

committee early in the process. Who would buy a minority piece of a troubled company controlled by another troubled firm?

The conversation quickly shifted to the share price. The $1.68 offer did not even represent a premium on the stock price, but in the end, Infogrames and BlueBay delivered the bad news through their advisor, Lazard: "Not a penny more." Lazard pointed out that it did provide a premium to Atari's trading price that existed five days and thirty days prior to the announcement, and BlueBay said, "We could have let it go into bankruptcy and perhaps bid on the assets as a creditor, but there was risk in that."

Back in the United States, the Atari directors knew BlueBay was the only source of funding and all the assets were pledged to them. If the offer were withdrawn, the alternative was bankruptcy, so $1.68 to the shareholders was better than nothing, which the advisors said they'd get in a bankruptcy. They were in a pincer and there was still the question of funding. Would BlueBay fund Atari's operating losses and working capital needs through the closing of the deal? The special committee also asked to change the no-shop provision so that the board had the ability to change its recommendation if a white knight appeared at the eleventh hour since the offer was now made public. Committee members also wanted to eliminate the termination fee if Atari backed out of the deal.

For the next several weeks, the two sides exchanged drafts of the purchase agreement and other terms. BlueBay and Infogrames agreed to extend a loan of up to $20 million to cover capital needs and limit Atari's obligations under the preclosing covenants. In the end, Atari directors retained the right to consider and recommend a superior proposal, although that turned out to be an academic point. It also reduced the termination fee from 15 percent to 5 percent of the purchase price.

Duff & Phelps was analyzing the terms of the deal for fairness and delivered its final results to the board on April 28. First, it reviewed historic performance and projections provided by Atari's management for the fiscal year that would end March 31, 2009. Duff analyzed Atari's closing price and trading volume during the prior twelve months. During the year, the stock had traded above and below the offering price, with a weighted share price of $1.45. During the period between Atari's most recent quarterly report on February 13 and April 22, the volume-weighted share price was $1.55. Duff also calculated the enterprise value for a small group of packaged media distributors and analyzed the outcome for shareholders if the company filed for Chapter 11.

While members of the special committee agreed that the price was fair, especially in light of the grim alternative, they faced threats on two fronts. First, on April 18, attorneys representing one shareholder sued, charging that Atari directors breached their fiduciary duties to shareholders by agreeing to an unfairly low price. The suit pointed out that the $1.68 represented no premium over the close on the day of the offer and that in light of Infogrames's 51.6 percent ownership, minority shareholders had no voice in deciding whether to accept the deal. Meanwhile, a letter came from a hedge fund which claimed to own 9.4 percent of Atari shares, charged that wrongdoing by Infogrames managers had depressed the value of Atari shares. The fund demanded that Atari directors start an action against the French parent to recover $72 million that had been "misappropriated."

In the end, Atari settled the first shareholder lawsuit by making additional disclosures in their proxy statement describing the sale process. As for the hedge fund's charges, the company appointed a special committee to look into the allegations, but found the case to be "entirely without merit," according to the proxy. The threat was dropped.

The final months leading up to the October 8 shareholders meeting dealt with procedural issues—drafting of the proxy and answering questions from the Securities and Exchange Commission (SEC). According to one committee member, "There were a lot of steps but we had to make it as bullet-proof as possible."

In the end, the acquisition of Atari turned out to be a major hassle—a complex process involving six sets of lawyers for a share buyback that cost only $15 million.

Things were looking up on the operations side as the board had recently hired a new CEO, Jim Wilson, who started on March 31. He had experience in digital media, games, and home entertainment businesses. He reduced the staff once again by more than twenty employees and cut other expenses associated with being a public company.

He reduced shipments of a game Infogrames had developed in Europe, *Alone in the Dark*, by 50 percent. The Europeans had high hopes but the Americans were skeptical, and it received low review scores in testing. Wilson decided to focus on successful games in the Atari catalog, such as *Dragon Ball Z*, *Test Drive*, and *RollerCoaster Tycoon*.

Once the tender offer closed, Atari returned to developing games. The parent company sold its European distribution business and dropped the Infogrames name. The combined company narrowed its losses to $27 million for the fiscal year ending March 31, 2010, on sales of $163 million versus a loss of over $300 million for the prior fiscal year. They expect to be at or above breakeven this year. Atari shares are traded on the Euronext Paris exchange.

The saga of Atari offered a nostalgic piece of Americana. As a board member said, "When I told people I was on the Atari board, everyone knew the brand name and there was always a smile." That nostalgia for the brand has led the company to a successful licensing of its original logo to a variety of items, including bags, hoodies, and even wallpaper.[9] Old games like *Asteroids* are being sold as movie plots. Digitally distributed games cost substantially less to produce, such as online games, played on social networks such as Facebook. Headquarters, previously split between New York and Paris, was combined in Los Angeles, near gaming talent. They even brought the founder, Nolan Bushnell, back on the board after a thirty-two-year absence.

Exiting

Upon successfully executing a turnaround and returning a company to health, the professional buyer will usually begin to contemplate an exit strategy. Three main opportunities exist: an IPO, a recapitalization, or a sale. IPOs, obviously, will only be available to larger companies, because the costs of being public are so prohibitive. Recapitalizations were a very popular method of increasing return for private equity firms during the credit boom, as they could simply pay off a company's debt (and hopefully increase its profitability) and then relever the company, taking the proceeds of the debt issuance as a special dividend to equity holders. So-called "dividend recaps" allowed PE firms to maintain their ownership of a company while taking a lot of money off the table and increasing their internal rate of return, which, as a time-weighted measure of profitability, benefits greatly from earlier returns of capital. However, the excesses of the 2002–2007 credit boom have left many lenders appropriately reluctant about extending debt financing for the purposes of a dividend recap, given how aggressively the concept was abused by some PE firms during the boom. (One lender tells a story, all too familiar to his peers, about an equity sponsor who paid off the debt of a portfolio company and took the maximum agreed-upon dividend recap of seven times EBITDA of $20 million for $140 million, then just one quarter later, when EBITDA had increased to $21 million, came back demanding another $7 million in debt financing to juice its IRR.) Although recapitalizations will be available to healthy companies, the "once bitten, twice shy" mentality of most lenders post credit-crunch will make them less realistic for companies whose past distress may make lenders gun-shy.

That leaves a sale of the company as the most realistic exit option. Stacks of books have been written on the mergers and acquisition process, so I need not go into excessive detail here about what it takes to sell a healthy company. However, the buyer of a distressed company will face one additional hurdle in attempting to exit after executing a turnaround. The very fact that the company was once distressed will deter many buyers, simply because it suggests the company is not infallible, is not recession-proof, is not operating in an industry with such attractive economics that it cannot encounter difficulties. To most rational human beings, it should be obvious that every company in the world fits that description, but many private equity buyers are under pressure from their investors to identify companies that cannot possibly miss. Taking that into account, a buyer of a distressed company must therefore provide a credible explanation as to why the company's past distress will not recur in the future. The causes of distress identified in the assessment process will help here, as it is far easier to convince a potential buyer that internal causes (now addressed by the turnaround) led to distress, rather than external causes that could arise again.

In addressing these concerns, buyers will often look to the holding period to determine the seriousness of the risk of repeated distress. An investor who has bought a distressed company and is attempting to sell it just twelve months later will find buyers a great deal more hesitant than one who bought a company four years ago and has seen three steady years of profitability. This can naturally extend holding periods for distressed investors, which compresses IRRs, but one hopes that the depressed purchase price at acquisition more than compensates for that irregularity. Sale to a strategic buyer usually yields the highest sale price.

Chapter Ten

A Different Fresh Start

To many executives, consultants, lawyers, and reporters, the turn-around and bankruptcy world is one more suited for Harry Potter: it has changed over the centuries, often in mysterious ways, and seems the exclusive province of wizards. John Pierpont Morgan Sr. took over bankrupt railroads and combined them to become one of the wealthiest men in the world. His legacy, J.P. Morgan Chase, has recently acquired large pieces of bankrupt companies, albeit unintentionally; they extended loans that went sour, and had to exchange their debt for equity.

If the turnaround is enacted in a timely manner, the bankruptcy policy of a fresh start can be avoided for a less jarring approach to a fresh start. The successful turnaround can then be indicated by a number of factors, such as

- Increasing, positive true cash flow for more than two quarters
- A cash flow forecast that shows a year of positive results coming
- The ability to service debt and make capital expenditures for the foreseeable future
- Gross margins improving
- Six-sigma performance metrics in quality, on-time delivery, and so forth
- Internal issues under control
- An internal culture that encourages and celebrates new ideas
- Managing to cash and reporting in GAAP

Even the pros aren't always perfect in their projections. During the 2006–2008 timeframe, the turnaround industry—made up of tens of thousands of turnaround professionals, investment

bankers, bankruptcy and restructuring lawyers, liquidation professionals, and auctioneers—were convinced that their ship was
about to come in, laden with gold, jewels, Gulfstream jets, and a
nubile crew. Their logic was reasonable; given the amplitude of
the highs we saw in an overheated economy, the amount of money
being shoveled at companies to increase their debt, and the multiples of earnings paid by the ravenous feeding of deal junkies,
the system was on too much adrenaline and had to crash. Couple
this with the massive bonuses paid out that encouraged the closing
of deals that made no economic sense, and everyone thought the
"great unwinding" would bring years of $1,000 an hour work for
them. (Yes, the top players in this field do charge that much.)
Thus, both the big turnaround and other consulting firms logi-
cally added to their payrolls, picking up multiple professionals
and staff to support them.

The trouble is, logic did not prevail. Those firms discovered
that all the expected restructurings through bankruptcies didn't
happen nearly as quickly as they anticipated. Part of it was the
severity of the credit crunch, which dried up DIP and exit financing, forcing companies such as Circuit City, Linens 'n Things, and
many others to liquidate and preventing the more lucrative reorganization work. Another element was the behavior of the lenders,
normally a huge source of work by forcing customers with broken
covenants to hire turnaround professionals. So deluged were such
lenders with defaulted loans, however, that instead of forcing
their borrowers to hire experts, they changed the due dates on
the payments. This became known as the "amend, extend,
and pretend" strategy, which simply pushes the problems out to
a later date.

That delay helps very few people if the underlying problems
are not fixed. It is true that sometimes an entire industry seems
to be stuck in the blinded-through-faulty-action phases for many
years, until finally they hit crisis and bankruptcy; newspapers are
the current poster children. I was asked to take the entire day of
the bi-annual summit of the heads of the fifty largest U.S. newspapers at the American Press Institute in Washington, D.C., and
discuss how best to fix newspapers. I introduced various ideas
at the summit, many of which are outlined in this book.
Unfortunately, not everyone will listen; despite overwhelming

evidence to the contrary, some still believed advertisers and sub-scribers would come back in full when the recession ends. They need to focus, however, on content people want to pay for. There are many ideas on how to fix newspapers. For example, readers should go to Newspaper Next 2.0 at www.newspapernext.org. As stated earlier, their core competency is really as a trusted infome-diary. They saw the Internet as an enemy rather than a new pipe-line for too many years before they woke up. All that time, it should have been *newspapers* that created Craigslist, Angieslist, and all the other alternatives that have eroded their revenue streams. Instead, far too many fired reporters and replaced them with more color pictures, which seemed to dumb down the product into a coloring book.

The press release from the API Summit covering my presenta-tion hit home to one additional newspaper fan, an author of erotic novels. She wrote about my thoughts on the subject on her blog as a way to support keeping newspapers alive. It caused me a bit of ribbing from friends, however, when it got picked up by the university PR Internet crawler. She quoted me and listed my affiliation with the university . . . right alongside advertisements for her books, which featured pictures and language far steamier than anything I use in working with distressed companies.

Comedy Central's *The Daily Show* had a great routine one evening wherein one of their reporters, Jason Jones, interviewed various editors at the *New York Times*.[1]

Jones: So why is aged news better than news?
Editor: No, we do publish news.
Jones: But it's yesterday's news.

The editor then admitted that some of the paper's more in-depth stories covered events even older than twenty-four hours versus the Internet's rapid updates. The interview ended with what seemed to be a joke:

Jones: OK, what's black and white and red all over?
Editor: That's a very old joke. It's a newspaper that's read all over.
Jones: No, that's your financial statements.

At my annual conference at Kellogg on Turnarounds and Corporate Renewal, we created a panel on turnarounds at newspapers. I put two "lifers" from the newspaper industry on it, Andy Davis, president of the American Press Institute (previously president of several newspapers), and Steve Gray, managing director of Newspaper Next (previously publisher of the *Christian Science Monitor*). Two others were professional bloggers, Rachel Sklar of Adams Research and Glynnis MacNicol of mediabistro.com's FishbowlNY (both formerly of the Huffington Post). The bloggers made it clear they thought newspapers had long served their purpose and should die a gracious death. The newspapermen wanted to know where the bloggers would steal their verified news from. Carlyn Taylor—the turnaround professional from FTI on the panel—had her own ideas, which mirrored mine. The standing-room-only crowd made it clear they could have listened to the debate rage for quite a while.

In the movie *State of Play*, Russell Crowe plays the obligatory grizzled newspaper reporter who shows the young blogger how to really do investigative work to uncover a story of corruption. While I enjoyed it, I listened to the crowd at the end. During the credits, footage of a newspaper plant was shown from the setting of type to the press run to bundling into trucks. I was amazed how many people of different ages said, "So that's how newspapers are made." Others said, "Maybe we still need investigative reporters."

We still don't know how many newspapers will survive in the future. The speed of change can catch any industry off guard, such as Bear Stearns and Lehman Brothers disappearing overnight and Facebook taking two years to reach a 50 million audience, a milestone it took television thirteen to reach.[2] That speed of technological, social, and economic change seems to accelerate every year, and clearly had reached a velocity great enough to bring even giants like the *New York Times* to seek emergency financing from the richest man in Mexico. If nothing else, it means that there will always be turnaround work, but it also means that healthy companies must remain even more vigilant—or in the more emphatic words of Intel's Andy Grove, *paranoid*—than they did in years past. As Grove pointed out, the day-to-day operations of a company can get in the way of thorough market environment analysis and its effect on the firm's priorities, thus masking the imminent, unforeseen technological change or commercial event that makes established products or processes obsolete. Such changes, he said, paraphrasing Carl Sandburg, "creep in on cat's feet"; that cat crept right past America's newspapermen.[3] Do not let it creep past you and your company.

Be careful whom you turn to for help. There are many consultants and advisors who purport to handle turnarounds. Too often, what they really give you is known as a WAGNER, a wild-ass guess not easily refutable. There are others who should not be giving advice so specific as that needed in a turnaround. As the oft heard phrase implies, anyone can wear a Speedo, but not everyone should wear one. Check the credentials of the actual people doing the work, not the reputation of the firm.

If your small company needs help, several chapters of the Turnaround Management Association have volunteers; go to www.turnaround.org to find the international chapter near you. Other sources of help include the volunteers at the Service Corps of Retired Executives (SCORE) who can help over the Internet or in person at www.score.org, the U.S. Small Business Association at www.sba.gov, and legal clinics at most law schools.

For do-it-yourself types, just follow the advice in this book. Determine the stage your company is in by using the external and internal warning signs, as well as trend analysis, benchmarking, Z-score, and whether your ROA is greater than your cost of capital. Even if you think you are doing very well, every executive should examine those factors periodically for their organization, as well as for their key suppliers and customers to see if they may have problems that will explode onto you.

No matter what stage they are in, all organizations need to periodically examine their strategy, whether they are for-profit, nonprofit, government, or U.S. or foreign entities. Core competencies should be determined and built upon or acquired. With this information, and what you learn from talking to customers about their plans, you can arrive at a new strategy for now and the intermediate future. Once those are determined, occasional reengineering will tell you how best to operate the group and figure out the people you'll need now, as well as for the future. Empowering your employees and understanding your fiduciary duties will help your management efforts. Finally, always remember that even if you have to report in GAAP or IAS to stakeholders, you should manage on a true cash basis.

If you have ever swum in Lake Michigan or some other body of cold water, you know what it's like to jump into a turnaround. You take a sudden deep breath to get your courage up, and then plunge in. You might enjoy it once you get used to it. Turnarounds are much more addictive, and you just might enjoy the fresh start. You'll never be bored.

Notes

Introduction

1. Miller, Steve, *The Turnaround Kid: What I Learned Rescuing America's Most Troubled Companies* (New York: HarperBusiness), 2008.
2. It is interesting to note that this trait sometimes shows itself as quiet confidence, as discussed in Chapter Four, but the ability to convince others and the willingness to change are critical.
3. Gonzalez, Gonzalo X., Ho, Darren, Jaegemann, Oliver, Hennegan, John, Juncker, David. *Saks Incorporated Turnaround.* May 18, 2009.
4. Asiyanbi, Susan, Byrro, Leonardo, James, Daniel, Johnston, Zachary, Schwartz, Tracy, Stott, David. *Imperial Sugar Turnaround.* May 18, 2009.
5. http://money.cnn.com/2004/05/07/news/midcaps/krispy_kreme/. Note that this often serves as a way for management to blame someone other than themselves, as discussed in Chapter One.
6. http://www.dothaneagle.com/dea/news/local/article/fuel_feed_prices_spike_for_dairy_livestock_producers/20817/
7. http://www.allbusiness.com/legal/labor-employment-law-wage-hours/5156476–1.html
8. 10-K Reports: Conagra May 27, 2007; General Mills May 27, 2007; Kraft December 31, 2007; Campbell Soup July 29, 2007; P&G June 30, 2007; Sara Lee June 30, 2007; Unilever December 31, 2007.
9. Shein, James B., "Sara Lee: Tale of Another Turnaround," Kellogg School of Management Case, Evanston, Ill. (March 2008).
10. Singh, Sudhir, "Toxic Convertibles: Catalysts of Doom or Financing of Last Resort?" *SAM Advanced Management Journal, Winter* 2005.
11. Thomas, C. William, "The Rise and Fall of Enron," *Journal of Accountancy, April* 2002.

Chapter One

1. Weitzel, W., and Jonsson, E., "Decline in Organizations: A Literature Integration and Extension," *Administrative Science Quarterly*, Vol. *34*, 1989.

2. Crown, Judith, and Coleman, Glenn, "The Fall of Schwinn," *Crain's Chicago Business*, October 11, 1993.

3. Austin, Robert, and Nolan, Richard, "IBM Corporation Turnaround," HBS Case No. 9–600–098, November 14, 2000.

4. Sara Lee 10-K Reports dated July 3, 2004, July 2, 2005, July 1, 2006, June 30, 2007.

5. Porter, M. E., "How Competitive Forces Shape Strategy," *Harvard Business Review, March/April* 1979.

6. Cole-Gomolski, Barb, "Client/Server Outsources Changing Pricing Methods," *Computerworld*, June 28, 1999.

7. Shein, James B., Teaching note: "A Tale of Two Turnarounds at EDS: The Jordan Rules," Kellogg School of Management Case, Evanston, Ill. (February 2010).

8. Lee, D., Ho Lee, M., Mahon, E., Matsuda, K., Meagher, E., and Miller, J., "Electronic Data Systems Corp. Turnaround," 2008.

9. Halkias, Maria, "Pension Fund Criticizes EDS, Michaels," *Dallas Morning News*, February 25, 1998.

10. Halkias, "Pension Fund Criticizes EDS, Michaels."

11. Salomon Smith Barney Equity Research, "EDS: Let the Transformation Begin!" May 19, 1999.

12. "EDS Swabs the Decks of NMCI Mess," *eWeek*, January 22, 2006.

13. "Morale: Marines 0, Geeks 1," *StrategyPage*, December 21, 2006, http://www.strategypage.com/htmw/htmoral/articles/20061221 .aspx (accessed February 8, 2009).

14. UBS Warburg Equity Research, "Electronic Data Systems: Texas Medicaid Contract Creates More Controversy," July 17, 2002.

15. Palmer, Jay, "Powering Up at EDS," *Barron's*, October 31, 2005.

16. Palmer, "Powering Up at EDS."

Chapter Two

1. http://www.theonion.com/articles/even-ceo-cant-figure-out-how -radioshack-still-in-b,2190/

2. http://www.usatoday.com/money/industries/retail/2006–02–20 -radioshack-ceo_x.htm

3. Van Jarwaarde, E., Turner, G., Virachanang, V., Wuellner, T., Zhang, Y., "RadioShack Turnaround: Restructuring for the Future," 2010.

4. In *The Core Competence of the Corporation*, C. K. Prahalad and Gary Hamel coined the term "core competencies," defining them as "the company's collective knowledge about how to coordinate diverse production skills and technologies," and made the now widely accepted assertion that a firm's idiosyncratic core competencies are the source of its competitive advantage.

5. Baron, Lloyd, Blitz, Kevin, Bloomfield, Matthew, Brosowski, Julie, Byrd, Monica, Carter, Jamail. "Harley-Davidson—In Need of Some Gas," undated.

6. Clifton, Rita, Simmons, John, and Ahmad, Sameena, *Brands and Branding: The Economist Series* (2nd ed.) (New York: Bloomberg Press), 2004, p. 106.

7. "Motorcycle Maker Harley Calls for End to Import Restraints," The Associated Press, March 17, 1987.

8. "Back from the Brink and Ready to Rumble," *Roanoke Times & World News*, June 12, 1993.

9. Sawhney, Mohanbir, Wolcott, Robert C., and Arroniz, Inigo, "The 12 Different Ways for Companies to Innovate," *MIT Sloan Management Review*, April 1, 2006.

10. Bryan, Lowell, "Just-in-time Strategy for a Turbulent World." McKinsey & Company, June 2002.

11. Chidester, Thomas, Christen, Alexander, Coles, John, Davidson, Aaron, Drew, Michael, Fitzgerald, Kevin. "Krispy Kreme's Turnaround," August 10, 2009.

12. Thomas, Oliver, *The Real Coke, The Real Story* (New York: Penguin, 1986).

13. "Wang to Describe Its New Focus," *CommunicationsWeek*, October 18, 1993.

14. "IT Metrics: IT Spending and Staffing Report," 2010, *Gartner*, January 22, 2010.

15. http://www.nytimes.com/2008/05/18/magazine/18rebranding-t.html

16. Moody's Investors Service, press release, "Moody's Lowered Ratings on Solo Cup Company One Notch and Changed Outlook to Negative," October 5, 2005.

17. Phone interview with David Garfield, February 27, 2010.

18. "Solo Cup Divests Japan Manufacturing Assets; Company Further Reduces Debt," *Business Wire*, October 25, 2007.

19. Phone interview with David Garfield, February 27, 2010.

20. Garfield, phone interview.

21. "Solo Cup Reduces Debt by More than $325 Million Year-to-Date; Company Closes Transactions and Announces Plans to Consolidate Certain Operations," *Business Wire*, October 16, 2007.

22. http://news.medill.northwestern.edu/chicago/news.aspx?id=65795&print=1, May 15, 2010.

23. "Solo Cup Divests Japan Manufacturing Assets: Company Further Reduces Debt," *Business Wire*, October 25, 2007.

24. "Solo Cup Divests Japan Manufacturing Assets."

25. Garfield, phone interview.
26. Robert Korzenski presentation at Kellogg School of Management Turnaround Conference, April 3, 2009.
27. David Garfield presentation at Kellogg School of Management Turnaround Conference, April 3, 2009.
28. Robert Korzenski presentation at Kellogg School of Management Turnaround Conference, April 3, 2009.

Chapter Three

1. Miller, Steve, *The Turnaround Kid* (New York: HarperCollins), 2008, p. 144.
2. "IBM Corporation Turnaround," HBS Case #9–600–098.
3. Dunlap, Albert J., with Andelman, Bob, *Mean Business: How I Save Bad Companies and Make Good Companies Great* (New York: Simon & Schuster), 1996, pp. 196–198.
4. "The Shredder: Did CEO Dunlap Save Scott Paper, or Just Pretty It Up?" *Business Week*, January 15, 1996.
5. http://www.portfolio.com/executives/2009/04/22/Al-Dunlap-Profile
6. Smith v. Van Gorkom, 488 A.2d 858 (Supreme Court of Delaware, 1985).
7. Shein, James B., "Trying to Match SOX: Dealing with New Challenges and Risks Facing Directors," *The Journal of Private Equity. Spring* 2005, 20–27.
8. "Directors' Duties in the Zone of Insolvency," Foley & Lardner LLP, 2007.
9. "The Fall of Schwinn, Part II," *Crain's Chicago Business*, October 4, 1993.
10. "The Fall of Schwinn, Part II," *Crain's Chicago Business*, October 4, 1993.
11. Wong, Anita, Ward, Justin, Surakanti, Jayanth, Wahi, Kartik, Zier, Martin, Tyler, Tiffany. "Analysis of the Turnaround of J. Crew," May 18, 2009.
12. Mueller, John M., "How to Create a Businesslike Family Business," *The Journal of Corporate Renewal*, January 1, 1997.
13. http://www.newsweek.com/1997/07/27/a-death-spiral.html
14. Shein, James B., "Out of the Frying Pan: Middleby Corporation," Kellogg School of Management Case, Evanston, Ill. (March 2009).

Chapter Four

1. Special thanks to Alan T. Handley, CPA, CIRA, for the insights into the 13-Week Cash Flow Model that he has passed on to my students

at the Kellogg School of Management, and for his permission to use a past client engagement (disguised as "Wolverine Tooling") for the purposes of illustrating the model's intricacies. Readers interested in a more hands-on experience with the 13WCFM can visit this book's Web site at www.reversingtheslide.com and download a fully flow-through Microsoft Excel spreadsheet version of this model.

2. "Do Other Firms Use Lehman's Accounting 'Dirug'?" *Market Watch*, March 12, 2010.
3. http://en.wikipedia.org/wiki/Gaap
4. http://www.fundinguniverse.com/company-histories/Itel
5. http://www.fundinguniverse.com/company-histories/Itel
6. Alan Handley presentation, April 20, 2009.

Chapter Five

1. Grover, V., and Malhotra, M. K., "Business Pieces Reengineering," *Journal of Operations Management*, 1997, *15*, 193–213.
2. Adam Smith's famous example from *The Wealth of Nations*.
3. "Reengineering Your Company," *Nation's Business*, February 1, 1994. See also Hammer, Michael, and Campy, James, *Reengineering the Corporation: A Manifesto for Business Revolution* (New York: HarperCollins), 2001.
4. "The '90s Imperative," *Computer System News*, December 11, 1989.
5. "The Cat That Came Back," *Booz Allen Hamilton Resilience Report*, August 17, 2005.
6. Kaplan, R. S., *Pillsbury: Customer Driven Reengineering*, Harvard Business School, April 26, 1995.
7. Kaplan, R. S., *Pillsbury: Customer Driven Reengineering*.
8. "Quality Isn't Just for Widgets," *Business Week*, July 22, 2002, *20*(2), 72.
9. "Quality Isn't Just for Widgets."
10. Jarman, M. "Companies Often Lose in Downsizing," *The Arizona Republic*, January 31, 1998.
11. "WARNing: Shareholders May Be Liable for Violating Act," *Journal of Corporate Renewal*, August 1, 2004.
12. "When the Laid Off Are Better Off," *Business Week*, November 2, 2009, 65.
13. "When the Laid Off Are Better Off," *Business Week*.
14. "Where Layoffs Are a Last Resort," *Business Week*, October 8, 2001.
15. "A New Calling: France Telecom Helps Employees Set Up Shop to Offset Rising Costs," *The Wall Street Journal Europe*, August 14, 2006.
16. "France Télécom Executive Resigns on Suicide Issue," *The Wall Street Journal*, October 6, 2009.

17. "A Head with a Heart," *Boston Globe*, March 12, 2009.
18. Rovzar, L., Schwieterman, L., Seifert, E., Shah, A., Shockley, R., Singh, R., "Greyhound Lines: A Bumpy Ride," 2008.
19. "Preserving Employee Morale During Downsizing," *MIT Sloan Management Review*, Winter 1998, *39*(2).
20. "RadioShack Uses E-mail to Lay Off Employees," Associated Press Newswires, August 30, 2006.
21. "Preserving Employee Morale During Downsizing," *MIT Sloan Management Review*.
22. "In Crisis, French Resort to 'Bossnappings,'" *International Herald Tribune*, April 3, 2009.
23. "At France Télécom, Battle to Cut Jobs Breeds Off Tactics," *The Wall Street Journal*, August 14, 2006, A1.
24. Nasseh, Nooshin, Manchon, Daniel, Martinez, Steve, Maya, Juan, Muehl, Alexandra. "Xerox: The Improbable Turnaround," 2009.
25. "Ready to Copy?" *Barron's*, May 29, 2000.
26. "Xerox Seeks to Survive on Tuna Sandwiches, Shared Cubicles, Layoffs," *The Wall Street Journal*, December 20, 2000.

Chapter Six

1. The U.S. Bankruptcy Code has more than 400 pages and hundreds of thousands of court decisions interpreting the law. This, along with the hundreds of Federal Rules of Bankruptcy Procedure, means that we can only highlight the parts of the Code and Rules that help explain the topic of this book.
2. This simple description is a fraction of the legal detail needed to ensure a lien is perfected. A typical law school introductory class in secured transactions involves 45 classroom hours and 90 hours of homework. Introduction to Bankruptcy is another law course of the same length and thus we can only highlight bankruptcy issues in this chapter.
3. http://www.slate.com/id/2219256
4. Baird, Douglas G., "Revisiting Auctions in Chapter 11," The University of Chicago Law School, Chicago Law & Economics Working Paper No. 7.
5. Agarwal, Vikas, Hall, Suzanne, Myhre, Thomas, Placek, Nick, Saigh, Neil. "Aladdin," 2006.
6. http://www.chicagobusiness.com/cgi-bin/news.pl?id=3131
7. Shein, James B., "Winn-Dixie Stores: Cleanup on Aisle 11," Kellogg School of Management Case, Evanston, Ill. (August 2008).

8. "Supermarket Industry Review and Outlook," J.P. Morgan Securities, 2006.
9. In one notable example, poor coordination led to a manufacturing plant committing to purchase more than three months' worth of packaging for the company's Thrifty-Maid ice cream brand despite the decision at headquarters to discontinue the brand in favor of the higher-priced Prestige line.
10. PRNewswire—First Call, August 19, 2004.
11. http://www.fool.com/investing/small-cap/2004/12/10/peter-lynch-named-supermarket-ceo.aspx, July 23, 2008.
12. "Background & Description of Winn-Dixie's Stores," *Winn-Dixie Bankruptcy News*, Bankruptcy Creditors' Service, Inc., February 23, 2005.
13. "Background & Description of Winn-Dixie's Stores."
14. Presentation by Holly Etlin of Alix Partners, 2008 Kellogg Turnaround Management Conference, April 23, 2008.
15. *Winn-Dixie Bankruptcy News*, Bankruptcy Creditors' Service, Inc., February 23, 2005.
16. Jan Baker presentation at 2008 Kellogg Turnaround Management Conference, April 23, 2008.
17. Prior to the agreement, for example, some creditors held claims only against individual entities such as warehousing facilities that lacked financial viability if separated from the larger organization.
18. Interview with Flip Huffard, July 25, 2008.
19. Prior to the Substantive Consolidation Agreement, joint-and-several liability made all of the related Winn-Dixie entities both collectively and individually liable for bondholder claims.
20. Id.
21. "Court Approves Winn-Dixie's Reorganization Plan," *bizjournals.com*, August 4, 2006.
22. The Bankruptcy Research Database shows food retailers that successfully emerge from bankruptcy spend an average of 392 days in Chapter 11.
23. Huffard presentation at 2008 Kellogg Turnaround Management Conference, April 23, 2008.
24. Interview with Flip Huffard, July 26, 2008.

Chapter Seven

1. http://www.eads.com/eads/int/en/investor-relations/private-shareholders/faqs_ir/shares.html

2. "In Place of Strief," *The Economist*, October 14, 2006.
3. Shein, James B., "Parmalat U.S.A. Turnaround," Kellogg School of Management Case, Evanston, Ill. (October 2008).
4. Chagas, Marcos, "Brazil's Ruling Party Insists: There Was No Monthly Allowance Scheme," *Brazil Magazine*, April 5, 2006.
5. http://www.internetworldstats.com/sa/br.htm
6. "French Rescue Plans Limit Creditors' Role," *Journal of Corporate Renewal*, January 2004.
7. "Protecting Investments in Challenging Environments: A Guide for Clients," prepared by the Salans Global Corporate Group, 2010.
8. "Spanish Courts Grapple with 'Preventative Attachment,'" *Journal of Corporate Renewal*, March 2008.
9. Lewin, Bryan P. "The Role of the Institutional Environment in Corporate Failure and Restructuring," September 2006.
10. Bonsall, Jim, "Inside a German Turnaround," *Institutional Investor*, Spring 2004.
11. "French Rescue Plans Limit Creditors' Role," *Journal of Corporate Renewal*, January 2004.
12. "French Rescue Plans Limit Creditors' Role."
13. "When Crisis Crosses Borders: A Guide to Bankruptcy, Insolvency Practices in the U.S., Europe," *Journal of Corporate Renewal*, April 2006.
14. "China's Enterprise Bankruptcy Law Is a Work in Progress," *Journal of Corporate Renewal*, January 2008.
15. "Turnarounds Down Under; How One Old-Line Company Survived," *Journal of Corporate Renewal*, April 2003.
16. Presley, Greg, "The Art of the European Turnaround," *Institutional Investor*, Spring 2004.
17. Shein, James, *Elan Corporation Turnaround*, Kellogg Publications Case # 5–210–262.
18. "Is Mexico Safe for Secured Transactions?" *Journal of Corporate Renewal*, April 2003.
19. Helgason, Gudjon, and Wardell, Jane, "McDonald's Closes in Iceland as Currency Collapse Takes a Bite out of Big Mac Profits," *The Canadian Press*, October 26, 2009.
20. Presley, Greg, "The Art of the European Turnaround," *Institutional Investor*, Spring 2004.
21. Presley, Greg, "The Art of the European Turnaround."
22. Zwaig, Melvin C., and Leonard, Bruce, "Cooperation and Coordination in Cross-Border Insolvency Cases," *Institutional Investor*, Spring 2004.

23. "Greece Adopts Legislation Based on UNCITRAL Model Law on Cross-Border Insolvency," States News Service, June 25, 2010.

24. "Fraud Is a Growing Threat in Worsening Economy," *Journal of Corporate Renewal*, November 2008.

25. "Little Elan Becomes a Big Deal," *Pharmaceutical Executive*, October 1, 2001.

26. "Research Partnerships Give Irish Drug Maker Rosy Financial Glow," *Wall Street Journal*, January 30, 2002.

27. Shein, James B., "Elan Corporation's International Turnaround," Kellogg School of Management Case, Evanston, Ill. (2010).

28. OECD, Trade Union Density, http://stats.oecd.org/Index.aspx? DataSetCode=UN_DEN (accessed April 13, 2010).

29. Whalen, Jeanne, "Elan's Chief to Step Aside," *The Wall Street Journal*, June 2010.

30. Oliver, K., Samakh E., and Heckman, P., "Rebuilding Lego Brick by Brick," *Strategy + Business, Autumn* 2007, *48.*

31. Greene, J., "How LEGO Revived Its Brand," *Bloomberg Businessweek*, July 23, 2010.

Chapter Eight

1. http://www.spah.org/index.php/faqs/25-about-spah

2. "Breathing New Life into Home Health Agency Turnaround Sets Not-for-Profit on Growth Track," *Journal of Corporate Renewal*, June 2003.

3. "Greenbacks and Humpbacks," *The Globe and Mail*, August 23, 1995.

4. Preston, Caroline, "Have 100,000 Nonprofit Group Failed in the Recession?" *The Chronicle of Philanthropy*, August 7, 2010.

5. Land, Jon, "Failed Refugee Charity Unable to Manage Its Affairs," 24dash.com, June 17, 2010.

6. Land, Jon, "Failed Refugee Charity Unable to Manage Its Affairs."

7. "Jewish Charities Go Under Hit by Madoff Scam," *Agence France Presse*, December 18, 2008.

8. Marks, Gerald M., "Charity Brawl: Nonprofits Aren't So Generous When a Name's at Stake," *The Wall Street Journal*, August 5, 2010, A1.

9. Johnson, Patrick, Karra, Arun, Koeninger, Brooke, Leffler, Jack, Macock, Courtland, and Maitra, Mona. "Big Brothers Big Sisters of Metropolitan Chicago." Turnaround Analysis. Undated.

10. "Food Depository Executive Makes FSB: Fortune Small Business' 'Best Bosses' List," PR Newswire, September 24, 2003.

11. http://www.nonprofitlawblog.com/home/2008/10/nonprofits -and.html

12. http://www.nonprofitquarterly.org/index.php?option=com
    _content&view=article&id=1568:chapter-11-why-not&catid=150:from
    -the-archives
13. Anderson, Lincoln, "St. Vincent's Postmortem: Why Village Hospital
    Died," *Chelsea Now*, July 13, 2010.
14. "Governance, Rehabilitation in the Nonprofit Sector," *Journal of
    Corporate Renewal*, October 2007.
15. Takagi, Gene, "California Attorney General Sues Charities, Directors
    and Fundraisers," *Nonprofit Law Blog*, June 2, 2009.
16. http://a-score.com/rbjarticle.htm
17. Delany, Leslie, Marathe, Nikhil, Stelter, Stephan, Tadsen, Brent,
    Vuren, Erik Van, and Wellehan, John. "Joffrey Ballet." Turnaround
    analysis of a nonprofit company. August 7, 2006.
18. Arguedas, Juan Perez, Nimmagadda, Venkata, Nyffeler, Patrick,
    Ochoa, Rafael, Phillips, Michael, and Rubin, Michael. "USPS: A
    Crisis in Action—Will Current Turnaround Efforts Be Enough?"
    November 9, 2009.
19. United States Postal Service website: http://www.USPS.com
20. Friedman, Thomas, *The World Is Flat* (New York: Farrar, Straus, and
    Giroux), 2005.
21. Nair, A., Niranvichaiya, Y., Palmer, N., Passero, L., Ramu, V.,
    "Turnaround of Indian Railways," 2010.
22. "New Orleans Public Schools Get Overhaul," *USA Today*, March 4,
    2006.
23. "New Orleans Schools Aim Higher," *USA Today*, June 11, 2006.
24. "This Is a Mess," *New Orleans Times Picayune*, July 24, 2005.
25. "This Is a Mess."
26. "Recovery School District Legislatively Required Plan," June 7, 2006.
27. "State Superintendent Paul Pastorek Recognizes Contractors Who
    Participated in Successful Opening of Schools," *US Fed News*,
    September 5, 2007.
28. "Economic Squeeze Pushes Local Governments Toward Chapter 9,"
    Journal of Corporate Renewal, June 2008.

Chapter Nine

1. http://www.themiddlemarket.com/news/HIG-Capital-Makes
   -Coachmen-Investment-199259–1.html
2. http://www.nytimes.com/2010/01/10/business/10digi.html?
   _r=1&hpw
3. Interview with Flip Huffard, July 25, 2008.
4. Laffer, Arthur B., Hass, William J., and Pryor, Shepherd G. IV, *The
   Private Equity Edge* (New York: McGraw-Hill), 2009, p. 193.

5. Laffer, Arthur B., Hass, William J., and Pryor, Shepherd G. IV, p. 210.
6. Russell, J., Stienstra, M., Sukhrani, D., Shore, J., Shen, E., Sikaria, P., "Gerber Plumbing's Turnaround Story," 2009.
7. Presentation by Michael Warner at Kellogg Conference on Corporate Renewal, April 7, 2010.
8. Shein, James B., "Atari: Between a Rock and a Hard Place," Kellogg School of Management Case, Evanston, Ill. (2010).
9. Fritz, Ben, "Ex-game Leader Looks to Reboot," *Chicago Tribune*, August 9, 2010, p. Business 1.

Chapter Ten

1. Jason Jones's interview of editors at the *New York Times*, June 10, 2009, *The Daily Show*, Comedy Central Network.
2. Murray, Alan, *The Wall Street Journal Essential Guide to Management* (New York: Harper Business), 2010.
3. Shane Greenberg presentation, "Managing Disruption: Paranoid Strategies at Intel," November 8, 2007.

Acknowledgments

This book started as a result of students, business leaders, and others asking if there were any good books on the subject of turnarounds and corporate renewal that could be used as a textbook as well as for general business reading. My course lectures were that mixture of experience as a CEO and board member of a number of firms, and of academic research in the field. Along the way, my students wrote papers that were invaluable to this book, and I always learn from the students in every class and must thank them for their inspiration.

In particular, I must thank Evan Meagher, who has been a part of this project since taking and recording my course, through various drafts as writer, researcher, and collaborator. It was his and Rebecca Frazzano Meagher's efforts that made this book get off to the right start and make it to the finish line.

A most important person in my academic life has been Steven Rogers, Professor of Finance at the Kellogg School of Management. His support for my hiring, case creation, and now book writing has been rock solid. It's no wonder his courses get oversubscribed and he is often voted Professor of the Year. Professor Rogers is also the Director of the Levy Institute for Entrepreneurial Practice, and the Associate Director, Scott Whitaker, has played a strong support and managerial role in all my efforts.

I had always wondered why anyone needed a literary agent, and now I know. Joy Tutela of the David Black Literary Agency has been a part of this project from the beginning. She had suggestions starting with the original book proposal. Her knowledge of which editors at what publishing houses would be most interested in the book was critical in generating interest in getting this book to you, Dear Reader. Each chapter went before her critical eye in advance of even going to the publisher.

My commanding general at the Jossey-Bass imprint of John Wiley and Sons Publishing is Kathe Sweeney, the wonderful editor who championed the book for approval, and then oversaw its creation every step of the way. Other key players on the publishing team were Mark Karmendy, production manager; Suzanne Copenhagen, the copyeditor who added some delightful praise to her many suggestions how to make the book less grammatically challenged; and Erin Moy from Marketing.

Financial support for the project came from the sponsors of my annual Kellogg Conference on Turnarounds and Corporate Renewal. These include Mesirow Financial, AlixPartners, Grant Thornton, Huron Consulting, FTI Consulting, Macquarie, and the Chicago Chapter of the Turnaround Management Association. Logistical support came from McDermott Will & Emery and from Wrightwood Capital.

Saving the best for last, I must thank my family for their support along the way. My wife Jane has not only put up with me for many years, she helped with the typing of the manuscript. My sons Justin and Jered have always been there for me, often giving sound advice, leading me to question sometimes who is the parent and which of us is the child. They bring me laughs, worries, and most of all, happiness.

About the Author

James B. Shein has decades of experience as a CEO and running, advising, purchasing, and reviving distressed companies. He is now a professor of Management & Strategy at the Kellogg School of Management at Northwestern University, where he teaches Managing Turnarounds and Entrepreneurship. Professor Shein is also a member of the boards of directors at several public and private companies where he serves on audit and governance committees.

He was counsel at McDermott, Will & Emery, with areas of practice in corporate governance, restructurings, acquisitions, and fiduciary duties of officers and directors. Prior to that, Professor Shein spent four years as the president and chief executive officer of R.C. Manufacturing and ten years prior to that as president and chief executive officer of Northbrook Corporation. During that time he purchased, turned, and sold underperforming companies.

Professor Shein has chaired programs at the Federal Reserve Bank of Chicago on the outlook for troubled industries, and conducts workshops on corporate restructuring and governance for the Bank Lending Institute and the American Press Institute. His work with corporate directors led to his article, "Trying to Match SOX: Dealing with New Challenges and Risks Facing Directors," published in *The Journal of Private Equity*. He has also published a number of cases for the Kellogg Case Collection on turnarounds and corporate renewal in large and small companies, for-profit and nonprofit organizations, and international companies. He is regularly quoted in major business newspapers and magazines.

A frequent lecturer and author on corporate renewal and governance, he was declared an expert on corporate governance by a Federal court and has been highlighted on National Public Radio programs as an authority on restructuring and downsizing. Professor Shein has earned engineering, MBA, PhD, and law degrees.

Index